Developing Strategic International Partnerships:

Models for Initiating and Sustaining

Innovative Institutional Linkages

Previous Titles in the Global Education Research Reports Series

U.S.-China Educational Exchange: Perspectives on a
Growing Partnership

Higher Education on the Move: New Developments in
Global Mobility

International India: A Turning Point in Educational Exchange
with the U.S.

Innovation through Education: Building the Knowledge
Economy in the Middle East

Who Goes Where and Why?: An Overview and Analysis
of Global Educational Mobility

Developing Strategic International Partnerships:

Models for Initiating and Sustaining

Innovative Institutional Linkages

EDITED BY SUSAN BUCK SUTTON AND DANIEL OBST

Sixth in a Series of Global Education Research Reports

New York

IIE publications can be purchased at: www.iiebooks.org

The Institute of International Education
809 United Nations Plaza, New York, New York 10017

Library of Congress Cataloging-in-Publication Data

Developing strategic international partnerships : best practices and innovative approaches / edited by
Susan Buck Sutton and Daniel Obst.
    p. cm. -- (Global education research reports ; 6th)
  ISBN 978-0-87206-344-0 (alk. paper)
1. University cooperation. 2. Education and globalization. 3. Technology--International
cooperation. I. Sutton, Susan Buck. II. Obst, Daniel.
  LB2331.5.D484 2011
  378.1'04--dc23
                                2011033485

Series editors:
Daniel Obst, Deputy Vice President for International Partnerships, IIE
Sharon Witherell, Director of Public Affairs, IIE

Cover and text design: Pat Scully Design

Table of Contents

Models for Managing and Sustaining International Partnerships

Community Partnerships and Capacity Building

Designing Research Partnerships

Partnering through Networks and Consortia

Meeting Challenges and Lessons Learned

Developing Partnerships with U.S. Institutions

Planting the Seeds for Partnerships: National Level Efforts in Europe

Appendices

Figures and Tables

Figures

Tables

Forewords

By Allan E. Goodman

In today's rapidly developing international education sector, partnerships that transcend borders and cultures can enhance both partner universities in indelible ways. The intercultural skills and connections gained through such linkages will assist students and faculty alike in navigating the global knowledge economy of the twenty-first century.

The Institute of International Education (IIE) is committed to fostering partnerships among higher education institutions worldwide. In recent years, IIE has undertaken a number of strategic initiatives to encourage academic linkages. In particular, we launched the IIE Center for International Partnerships in Higher Education in 2009 to assist higher education institutions in initiating and nurturing partnerships across the globe. Since its founding, the Center has helped higher education institutions around the world to develop or enhance their international partnership strategies.

Two key programs of IIE's Center are the International Academic Partnership Program, launched with support from the U.S. Department of Education's Fund for the Improvement of Postsecondary Education, and the U.S.-Indonesia Partnership Program for Study Abroad Capacity, funded through a grant from the U.S. Department of Education's Bureau of Educational and Cultural Affairs. These two programs help build academic linkages in key countries such as China, India, and Indonesia. IIE's Center is also dedicated to producing timely research on critical issues, such as a recent White Paper on "Building Sustainable U.S.-Ethiopian University Partnerships." This White Paper recounts key findings from a U.S. Embassy-sponsored conference in Addis Ababa in December 2010 that brought together a wide range of both U.S. and Ethiopian universities interested in forming partnerships.

Institutional partnership arrangements take many forms—the signing of Memoranda of Understanding (MOUs), exchanges of students and faculty members, creation of dual and joint degree programs, and interdisciplinary joint research initiatives to name a few—but their common link is that they require formal institutional commitments between higher education institutions. This book, produced in partnership with the AIFS Foundation, is intended to serve as a resource to institutions that wish to build or expand strategic institutional linkages. The chapters provide useful models from all world regions for higher education institutions that are seeking information on how they can initiate and strengthen their global linkages.

It is our hope that this book will provide lessons and best practices in developing partnerships from authors who have been instrumental in helping their institutions and organizations form lasting linkages across international boundaries. Other useful partnership resources can be found on our website at www.iie.org/cip.

Allan E. Goodman
President & CEO, Institute of International Education

By William L. Gertz

There is an art to developing and sustaining a successful strategic partnership. For every partnership that bears fruit, there are many that fail due to poor planning or execution. When contemplating an institutional relationship, it is important to assess the compatibility of the organizations and their respective missions, avoiding being swayed by the "prestige" of working with a certain institution.

In the field of education, there has been a marked increase in the number of institutional partnerships, fueled by the knowledge that to accomplish a globally-minded academic mission one needs to reach out and expand program offerings. Also, institutions can share best practices, increase recruitment, and become more attractive to students as they broaden their scope.

Throughout its history, AIFS has partnered with dozens of international institutions in creating study abroad programs for U.S. students. In each of its locations, AIFS first identifies an academic partner that has the ability to develop and deliver a strong academic program for visiting students. AIFS handles the recruitment of students, flights and transportation, insurance, housing, meals, and logistics, while the international university or college provides the venue, teaching, and academic transcripts. At each location, AIFS employs a Resident Director who provides student services, excursions, and activities designed to help students adjust to life abroad and safely maximize their time. This model, while revolutionary in the 1960s when we developed the concept, is now the norm.

AIFS also partners with U.S. institutions that bring groups of students abroad with their own faculty and curriculum. Again, AIFS handles all the logistics, including securing classroom space, providing academic support services, arranging housing and meal options, and developing field activities and excursions. These "three way" partnerships are much easier to arrange than they were a decade ago, with such tools as email, Skype, and video chat now available. In addition, the rise in English language proficiency makes the old adage that you should "sell in the language of your customer" almost trite.

Even with these new tools, the work in engaging a successful partner needs to be approached with exceeding care to make up for any potential cultural or technical misunderstandings. We have found that sometimes a partnership can take years of cultivation by both institutions and a series of visits before an agreement can be fashioned. Once an agreement is made, the real work begins. The measure of success needs to be identified before the agreement is finalized. A multiyear analysis needs to be conducted. There is a lot of work required, but the perseverance will pay off when there is a relationship that works seamlessly and is a benefit to both parties.

The AIFS Foundation is once again pleased to partner with IIE. This is our sixth Global Education Research Report, which we hope leads to new initiatives for your institution.

William L. Gertz
President & Chief Executive Officer, American Institute For Foreign Study (AIFS)

THE CHANGING LANDSCAPE OF INTERNATIONAL PARTNERSHIPS

SUSAN BUCK SUTTON, SENIOR ADVISOR FOR INTERNATIONALIZATION,
BRYN MAWR COLLEGE

DANIEL OBST, DEPUTY VICE PRESIDENT OF INTERNATIONAL PARTNERSHIPS,
INSTITUTE OF INTERNATIONAL EDUCATION

This is a dynamic moment for international academic partnerships, a time of renewed vitality and broadened scope. For many colleges and universities, such partnerships are no longer simply one tactic of internationalization among many, but rather a core, driving philosophy. Institutions are rethinking their reasons for pursuing international partnerships and the processes by which they form them. The result is a fascinating, constantly changing landscape of new partnership forms, policies, and procedures.

The forces impelling this embrace of international partnerships can be grouped into two overarching themes: 1) growing recognition that academic internationalization is as much a process of outward engagement as internal restructuring, and 2) the increasing need for academic institutions to position themselves within emerging global systems of higher education. The first theme reflects a view of student learning as advanced by bringing multiple voices into the classroom and curriculum; cutting-edge scholarship as advanced by collaboration among the best minds no matter where these are located; and community engagement as having global dimensions. The second theme revolves around what Jane Knight (2008) accurately describes as the now tumultuous global arena of higher education, with its jumble of confusing, often conflicting trends, including global rankings, new patterns of student mobility, the increasing reach of distance education, the emergence of regional networks and education hubs, financial restructuring, international patterns of brain drain and gain, and the dawning understanding that internationalization can have negative as well as positive consequences (see also Egron-Polak and Hudson 2010).

The first of these two themes argues unequivocally for greater and more creative use of international partnerships by institutions of higher learning. The second theme has evoked a range of responses, including some that pit institutions, nations, and organizations against each other for status and market share. Other responses to the second theme, however, take a more collaborative direction and give added impetus to international partnership formation.

The more collaborative response to the second theme posits that colleges and universities in different nations have much to gain from each other, not only in terms of their long-standing goals of internationalization but also in terms of institutional positioning on a global stage. International collaboration brings international recognition to those thus engaged and sets the stage for further international work and outreach. Within the emerging global systems of higher education, international academic partnerships are thus seen to convey what Rosabeth Moss Kanter (1994), referring to international business, has labeled "collaborative advantage"; that is, the locally-knowledgeable partners, significant resources, transformative dialogues, and unexpected opportunities that accrue to institutions skilled at developing and sustaining effective international collaborations.

In short, international academic collaborations reflect a variety of motivations. They also take a variety of forms. This volume focuses on just one of these: partnerships among a pair or small set of institutions of higher learning. Networks, consortia, associations, and partnerships with other kinds of organizations, businesses, and local communities parallel and sometimes overlap such one-on-one partnerships among colleges and universities, but are beyond the scope of this discussion (see Stockley and de Wit 2010 for an introduction to these others). We focus instead on formal cooperative agreements between two (or sometimes several) colleges and universities located in different nations (see Kinser & Green 2009 for basic definitions of partnerships).

More specifically, this volume attempts to capture the current dynamism and range of what is happening with international partnership development among colleges and universities. International academic partnerships are a work in progress, a conversation that needs many voices and points of entry. Different institutions are exploring the potential of international partnerships in different ways. They are also confronting the many challenges that make such work daunting. There is value in compiling and learning from their varied experiences, and the chapters that follow provide just such a panorama. This volume elaborates the U.S. experience, in its many forms, but entries from the UK, France, India, and Ethiopia clearly indicate that what is happening in the U.S. is not unique. The institutional types covered in the volume range from HBCUs (Historically Black Colleges and Universities) to community colleges to research universities, and the academic fields are as diverse as engineering, business, education, health, and liberal arts. The resulting image is a complex, multifaceted, and dynamic landscape of new ideas and bold moves.

What Partnerships Are Being Asked to Do

A conclusion that quickly emerges from scanning this landscape is that international academic partnerships are being asked to do more than has been the case in the past. Twenty years ago partnerships were almost exclusively about student exchange, with only the occasional example of collaborative research or cooperative capacity-building or community development (Klasek 1992). While exchange partnerships continue strong, their goals have multiplied, their geographical span has widened, and—most importantly—they have been supplemented with other forms.

The partnerships documented in this volume pursue goals as varied as:

- Student learning, as global citizens and as future members of a global workforce;
- Curriculum building and course enhancement;
- Providing international learning experiences even for students who do not study abroad and even in disciplines that have historically had few such opportunities;
- Developing the international capacity of faculty and staff;
- Advancing research by connecting institutions and scholars with those who have similar strengths and interests;
- Connecting to key parts of the world;
- Supporting and enhancing the international ties and interests of the surrounding community;
- Tackling pressing global issues of health, education, economic development, environment, energy, conflict, inequality, human rights, and social justice;

- Promoting the overall mission of the institution, giving it distinctive qualities, and enhancing its international positioning and reputation;
- Generating revenue through tuition and grants;
- General institutional capacity building;
- Pursuit of public diplomacy and other national priorities; and
- Shaping the global system of higher education in beneficial ways.

These partnerships also employ a wide range of methods and strategies to achieve their goals. Some develop short-term, deeply-embedded study abroad programs that attract a wider range of students than those who study overseas for the whole year (e.g., Asgary & Thamhain). Some use international faculty, laboratories, and internships to introduce international learning to curricula in the professions and STEM fields (e.g., Haller & Groll, Valentine et al., Louime et al., Owusu-Ofori & Mayes). Dual degrees and joint educational programs have emerged that foster blended cohorts of students from different nations (e.g., Lavakare, Lacy & Wade, Foster & Jones, Harrell & Hinckley). Information technology and social media are used to create globally interactive classrooms (e.g., Haller & Groll, Chia et al., Valentine et al., Tedeschi et al., Harrell & Hinckley). International research teams compare perspectives and pool resources in exploring questions of mutual interest (Kuchinke, Lacy & Wade, Harrell & Hinckley), while similar teams collaborate on community development and institutional capacity building, such as spreading the community college system (Spangler & Tyler) and introducing innovative modes of English language instruction (Shull). (See Appendix A for a broad list of the many kinds of activities now undertaken by international partnerships.)

Transaction and Transformation

Whatever their goals and forms, the partnerships discussed in this volume invoke the power of collaboration and an ethos of mutuality. There is something to be gained by working together that cannot be accomplished by either institution alone. The pursuit of mutual benefit, in which all partners gain from the engagement, is a near universal theme of these chapters. Some also articulate an additional benefit: they see mutuality as the mutual construction of goals and projects, the changes in thinking that result, and the benefits that occur as these collective efforts move forward with a momentum of their own (e.g., Cunningham et al., Carbonell).

This range of meaning for mutuality resonates with what can be seen as two poles of collaboration. Borrowing terminology from the field of service learning (Enos & Morton 2003), there appears to be a continuum of international academic partnerships from what might be called "transactional" to what might be called "transformational" (Sutton 2010, Sutton, Egginton & Favela Forthcoming). Partnerships focused exclusively on student exchange are at the transactional end because students are traded in a manner that resembles transactions in a marketplace. The individuals who travel from one institution to another are changed as a result of the partnership, but the institutions themselves remain largely separate and unaffected. Transformational collaborations, in contrast, are those that change or transform entire departments, offices, and institutions, through the generation of common goals, projects, and products. Both sides emerge from the relationship somewhat altered. Transformational partnerships combine resources and view linkages as sources of institutional growth and collaborative learning. They often produce new initiatives that go far beyond what was originally planned.

Whether expressly articulated or not, it is clear that the partnerships discussed here demonstrate a movement toward the transformational side of this continuum. As already stated, more is expected of academic partnerships than in the past. There is increasing confidence that international collaboration— with carefully selected and strategic partners—can be an important element of institutional growth. What happens outside institutions can change what happens within them. Resources can be shared or created. Joint projects can take institutions to new places. The partnership itself becomes a kind of bi-national academic unit. And it is in this manner that transformative, strongly committed, strategic partnerships can be seen as important actors in the emerging global system of higher education.

Developing an Institutional Approach to Partnerships

The desire to form more strategic international partnerships has led many colleges and universities to develop overall partnership plans and policies. These documents guide the establishment of new partnerships and reposition partnerships within institutional goals and missions. They move colleges and universities from "incidental" collaborations to "intentional" ones (Barnes) and produce "real" agreements rather than "feel good" ones (Aw & Dunsmore).

Several recent discussions (especially Van de Water, Green & Cook 2008, Kinser & Green 2009), as well as the contributions to this volume make clear that developing an institutional partnership program is a multipronged, long-term project encompassing at least the following elements:

- Taking stock of existing affiliations (creating a registry, assessing levels of activity, identifying gaps);
- Establishing a partnership approval process (developing application procedures and criteria for approval, identifying lines of decision-making);

- Articulating overall partnership goals and strategies (setting targets for number, types, and location of partnerships, activities they will pursue, impact they are expected to have, and the resources, opportunities, and challenges involved);

- Spreading a culture of partnership (promoting the value of partnerships, connecting to institutional and departmental mission, developing faculty capacity and supporting faculty in becoming involved);

- Developing policies, procedures, and organizational structures for managing partnerships (establishing steering committees, hiring staff, articulating principles for participating, tackling procedural roadblocks);

- Providing baseline financial and other support (equivalent to what is provided for other key institutional functions, such as personnel, IT, and travel funds);

- Developing effective practices for initiating partnerships (requiring multiple conversations, engagement of relevant decision-makers, and patience to let relationships and understandings mature);

- Drafting well-crafted Memoranda of Understanding and Implementation Plans (the first setting general parameters of the partnership and the second identifying specific activities, the financial and other responsibilities of each institution, outcomes expected, and when and how these will be assessed; see Appendix B);

- Pursuing effective practices for sustaining partnerships over time (providing the organization, support, and leadership to insure valued partnerships endure even when their original proposers are no longer active in them); and

- Establishing procedures for reviewing, revising, and/or terminating partnerships (including periodic assessment of activity levels and quality, number of students and faculty involved, effectiveness of the working relationship, cost, and impact).

Several of the chapters in this volume provide cogent discussions of how their institutions developed partnership plans, all closely connected to institutional mission and goals. Radwan's university, for example, found it useful to identify three tiers of partnership, each meriting a different approach. The University of Nottingham decided to focus on international teaching partnerships (Foster & Jones). Step one for Ethiopian institutions may well be identifying what they have to offer partners, since they are more used to seeing themselves as less developed than their international counterparts (Francisconi). Harrell & Hinckley give a particularly illuminating account of modifying their institution's original plan as a result of on-the-ground experiences.

Challenges to Be Met

No matter how good the plan may be, international partnership work is not without its challenges, and many of these chapters take up this point as well. Many of these difficulties derive from the relative newness of such collaborations, at least in the robust multifaceted form presented in this volume. Administrators, fiscal officers, and faculty need to be convinced of the value of this new form, avenues of support must be identified, and procedural and structural roadblocks that limit what can be done overseas must be addressed (Lavakare, Kuchinke, Asgary & Thamhain, Osuwu-Ofori & Mayes). International work has to earn its place alongside other priorities with regard to institutional mission (Valentine et al.). Policies that come from older, more inward-looking administrative forms need to be rethought (Delisle).

Other challenges reflect the turbulent changes occurring in higher education in general: from funding difficulties to online delivery of degrees, branch campuses, the possible rise of a small set of dominant global universities, significant differences in educational resources across nations, and political unrest both within and among nations (Altbach & Knight 2010, Knight 2008, Wildavsky 2010). These can create a tension between institutional advancement and collaborative advancement in international partnerships (Haller & Groll). Issues of brain-drain and gain, of educational and economic inequalities between the Global North and Global South can also strain partnership goals of reciprocity (Francisconi).

Other chapters in this volume discuss the challenges involved in engaging U.S. students, many of whom lack fluency beyond English, find the cost of studying abroad too high, and may be majoring in disciplines not historically engaged in international work (Asgary & Thamhain, Valentine et al., Baker). International partnerships that involve student exchange are often unbalanced, with fewer U.S. students going out than their counterparts coming in (Klahr, Asgary & Thamhain).

Finally, these chapters discuss the challenges of meshing institutional policies, procedures, and accepted business practices across nations, as well as different educational cultures and accreditation systems (Baker, Shull, Harrell & Hinckley). In a similar vein, many a partnership has foundered on false assumptions that both sides understood the meaning of partnership in the same way, and overly ambitious but unrealistic proposals (Harrell & Hinckley).

Developing and Sustaining a Partnership

What these chapters provide are stories of partnerships that have overcome these and other challenges. In so doing, they identify factors that have proven effective both for selecting partners at the outset and sustaining collaboration in the long run. Klahr,

Barnes, Louime et al., Delisle, and Aw & Dunsmore devote particular attention to partnership selection, assessing what makes a good institutional match, what must be learned about potential partners in order to evaluate the match, the kinds of candid conversation and careful listening that must occur, and the need to make sure that institutions have the same understanding of what partnerships mean in general and what the specific one being proposed might achieve. Cunningham and her colleagues see this as a dialogical process in which positions and understandings are modified as conversation proceeds. Relevant decision-makers must be involved, and faculty champions identified and supported (Lacy & Wade, Kuchinke). Patience, flexibility, and attention to building relationships, trust, and rapport are critical (Shepherd, Baker). So is identifying early achievable projects that can move the partnership forward (Tedeschi et al., Lavakare).

These chapters also identify factors that distinguish long-lived and productive collaborations from those that fade more quickly. (See Duval 2009, Hartle 2008, Kellogg 2009, Chan 2004, Prichard 1996, Kinser & Green 2009, Wiley 2006, de Wit 2004, Van Ginkel 1996, Van de Water, Green & Koch 2008, Sutton, Egginton & Favela Forthcoming for general discussions of what builds strong partnerships.) In all such cases, mutual benefit must be achieved, and there must be a balance of success in partnership projects (even if some fail). Operating with integrity, trust, and genuine reciprocity is essential, as is developing a system that fosters frequent, candid, open-ended communication that attends to cultural, linguistic, and institutional differences (Baker, Shepherd). Difficulties and crises must be handled openly and with a sense that the institutions are committed to each other for the long-run (Delisle, Baker, Lacy & Wade). Adaptability, flexibility, and willingness to change course keep collaboration active and real (Owusu-Ofori & Mayes, Harrell & Hinckley). All relevant constituencies should be engaged on both sides and structures put into place to manage the partnership and make key decisions (Carbonell, Radwan, Asgary & Thamhain, Foster & Jones, Barnes).

Long-lived partnerships also develop an ethos that the partnership is as important as any particular sub-project or individual (Shull) and develop activities that build relationships across participants while also bringing in newcomers (Cunningham et al., Harrell & Hinckley, Tedeschi et al., Brustein & Miller). They become integrated with institutional mission and core curricula (Louime et al., Klahr, Valentine et al., Owusu-Ofori & Mayes) and are also advanced when they broaden their reach to connect to local communities and businesses (Louime et al., Asgary & Thamhain, Brustein & Miller, Harrell & Hinckley). And they require regular assessment and reworking (Louime et al., Baker, Carbonell, Radwan, Tedeschi et al., Harrell & Hinckley).

Finally, long-lived partnerships are given base-line support by their institutions to keep them moving forward, but simultaneously generate new resources and external funding. Seed monies for faculty engagement, staffing to manage the partnership, programs to orient newcomers and provide the needed cultural background are all very useful (Klahr, Barnes, Kuchinke, Radwan, Foster & Jones, Haller & Groll, Lacy & Wade). The Ohio State University has even moved to opening international offices in key countries to manage their partnerships on the ground (Brustein & Miller). At the same time, successful partnerships bring new resources both to their constituent institutions and to the partnership as a whole through external grants, resource-sharing, and tuition generation (Shepherd, Haller & Groll, Harrell & Hinckley).

The Era of International Educational Partnerships

The challenges faced in constructing and sustaining international academic partnerships could, of course, ultimately prove stronger than the forces favoring such collaborations. At the present moment, however, such affiliations are experiencing a tremendous growth and elaboration, what might even be called a flowering. The forms are many and the goals ambitious. A sense that institutions can do more together than they can do alone is taking hold, coupled with the realization that learning, research, institution-building, and community engagement are now global endeavors. International partnerships are playing an important role in the global systems of higher education that are now emerging, operating as bi- or multi-national nodes within these systems.

It is for such reasons that several governments and organizations have recently developed programs that support the establishment of international academic partnerships. For example in the United States, the U.S. Department of Education has for many years provided funding for innovative academic linkages or small consortia through programs such as the U.S.-Brazil Higher Education Consortia Program, the European Union-United States Atlantis Program, the Program for North American Mobility in Higher Education, and the U.S.-Russia Program, although these programs have tentatively been suspended because of the financial crisis. In 2010, the U.S. Embassy in Iraq launched a multimillion-dollar University Linkages Program that will fund partnerships between five Iraqi universities and five U.S. universities, with a focus on curriculum review and reform, career center development, and student and faculty exchanges. In June 2011, India's Minister of External Affairs, Shri S.M. Krishna, and the U.S. Secretary of State, Hillary Rodham Clinton, announced the launch of the Obama-Singh 21st Century Knowledge Initiative, which aims to strengthen academic collaboration between U.S. and Indian higher education institutions by providing U.S.-India Institutional Partnership Grants. And the U.S. Department of State's Bureau of Educational and Cultural Affairs provided grant funding to the Institute of International Education to launch the U.S.-Indonesia Partnership Program for Study Abroad Capacity, an initiative that brings together six U.S.

and six Indonesian institutions. Francisconi's chapter describes a U.S. Embassy in Ethiopia–sponsored workshop and seed grant competition to promote academic partnerships between U.S. and Ethiopian institutions.

Other governments and private foundations and organizations have also recently launched initiatives to support international linkages. The chapters by Delisle and Shepherd recount such efforts in France and the UK, respectively. Appendix C describes IIE's Center for International Partnerships in Higher Education, which assists institutions in developing or expending international partnerships through initiatives such as the International Academic Partnership Program. These initiatives may well be harbingers of more to come.

As demonstrated by the chapters in this volume, we have entered an era of international collaboration among colleges and universities. The partnerships thus formed enhance, even transform, the institutions that engage in them, produce enduring insights and relationships across national boundaries, and are creating a globally collaborative conversation on the forms and future of higher education that is likely to continue well into the future.

SELECTED BIBLIOGRAPHY ON INTERNATIONAL ACADEMIC PARTNERSHIPS

Altbach, P. G., & Knight, J. (2010). The internationalization of higher education: Motivations and realities. *Journal of Studies in International Education,* 11, 290-305.

Altbach, P. G., & Teichler, U. (2001). Internationalization and exchanges in a globalized university. *Journal of Studies in International Education,* 5, 5-25.

Bhandari, R. (2010). International India: A turning point in educational exchange with the U.S. New York, NY: Institute of International Education.

Chan, W. Y. (2004). International cooperation in higher education: Theory and practice. *Journal of Studies in International Education,* 8, 32-55.

De Wit, H. (2004). Academic alliances and networks: A new internationalization strategy in response to the globalization of our societies. In Theather, D. (Ed.) *Consortia, international networking, alliances of universities.* Melbourne: University of Melbourne.

Duval, J. (2009). Crafting strategic partnerships. Presentation at Annual Conference, International Commission, Association of Public and Land-grant Universities, Colorado Springs.

Egron-Polak, E., & Hudson, R. (2010). Internationalization of higher education: Global trends, regional perspectives. Paris: International Association of Universities.

Enos, S., & Morton K. (2003). Developing a theory and practice of campus-community partnerships. In B. Jacoby (Ed.) *Building partnerships for service learning* (pp. 20-41). San Francisco, CA: Jossey-Bass.

Hartle, T. (2008). Expanding partnerships to strengthen Africa's higher education institutions. Washington, DC: U.S. AID and Higher Education for Development.

Institute of International Education (2011). Building sustainable U.S.-Ethiopian university partnerships: Findings from a higher education conference. New York, NY: Institute of International Education.

Kanter, R. M. (1994). Collaborative advantage: The art of alliances. *Harvard Business Review.* July-August.

Kemp, N., & Humfrey, C. (2010). UK-US higher education partnerships: Realising the potential. London: The British Council. Retrieved from http://www.britishcouncil.org/uk-us_higher_education_partnerships_realising_the_potential.pdf

Kellogg, E. D. (2009). Partnerships for development. Presentation at NAFSA Annual Conference, Minneapolis.

Klasek, C. B. (1992). Inter-institutional cooperation guidelines and agreements. In C. B. Klasek (Ed.), *Bridges to the future: Strategies for internationalizing higher education* (pp. 108-128). Carbondale, IL: Association of International Education Administrators.

Kinser, K., & Green, M. F. (2009). The power of partnerships: A transatlantic dialogue. Washington, DC: American Council on Education.

Knight, J. (2008). Higher education in turmoil: The changing world of internationalization. Rotterdam: Sense Pubs.

Laughlin, S. (2008). U.S.-China educational exchange: Perspectives on a growing partnership. New York, NY: Institute of International Education.

Linkages: Engaging in Global Partnerships (Spring 2007). *IIENetworker Magazine.*

Obst, D., & Kuder, M. (2009). Joint and double degree programs: An emerging model for transatlantic exchange. New York, NY: Institute of International Education.

Stockley, D. & de Wit, H. (2010). Global trends in higher education and the significance of international networks. In Advancing Australia-Europe Cooperation in International Education. Proceedings of a joint IEAA-EAIE Symposium. IEAA-EAIE, "Advancing Europe-Australia cooperation in higher education," Sydney, 11-12 October 2009.

Sutton, S. B. (2010). Transforming internationalization through partnerships. *International Educator,* 19(1), 60-63.

Sutton, S. B., Egginton, E., & Favela, R. (Forthcoming). Collaborating on the future: Strategic partnerships and linkages. In D. Deardorff, J.D. Heyl, T. Adams, & H. de Wit (Eds.), *Bridges to the Future: New strategies for internationalizing higher education in the 21ˢᵗ century.* Thousand Oaks, CA: Sage Publications.

Thullen, M., Tillman, M. J., Horner, D. D., Carty, S., and Kennedy, S. (1997). Cooperating with a university in the United States: NAFSA's guide to interuniversity linkages. Washington, DC: NAFSA.

Van de Water, J., Green, M. F., & Koch, K. (2008). International partnerships: Guidelines for colleges and universities. Washington, DC: American Council on Education.

Van Ginkel, H. (1996). Networking and strategic alliances: Dynamic patterns of organization and co-operation. CRE-Action 109. Geneva: CRE.

Wildavsky, B. (2010). The great brain race: How global universities are reshaping the world. Princeton, NJ: Princeton University Press.

Wiley, D. (2006). Best practices for international partnerships with higher education institutions in Africa. Lansing, MI: Michigan State University, African Studies Center.

Chapter One

Intentionality in International Engagement: Identifying Potential Strategic International Partnerships

Tim Barnes, Director, Illinois Strategic International Partnerships initiative, University of Illinois at Urbana-Champaign

As with many public research universities across the United States and around the world, at the University of Illinois at Urbana-Champaign we are re-examining our efforts at international engagement. We have worked to more clearly articulate our goals and desired outcomes, more carefully consider our modes and models of collaborating with partner institutions abroad, and more creatively imagine the ways in which our efforts at international engagement can be thoroughly integrated into our core institutional missions. Such self-examination seems inevitable, and not without value, during these times of ever-diminishing dollars in public funding for higher education. We are all seeking to do more with less, and to leverage any resources we may have to maximum advantage.

In fact, to suggest that we are "re-examining" our international engagement efforts may be somewhat disingenuous, as it implies that we as an institution previously had approached interactions with the world with some measure of deliberation and coordination. I would suggest that, to date, our university's international engagement has been largely *incidental,* in that our activities have grown organically, based on the particular interests and efforts of individual faculty, research groups, or academic units. I suspect that we are not alone among our peer institutions in relying almost exclusively on this decentralized approach; nor are we alone in taking initial steps toward a more strategic, or *intentional,* approach to internationalization.

The incidental model of international engagement is obviously of great value—individual faculty, research groups, and academic departments are in the best position to identify international partnerships that can answer their immediate needs and enhance their particular research and educational activities. The result is a large number of highly specialized and often short-lived collaborations, of the sort aptly characterized by Susan Buck Sutton as "transactional" relationships, with institutions abroad. Yet, by its very nature, this incidental model all but precludes any sort of long-range, strategic planning for international engagement at the institutional level. Strategic international engagement, whatever the particular model employed, must rely on deliberation, coordinated implementation, and quantifiable assessment for its success. In short, it must be intentional, rather than incidental.

The emerging Illinois Strategic International Partnerships (ISIP) initiative at the University of Illinois at Urbana-Champaign is a first step toward such intentionality. We seek to identify peer institutions around the world that, for various reasons including geographic location, historic collaborations, and current synergies or complementarities in our research and educational priorities, offer particularly strong opportunities for institutional collaborations that are both broadly and deeply impactful. In conjunction with this identification process, we are working to develop administrative structures, budget forecasts, and funding models that can provide the necessary "start-up" support for developing new strategic partnerships, and gain support for these new partnerships from our central campus leadership.

Defining the "Strategic" in Strategic International Partnerships

Having an ambitious, clearly articulated goal for this new model of strategic international partnerships is a critical first step, akin to the vision statement that informs a good strategic plan. We concluded that strategic international partnerships should be distinguished from our traditional, focused partnerships based on five key criteria:

- <u>Breadth of impact</u>. Strategic international partnerships should be broadly impactful on two fronts. First, they should cross discipline, college, and department boundaries to involve faculty and students at all levels, and throughout the institution. Ideally, they should foster true interdisciplinarity in research and in learning. Second, they should involve activities directly related to all of the institution's core missions (for example, research, education, engagement, economic development).

- Depth of impact. Strategic international partnerships should provide opportunities to move from simple to complex interactions between institutions. With regard to research, this might range from specific collaborative research projects, short-term exchanges of research personnel, and shared physical plant resources, to ongoing "laboratories without borders" and jointly-managed, offsite physical research facilities. Likewise, educational activities should run the gamut from simple reciprocal study abroad arrangements and short-term study abroad programming to 3+2 and sandwich programs, jointly taught courses, co-development of new curricula, and joint or dual degree programs.

- Strong faculty support. While some central coordination of activities in a strategic international partnership is necessary and desirable, there must be significant and ongoing interest among faculty across the campus if any meaningful collaboration is to develop. Identify key individual faculty at both partner institutions to spearhead the initial efforts and champion the partnership among their colleagues. Alumni of one institution who are working at the other can be strong advocates, particularly if they are alumni of Ph.D. programs, as the research relationships forged during their doctoral studies will often continue in their professional careers. However identified, these faculty coordinators and advocates should be recognized by the central campus administration for their efforts to promote the emerging strategic partnership.

- Demonstrable mutual benefit. Strategic international partnerships must offer ongoing mutual benefits to both institutions. They should add value to both institutions involved by increasing their capacity to do cutting-edge research, providing unique educational opportunities for their students, opening new funding streams, leveraging existing and creating new corporate relations, and enhancing their brand names and recognition around the world. Such benefits need not be financial, or even tangible, but they should be measurable and demonstrable. As with any strategic planning exercise, metrics for success should be developed, along with baseline and future goal levels for these metrics. Some of these may include numbers of students and faculty directly participating in the partnership, increased student diversity and inclusion of demographic groups traditionally underserved in international education, numbers of joint grant proposals and funded joint research awards, co-authored publications in peer-reviewed journals or presentations at national and international scholarly conferences, and joint patent applications.

- <u>Sustainability.</u> Successful strategic international partnerships will evolve over time. The various collaborative activities undertaken should eventually be self-sustaining. Collaborative research should continue through external funding, ideally from sources that are available because of the partnership. Cooperative educational activities should be sustained by fees assessed to the participants, paired where possible with potential subsidies by government direct financial aid programs, student mobility grants, or foundation and donor scholarships. Initial investments by the central administrative leadership at the partner institutions should come in the form of seed funding to facilitate initial interactions between faculty and international education administrators at the partner institutions. This central financial support should scale down over the first five years or so, as the institutional relationship matures; it can then be shifted to support other emerging strategic partnerships.

Identifying Potential Strategic Partners

Having established goals and expectations for this new model of strategic international partnership, we can look toward identifying partners. We can do this by taking two distinct but related inventories.

First, we should consider the various modes and models of international collaboration that have been employed across our campus. These various collaborative activities can be catalogued based on the core missions of the institution. Thus we consider the various types of collaborative research activities and faculty mobility programs; study abroad, student exchange, and cooperative education programs; outreach initiatives through institutional development, capacity building, and professional training programs, as well as community outreach activities of area studies centers; and corporate partnerships and relationships with strong international components. We identify activities and programs that have been sustained over time, and those that were short-lived, with an eye toward discerning the key factors in their long-term success or failure.

Next, we should review our current and recent-past portfolio of international partnerships. Here we consider the various types of institutions with which we have partnered, the typical length and outcomes of these partnerships, the geographic distribution of the partner institutions, and the number of disciplines/departments, faculty, and students participating in collaborative activities within the partnerships. The goal of these reviews is a set of criteria to be used in identifying potential strategic partners. These criteria will vary from one institution to another, based on particular institutional strategic plans, core missions and values, and current priorities and foci. Characteristics of strong potential partners for strategic collaboration should align with the criteria proposed above, for defining a strategic partnership more generally. They may include:

- Similar scope of activities. Potential partners should be relative peer institutions, similarly focused or comprehensive in their research and educational programs, with at least some shared strengths, as well as some complementary strengths in particular disciplines.

- Historical and existing connections. A survey of past interactions between potential strategic partners will often reveal surprisingly long, if sometimes sporadic, relationships.

- Mutual interest and commitment. The central administrations of potential partners should be equally vested in developing a strategic partnership, and willing to allocate relatively equal amounts of human and financial resources to ensure the partnership's success.

- Compatible administrative structures. The international offices at the partner institutions must be similarly responsive and proactive in advocating for the emerging strategic partnership.

- Faculty connections. Without significant faculty interest and support, the partnership has little chance of success. Initially, these connections can be fostered by holding joint seminars to bring groups of faculty together. Funding travel to enable 15 or 20 key faculty from each side to spend two or three days together, introducing one another to their research, can be fruitful.

- Student interest. The study abroad administrators at potential partner institutions should gauge the level of interest among their students in studying abroad at their particular locales.

- Potential for consortial activities. Strong candidates for potential strategic partnerships will often share other institutional partners in common, providing a facilitated path for developing consortia of institutions with shared collaborative activities. This can be particularly valuable today, when national and transnational government organizations (such as the European Commission) have developed funding programs specifically aimed at supporting consortia of three or more institutions.

- Potential for thematic focus. In addition to considering the geographic distribution of a portfolio of strategic international partnerships, it may be useful to consider focusing particular strategic partnerships on specific themes. These themes should be multi-disciplinary and inclusive enough to maintain a breadth of activities, but they can often focus the attention of both students and faculty who otherwise might not naturally seek to engage with the partner.

- <u>Logistics and practical considerations</u>. Do the academic calendars of the potential partners correspond sufficiently? Are there sufficient language competencies among both students and faculty to make collaboration practical? Is the time difference between the locations of partner institutions conducive or prohibitive for synchronous distance learning/interactions? Is the difference in cost of living between the locations prohibitive for student mobility? Are there safety and risk management concerns?

Conclusion

Defining our concept of strategic international partnerships, and then identifying potential candidates for such partnerships, is central in moving toward intentionality in our international engagements. The specific definitions and identifying criteria can and should vary from institution to institution. The successful strategic partnership profile for a small, private, liberal arts college will look different from that of a large, public research university. But the end goals will likely be similar. We seek to build broad, deep, lasting relationships with true peer institutions around the world. We look for partnerships that infuse all aspects of our institutional cultures and inform all of our core missions and values. We strive for flexible, organic linkages that are responsive to the changing needs, priorities, and opportunities of both the partner institutions and the constituents they serve.

It is commonplace among international education administrators to speak of the transformative nature of international experiences in the lives of our students and faculty. Thoughtful, deliberate, and strategic international partnerships are a means of scaling this transformation up to the level of the institution as a whole. The ideal of a truly transnational university, conducting research that addresses complex global problems and preparing students to be good global citizens and stewards, is within reach. Intentionality in institutional engagement can be a valuable means of attaining that lofty goal.

Chapter Two

MANAGING PARTNERSHIPS OF STRATEGIC IMPORTANCE

ANN B. RADWAN, ASSOCIATE VICE PRESIDENT FOR INTERNATIONAL AFFAIRS,
ST. CLOUD STATE UNIVERSITY

St. Cloud State University (SCSU) began to develop meaningful international institutional relationships about a decade ago. The expansion of the relationships was based on the identification of common interests, mutual benefits, and individuals in each institution who were willing to invest their time and intellectual energies into creating the programs and consequently giving the necessary shape to the relationship.

Initially, all institutional relationships were referred to as "partnerships," a usage that did not recognize the varying depths and breadths of existing relationships, nor were there systematic approaches for determining the potential of the relationships. Consequently, the creation of an operational strategic framework for expanding any relationship to the next level was needed. The categories that St. Cloud State University chose are: Relationships for Specific Purposes (RSP), Partnerships, and Strategic Partnerships. A strategic partnership is officially designated by the Office of the Provost. The factors for distinguishing a "strategic partnership" from a "partnership" include, but are not limited to, the duration of the active relationship, the quality and number of programs/activities developed and implemented with the partner institution, the centrality of the activities to SCSU curricular priorities, and the involvement of diverse disciplines/colleges.

With the categorization of institutional relationships, it has become possible to identify those relationships that have the potential for further development and those that do not. A strategic partnership designation allows each institution to evaluate its international relationships in ways that highlight opportunities and enable both members of the relationship to develop strategies for satisfying their emerging priorities and to identify specific areas for future cooperation. This process allows for new programs to be developed that are mutually satisfying, thereby increasing the probability of sustainability and growth.

According to our definitions, partnerships that have advanced to the next level are strategic partnerships. The processes by which an institutional relationship matures into a complex partnership are dependent on a multiplicity of factors both internal and external to the institutions engaged in the relationship. An external factor that is both relevant and potent is the economic-political relationship between the partner countries. Positive national political and economic relationships often create an environment of interest at both institutions, an environment which includes senior administration and the faculty, enhanced potential for external funding, and expanded opportunities for ancillary grants and research opportunities.

Internal factors and forces also play a role in determining the programmatic composition of the strategic partnership. As universities undergo strategic planning processes, with changes in academic leadership and the redesign of colleges and departments, it is necessary to factor these changes into the design of how the strategic partnership will be administered so that each realignment within the institution does not endanger the sustainability or the vitality of the international relationship. Additionally, positive relationships between senior institutional administrators and a broad base of engaged faculty are required.

Designing a Governing Structure for Strategic Partnerships

A factor to consider: How are the strategic partnerships to be governed? As is often the case, international activities, including institutional relationships, are created and nurtured by one or two faculty members who use their academic interests as the foundation for institutional activities and programs. These relationships are often idiosyncratic and always dependent on the energy and interests of individuals. The challenge is moving from a complex relationship referred to by the name of an individual professor to a relationship focused on the institutional identity.

In response, an International Vision Task Force at SCSU developed a mechanism that is now being piloted. A *Bi-national Steering Committee* has been formed (its structure was extrapolated from that used successfully in countries where the Fulbright program is administered by a bi-national commission or foundation). The bilateral structure of such a governing body will ensure that the interests and priorities of each institution are taken into consideration in the development of programs, and that a senior/junior partner relationship will not emerge. By responding to the priorities of both partners, supportive decisions from senior administrators will be easier to procure, and participating faculty will more readily identify with the academic relevance of the partnership. In turn, they will become willing and creative participants in the development of *next level* programs and opportunities.

The Bi-national Steering Committee should consist of equal numbers of representatives from each strategic partner. The committee should develop its own operational regulations, should be responsible for administering a modest budget funded by both universities by contributions of money or in kind services, and should also conduct program assessments on a regular basis. The Bi-national Steering Committee has two components: an executive committee and a full committee. The executive committee consists of two members from each partner university and includes both administrators and academic faculty. The full committee consists of representatives from colleges/schools/departments/programs/disciplines actively participating in the partnership. The members serve for limited durations to allow for the full integration of an expanding number of campus elements involved in the relationship. Although the members will be chosen on the basis of current activity, their mandate is to represent the strategic partnership, not just a component thereof.

Of constant and seemingly increasing importance is the partners' commitment to providing funding. The acquisition of external resources for sustaining the relationship should be relegated to a position behind the allocation of partner funding for sustaining and growing the relationship. The contributions made to the strategic partnership can and perhaps should take many forms, including but not limited to the allocation of no-cost residential accommodations for the exchange of students and scholars, university-funded travel grants for appropriate faculty and staff, and adjustments to fee structures so that the exchange experience is affordable for the students. Without these supportive commitments, the strategic partnership will become less a dynamic relationship and more of a burden for the partners.

Technology will allow for regular and cost effective meetings of the whole committee and, if funding allows, an annual meeting in alternate countries. Essential to the process is the development of the strategic identity by both institutional partners and the members of the committee. The challenge is to create a working environment that will change particular interests to strategic development.

An essential component of developing an appropriate governance structure aimed at institutionalizing the strategic relationship is the process used to create the structure. In the initial draft of the proposed structure, the partners should review and redraft the documents so that the resulting structure is compatible with the administrative structures of both institutions. This consultative approach underscores and reinforces the nature of the relationship: a strategic venture of co-equal partners. An indirect and somewhat unanticipated benefit of the negotiations is a greater understanding of the internal decision-making processes of each partner university. In the long run, such awareness will have positive repercussions as the strategic partnership progresses, including the evaluation of current programs, the development of new programs, and the positioning of the strategic partnership on the list of priorities of both partners.

During the pilot phase, the Bi-national Steering Committee is principally responsible for identifying an appropriate assessment instrument and conducting an assessment of administrative structures, academic programs, and experiential learning activities. The analysis includes addressing the effectiveness of the identified governance structure: Did the structure allow for institutional responsiveness to opportunities? Was the structure cost effective, and did the structure increase the active participation of faculty/departments/colleges and schools? Even during the early phases of implementing the governance structure, the "corporate cultures" of each partner are such that the choice of the assessment instruments and their implementation will require negotiations between the partners. It is also anticipated that there will be negotiations centered on transparency.

The development of structures designed for supporting strategic partnerships raises the issue of the relationship between those governing the strategic partnership and those governing the partner institutions. Strategic partnerships must be perceived as adding value to each of the partner institutions and to senior administrators who represent each university and who report to boards of trustees and other umbrella entities. Strategic partnerships that become a component of the institutional brand will have a stronger foundation, be more resilient to internal changes in personnel, and enable the academic cone to begin strategic curricular development and scholarly capacity planning. While the benefits of identifiable academic activities will be easier to observe, the benefits of administering complex programs across cultures and within different legal environments will be difficult to measure. As we strive to internationalize U.S. universities, the creation of egalitarian, consultative, and mutually compatible administrative structures is a challenge that ultimately will allow universities to appreciate the different ways in which they can achieve their agreed-on goals.

Chapter Three

MOBILIZING YOUR INSTITUTION FOR STRATEGIC INTERNATIONAL PARTNERSHIPS

HELEN FOSTER, HEAD OF PARTNERSHIP DEVELOPMENT,
THE UNIVERSITY OF NOTTINGHAM

IAN JONES, INTERNATIONAL OFFICER FOR PARTNERSHIP DEVELOPMENT,
THE UNIVERSITY OF NOTTINGHAM

Background

With campuses in China and Malaysia and almost 10,000 international students representing 142 countries at its campuses in the UK, The University of Nottingham has one of the largest groups of international students of any UK university and has a very innovative internationalization strategy.

Despite its global focus, international teaching partnerships did not play a significant part in the university's internationalization strategy until 2008. While university staff taught on its campuses in the UK and in Asia, they tended not to offer Nottingham degree programs in partnership with other institutions, and off-campus delivery was limited to a few self-selecting individual academics. A new internationalization strategy, which launched in 2008, highlighted partnership activity as a priority. In 2007, the University had just seven teaching partnerships worldwide; by March 2011, that number had increased significantly.

This chapter examines how The University of Nottingham has developed its international teaching partnerships' portfolio. It looks at some of the internal barriers to developing international teaching partnerships, including difficulties in securing "buy in" from academic colleagues, and shows how some of these were overcome. Using Nottingham as a case study, this chapter highlights areas of good practice in international teaching partnership development.

Initial Steps

The University of Nottingham recognized that, although a number of successful teaching partnerships had been in operation for many years—particularly off-campus delivery of the Executive MBA and a 2+2 undergraduate Engineering "twinning" program—there was, despite central institutional support, no team dedicated to teaching partnerships.

In 2008, the Partnership Development Team was established and located in the International Office. While the staffing of the Team was limited to a senior manager, an officer, and a part-time administrator, working within a large International Office allowed them to secure support and advice from a range of colleagues with student mobility and international recruitment expertise. The Team's remit is to source, develop, and seek institutional approval for teaching partnerships with educational and/or commercial partners overseas and any of the university's campuses in the United Kingdom, Malaysia, and China. It also seeks to increase opportunities for international teaching partnerships among academic and administrative staff.

At the same time, the University's Management Board decided to transform the existing Collaborative Courses Committee into The Transnational Education Committee. The Pro Vice Chancellor for Internationalization chairs the Committee and reports to the University's Teaching and Learning Committee. Members of the Committee are drawn from faculties and professional services, such as Registry and the Management Information Division. The Committee's terms of reference include both a strategic and operational remit.

The Partnership Development Team and the Transnational Education Committee adopted a three-pronged approach to developing partnerships: "central management-led," "grassroots," and "external profile-raising" initiatives. These measures began in 2008 and implementation remains ongoing.

Central Management-led Initiatives

The establishment of the Transnational Education Committee sent a message to the university community that the development of international teaching partnerships was an institutional priority. The Committee's first job was to devise an overarching set of Transnational Education Guiding Principles that outlined the types of international teaching partnerships the university would concentrate on developing. At the same time, it took on the work of the Collaborative Courses Committee in approving new partnerships with a focus both on academic quality assurance and wider due diligence, including legal and financial approvals.

In order to assure and enhance the quality of partnerships, a dedicated section of the University's Quality Manual was established, complying with the guidelines outlined in the UK's Quality Assurance Agency's Code of Practice on Collaborative Provision. At the same time, the Pro Vice Chancellor proactively led the development of an articulation agreement with a university in China across the Faculty of Arts and the Faculty of Law & Social Sciences. This paved the way for similar, school-led agreements, and again sent a signal to the university community that partnerships were supported and encouraged.

Grassroots Initiatives

The Partnership Development Team undertook a number of internal promotional activities to engage academic staff in schools with the concept of, and approval mechanisms for, international teaching partnerships.

An intranet site was developed that includes: details of the various types of teaching partnerships that the university may seek to enter; a database of all approved partnerships, searchable by country, institution, or school; guidance notes on the establishment of new partnerships; examples of successful partnerships; and podcast interviews with academic staff already involved in partnerships.

Briefing sessions were arranged with senior school management teams to outline the range of international teaching partnerships available and to promote institutional priority markets. The sessions not only were designed as a source of information for the schools, but also gave the Partnership Development Team insight into the priorities of each school and the academic, financial, and administrative barriers to partnership development. Although time consuming, the Team felt that this was one of the best ways to engage senior academic staff. Similarly, the Team attended a number of school "away days" in order to engage the wider academic community.

Internal press releases on new partnerships were disseminated to demonstrate the success of such arrangements and the multiplicity of benefits for both staff members and students. The university's commitment to international teaching partnerships was further exemplified through pump-prime funding that was made available. The Partnership Development Team delivered central information sessions on this type of funding, along with details of funding from external sources such as the British Council and Erasmus Mundus.

Another mechanism for engaging the academic community was the establishment of country/region groups—for example, a Middle East Group, a Europe Group, and a Latin America group. The groups act as informal fora for academic staff interested in research and teaching in particular geographic areas, including discussions on international teaching partnerships.

External Profile-raising Initiatives

As well as working to involve internal stakeholders with teaching partnerships, the Partnership Development Team established a UK-wide International Partnership Development Forum, which is now in its third year. The aim of the Forum is to engage internal audiences with external practitioners in the field in areas of best practice, and also to develop a UK-wide platform for knowledge-sharing. The Forum meets twice a year and has included a range of workshops on the practicalities of developing international partnerships, as well as presentations from guest speakers, including an education lawyer, a country-specific expert, a leader in international quality assurance, academic staff involved in the delivery of international partnerships, and an international speaker with expertise in double/joint doctoral programs.

The International Partnership Development Forum now has a membership of more than 160 practitioners, representing almost all British universities. A spinoff from the Forum has been the development of a UK-wide group on the professional networking website, LinkedIn.

In addition to the Forum, the Team has raised its profile through attending assessment panels for external funding and externally organized study tours in specific countries, speaking at external events, and contributing articles.

The Future

Teaching partnerships between Nottingham and institutions overseas have increased more than five-fold in three years. The vast majority of the partnerships are with the United Kingdom campus only, or with the United Kingdom campus and one or both of the international campuses. None of the partnerships are between an external institution and only the Malaysia and/or China campuses, without involvement from the United Kingdom. One of the challenges facing the Team in the years ahead—and one that many institutions will likely face as the global sector sees a significant increase in international branch campuses—is ensuring that international campuses are fully included in international partnership developments.

The Partnership Development Team at The University of Nottingham sees the key factors for success in developing international teaching partnerships as being:

- Senior management buy-in and support
- Examples of early success
- Clarity about what kinds of partnership the university is willing to develop
- An understanding of the benefits of teaching partnerships, beyond income generation
- The development of clear and quick processes for making decisions on teaching partnerships
- Financial (pump prime) support for partnership developments
- Clear administrative support for partnership developments

Chapter Four

FROM GRAND PLAN TO WORKING WEB, WITH PATIENCE AND FLEXIBILITY: THE UNIVERSITY OF WASHINGTON'S PARTNERSHIP WITH SICHUAN UNIVERSITY

STEVAN HARRELL, PROFESSOR, DEPARTMENT OF ANTHROPOLOGY, UNIVERSITY OF WASHINGTON, SEATTLE

THOMAS M. HINCKLEY, DAVID R.M. SCOTT PROFESSOR OF FOREST BIOLOGY, UNIVERSITY OF WASHINGTON, SEATTLE

The Plan

In 1999, Gretchen Kalonji hatched a grand plan for international collaboration. A theorist of defects in crystalline materials in the University of Washington College of Engineering, Kalonji had recently been appointed by UW President, Richard McCormick, as head of a newly formed International Faculty Council, designed to foster expansion and innovation in UW's relationships with universities in other countries. Kalonji instructed one of the Council's working subcommittees to consider relationships with China, a nation where the University of Washington had a distinguished history of study and research, but few formal institutional partnerships. Relationships developed with Chinese universities would ideally become models for partnerships with universities worldwide.

Working together with members of the China subcommittee, Kalonji resolved to begin with one or two willing partner institutions in China to integrate faculty research, graduate training, and undergraduate education in fields where UW and the partners had similar or complementary strengths. The Chinese university that expressed the strongest support was Sichuan University (SCU) in Chengdu, a university remarkably comparable to UW: both are regional flagship comprehensive universities with many strong programs, particularly in the health sciences, but overall reputations just below those of the elite universities of their respective countries.

Many meetings followed throughout 1999 and 2000 with interested faculty and upper- and middle-level administrators. The plan that emerged was centered on environmental study and research, involving multidisciplinary, multinational, multilevel collaboration to address pressing environmental issues. Faculty would engage in joint research projects with funding from both sides, and these projects would include students from an international exchange at both the undergraduate and graduate levels.

On the undergraduate level, each university would recruit 25 freshmen students for a special program, five each specializing in Materials Science, Civil and Environmental Engineering, Plant Biodiversity, Forest Ecology, and Environmental Social Sciences. In their first two years, students would study their subject areas with a focus on international implications, communicate with each other over the Internet to address research issues, and establish working groups under the direction of program faculty. In their junior years, beginning in 2002-03, students would travel to the partner institution, and in addition to coursework would participate actively in research projects as members of groups that would include faculty, graduate students, and undergraduates from both institutions. Students would pay their home-institution tuition only, essentially funding the education of a student who was visiting their university.

Kalonji secured financial support from the U.S. Department of Education's Fund for the Improvement of Post-Secondary Education (FIPSE), the National Science Foundation (NSF), and the Tools for Transformation Program administered by UW Provost's Office. SCU counterparts secured funding from the Ministry of Education. Classes of freshmen were recruited in 2000; presidents, vice-presidents, administrators, and faculty exchanged visits; and the UW Worldwide Program, designed to be a pilot for a new kind of undergraduate degree, was launched. It achieved orbital velocity when the first class of UW students traveled to Chengdu in June 2002 and the first class of SCU students arrived in Seattle in September.

The graduate level plans were equally visionary. A group of UW faculty, with Kalonji as principal investigator, applied to the NSF for an Integrative Graduate Education and Research Training (IGERT) grant, entitled Multinational Collaborations on Challenges to the Environment (MCCE). Doctoral students in any field could apply for two-year traineeships through this program, as long as their research addressed environmental questions. The grant named SCU as one of nine partner universities, from China, Japan, Vietnam, New Zealand, Namibia, South Africa, and Mozambique.

Trainees in their first year would participate in an interdisciplinary seminar entitled, "Coupled Human, Natural, and Engineering Systems," led by Kalonji with active participation of five co-principal investigators and several other faculty. In the second year, trainees would travel to one of the partner universities to conduct research under the joint direction of UW and host university faculty. Because IGERT funds only U.S. citizens and permanent residents, it was hoped that partner universities or less restricted research grants obtained by UW faculty would fund graduate student participants from partner universities.

Funding for the IGERT was approved in early 2004, and a hastily recruited cohort of doctoral students from Civil and Environmental Engineering, Materials Science, Anthropology, Social Work, Forest Ecology, Earth and Space Sciences, and Biology began their year with an international conference at Friday Harbor Marine Laboratories. It was attended by program directors and, in some cases, rectors or chancellors of the partner universities. After the conference the trainees began their interdisciplinary seminar.

This project would all be held together at the research level, as UW and SCU faculty would apply jointly for regular research grants, which would add to their ability to support graduate students and offer research opportunities for undergraduates. As a pilot project, UW and SCU linked with Jiuzhaigou National Park, a site in northern Sichuan that combined the research interests of biologists, interested in biodiversity and conservation; geologists and hydrologists, interested in travertine landscapes; environmental engineers, interested in sustainable infrastructure that could support almost three million tourists a year; archaeologists, interested in the history of the landscape and its human uses; and cultural anthropologists, interested in the culture of the area's native Tibetan community and its confrontation with the aforementioned tourists. UW also approached North Cascades National Park in Washington as a possible partner in what would become the Jiuzhaigou International Laboratory. Jiuzhaigou would become an example for similar multinational, multidisciplinary collaborative team research, which could be extended to other sites in China and eventually to other countries.

Despite our planning, neither the undergraduate nor the graduate program turned out the way it was envisioned. Nevertheless, our partnership with Sichuan University turned out to be sustainable. We worked through problems, evolved new structures, built confidence in each other, and ended up with a workable web of long-term relationships.

Problems and Compromises

The original plan was not practical for five reasons. These problems moved both the undergraduate and graduate wings of the program away from their original conceptions, but allowed at least the undergraduate portion to sustain itself, and to establish a foundation from which other avenues of cooperation have radiated.

Differences in Undergraduate Educational Systems

The idea of undergraduates' participation in research has been growing at American universities; for example, UW's annual undergraduate research symposium, initiated in 1998 with 70 participants, has grown to over 800 posters and presentations in 2011. Indeed, the trend toward undergraduate research was one impetus behind the idea of the exchange program. But the idea was foreign to the Chinese system, in which undergraduate education involves little research. SCU faculty were, however, surprisingly receptive to the idea of involving undergraduates in their laboratory, field, and museum research work.

A bigger problem was the expectations of students from the two countries. American students expected to be led through a series of assignments and heavy readings throughout the semester. Chinese students, in contrast, were accustomed to listening to lectures and memorizing the maximum amount of material to recite on a final examination, with no assignments, no reading, and no writing. In other words, American students worked more, but tended to slack when there was nothing due, while Chinese students were overwhelmed by the amount of work expected in an American class, but did not procrastinate.

The final problem was that Chinese students, particularly those in biology and engineering, could enroll in regular classes at UW, but very few UW students had the linguistic ability to enroll in regular SCU classes. They spent most of their class time studying Chinese languages, making the experience more like an ordinary overseas language-and-culture program than the research-centered program we had originally envisioned. In spite of these compromises, students on both sides of the exchange regularly participated in either faculty-supervised or independent research.

Differential Interest in and Ability to Fund Study Abroad

In 2000, studying abroad was a dream for most college students in China. It was considered a ticket to elite status in China or abroad. But even with the home-tuition exchange, few Chinese families could afford to pay the expenses of a year's study in America or Europe. As a result, we offered travel stipends and living scholarships for SCU students coming to Seattle. In these circumstances, SCU selected 600 incoming students, gave them an English test, and selected 60 for oral interviews, finally choosing 30 to compete for the 25 places promised by UW.

By contrast, most American students rarely thought about spending a year studying in China, even though it was within the financial reach of most American college students. And few of them knew any Chinese languages. Through a mailing by the UW admissions office, we managed to find about 18 among the 3,000 entering freshmen who expressed interest in a year-long China adventure. We funded a special section of Chinese 101 in addition to teaching a seminar entitled "Learning about China through the Environment." But we were still short of the 25 students that we needed to make the home-tuition exchange work.

In the first year of the exchange, the UW side was so determined to have enough students pay UW tuition that students originally signed up to go to Sichuan in 2003 ended up going a year early, and other students were recruited who had not been through the two years of preparation. The SARS epidemic in spring 2003 further discouraged U.S. students and their parents, so that only five qualified students were interested in going to Sichuan in 2003-04. Similar imbalances continued through the years, with the numbers of UW students varying from five in 2003-04 to sixteen in 2007-08, the year of the Sichuan earthquake. Eventually, the solution was to reduce the expectations of SCU, supplement home-tuition with tuition waivers obtained through other channels at UW, move the numbers in the program to a more sustainable basis of an average of 12 per year in each direction, and begin to draw home-tuition money from UW students participating in a summer language program at SCU, jointly administered with Arizona State University.

Unsustainable Funding

For UW Worldwide to become a permanent feature of UW education and research, it would have to be funded permanently. But all the funds secured for both the undergraduate and graduate programs were one-time, nonrenewable federal and internal grants. Despite the fact that the applications for each of them made vague promises that funding would be picked up locally, this became increasingly unrealistic as UW's state support continued to diminish throughout the decade. It is possible that if Kalonji had remained at UW, she would have been able to devote the time and energy to securing continued outside support from other sources. However, she left UW in January 2005.

By this time, most of the funds for the undergraduate program and for the institutional relationships had been spent, even though the IGERT was just getting going. IGERTs are notoriously difficult to renew, particularly when the home institution does not provide much support from its own funds. The associated faculty members who took over the programs—Thomas Hinckley for the IGERT and the Jiuzhaigou International Laboratory, and Stevan Harrell for the undergraduate exchange—had full schedules of teaching and research, and little time to spend on writing proposals. The IGERT program ceased to exist when the funding ran out in 2010. The undergraduate program continues on a shoestring budget, with no guarantee that it can continue beyond the 2011-12 academic year, though there are possibilities for continued funding. Research continues at Jiuzhaigou, though on a much looser model.

Lack of Faculty Incentives

It is fair to say that university faculty are driven primarily by their own research interests, and are attracted to any program on the basis of whether it increases their opportunities to pursue and fund those interests. At the beginning, faculty at both UW and SCU saw possibilities for funding in the UW Worldwide initiative. There were, however, two problems. One was with the top-down nature of the initiative. In order for multinational, multidisciplinary research teams to work, these teams needed to emerge out of the research interests of the faculty who formed them. Despite the willingness to attend a few meetings and take trips to Jiuzhaigou and other possible research sites, few faculty members found opportunities to further their own research, and few if any were interested in switching research directions in order to participate in this program.

The second was that this program took time that was not directly connected to faculty research interests. Participating faculty would need to spend more time mentoring undergraduate students and participating in joint meetings, classes, and seminars than the commitments to research, publication, and promotion would allow. As a result, faculty involvement fell off over the years. There were five co-PIs and fifteen associated faculty on the original IGERT, of whom eight participated in some its activities, and only two saw the program through to its end.

Inconsistent University-level Support

Before Kalonji left, the original co-architect of the International Faculty Council, University President Richard McCormick, had in late 2002 assumed the Presidency of Rutgers University in New Jersey. In June 2004, there was a new President (Mark Emmert) and, in June 2005, a new Provost (Phyllis Wise) was appointed. Both President Emmert and Provost Wise were interested in China and often highlighted the UW Worldwide Program as an example of a future direction they sought. They were not, however, in a position to offer further internal funding for any of the programs.

A newly formed office of Global Affairs was initiated in late 2004; however, this office had minimal funding and observed that the Worldwide program was surviving, however precariously, on its own. Campus-level interests in UW Worldwide waned as other more pressing issues emerged. The Office of Global Affairs did, however, supply funding for the 2011 Healthcare Disparities Institute. As this article goes to press, the role and the existence of the Office of Global Affairs are undergoing a university-wide review, and the outcome is uncertain; one thing that is certain is that the Worldwide Program will have to rely on external funding. Possibilities include the Confucius Institute of Washington.

What Happened Instead

Despite these problems, UW Worldwide has established a strong and multi-stranded relationship with Sichuan University. This has happened because the relationship has shifted from a top-down to a bottom-up orientation, because a few individual faculty at both institutions have managed to combine undergraduate and graduate education with research in creative ways, and because the original programs have resulted in growing institutional trust between the two universities. In these conditions, the original three programs have survived in modified form, and other exchanges between the universities have developed.

<u>Modifications of the Original Programs</u>

MCCE IGERT. After Kalonji left UW in 2005, the new principal investigator, Thomas Hinckley, made the radical decision to abandon the model of the IGERT as a comprehensive institutional bridge at the university level, and to redirect funds and efforts to individual trainees' experiences at partner institutions abroad. Although it took until the third and final cohort of IGERT trainees, recruited for the 2006-07 academic year, to get the model right, the process resulted in important pedagogical insights that can be applied elsewhere. The expensive, high-level meetings were cancelled, and the money that was saved was put into a fund that would support individual trainees' exploratory travel to partner institutions and eventually aid in their longer research stays at any university outside the U.S., not just the original partners.

In addition, funds were saved for three group trips to conduct short-term interdisciplinary research abroad, two led by Hinckley and SCU faculty in Jiuzhaigou, and one led by limnologist Michael Brett and native education activist Linda Tuhiwai Smith at the University of Auckland and other sites in New Zealand. The original model of the interdisciplinary seminar led by multiple faculty was replaced in the third year with a three-quarter seminar organized and led by graduate students from an earlier cohort with guidance from the two lead faculty.

The majority of MCCE fellows completed research projects overseas; three of them did significant research through SCU advisers, two at Jiuzhaigou and one at another site in Sichuan. MCCE thus provided a valuable interdisciplinary and international component to the education of graduate students in many fields, even though it did not, as originally intended, serve as groundwork for a large multi-institutional structure.

Jiuzhaigou International Laboratory. The Laboratory was formally established in 2005, with SCU, University of California, Jiuzhaigou National Park (JZG), and Yosemite National Park as partners. The University of Washington was added at our request. Sichuan University Faculty, particularly Professors Tang Ya and Zeng

Zongyong of the College of Life Sciences, have been tireless in promoting international research at JZG. Two teams of Jiuzhaigou staff members have been hosted for months-long traineeships in the U.S. A UW post-doctoral scholar and MCCE IGERT alumna recently spent six months in Jiuzhaigou carrying out research on historical geomorphic processes. Hinckley's three short-term team visits to JZG produced significant research initiatives on meadow ecology, bamboo growth, and particularly on archaeological research that has thoroughly revised our understanding of the history of human habitation in the area. Professor Tang has provided partial funding for many of these joint and individual efforts.

The Jiuzhaigou International Laboratory has thus provided another example of adaptive collaboration and institutional trust-building, resulting in significant research experiences for faculty, graduates, and undergraduates, despite (or perhaps because of) the fact that it has deviated from the original plan. Research visits in 2008 and 2010 further cemented the relationship and have led to expanded research programs, including one between Professors Tang Ya and Dan Jaffe (UW – Bothell), who works on environmental pollution.

Undergraduate Exchange Program. The undergraduate exchange program continues, with the tenth cohorts of students scheduled to travel to Chengdu and Seattle in September 2011. It is, however, a different program from what we initially envisioned. We had originally committed unprecedented amounts of faculty time and effort to the first exchange class in 2000. As we began to cultivate the second exchange class, we realized that we had committed unsustainable amounts of faculty resources to the program—teaching loads would increase with little or no increase in either student credit hours or student numbers, an untenable pattern in a public university that allocated funds according to the number of students taught. We thus curtailed our recruitment and training program.

It had also become clear by the time of Kalonji's departure in 2005 that the original model was unsustainable, primarily because it did not recognize the international asymmetries discussed earlier. The current program has settled into a comfortable, low-cost model that takes advantage of the asymmetries rather than fighting them. SCU continues to recruit its classes as freshmen, taken from their Honors College. Because SCU exchange students take regular classes at UW, and because UW class enrollments are being squeezed by the lack of state support for the university, we are not always able to accommodate the students from fields where SCU would like to send them. This has resulted in negotiation and compromise, but students from archaeology, civil and environmental engineering, materials science, urban planning, and various fields of biology have continued to be successful in Seattle. Students take regular UW classes and attach themselves to laboratories or field-research projects run by UW faculty. In addition, because scholarship support has run out, only students whose families can support their living expenses for a year in the U.S. are currently able to join the program. We are working toward permanent scholarship funding that will remedy this situation.

UW cannot realistically recruit freshmen, because U.S. students rarely plan anything two years in advance. Rather, we recruit students in fall and winter quarters of the year before they plan to go to Chengdu, and allow students from any major to go, as long as we judge that they will be able to benefit from the experience and not cause trouble. They take a one-quarter introductory seminar where they write proposals for their research projects. There were not enough students who had our original requirement of two years of Chinese language, but we also had disastrous results sending students with no previous language study. Hence, we compromised on a requirement of one year previous to departure.

Results of this modified strategy have been surprisingly positive. In immediate terms, approximately 58 students from SCU and 27 returned students from UW have presented their research at UW's annual Undergraduate Research Symposium, while 45 SCU students have gone on to master's or doctoral programs in China, Hong Kong, North America, and Europe, and several have received their doctorates, four of them from UW. A milestone was reached in fall 2010 when Dr. Wang Yuanyuan (Ph.D., Hong Kong Chinese University) returned to Sichuan University as a junior faculty member in the College of History and Humanities. U.S. students pursue a slightly less direct career trajectory on the whole, but two have obtained their doctorates and several their master's degrees. Others have gone on to medical and legal education, or to careers in China or involving China.

A positive secondary spinoff from the undergraduate exchange has been research activity in southern Sichuan Province in the Baiwu watershed. Some twenty UW undergraduates, several UW graduate students, two faculty members, and several undergraduate and graduate students from Sichuan University have spent anywhere from days to months completing both individual and joint research projects. These projects have formed the foundation for undergraduate theses, honors projects, and several refereed publications.

Spinoffs

At least as significant as the survival, albeit in modified form, of the three original components of UW Worldwide is the reservoir of mutual confidence and the web of connections between UW and SCU that have allowed other exchanges and collaborations to take place. These are possible because of the working relationships we have established among faculty and middle-level administrators at the two universities. Presidents, vice-presidents, and provosts have traveled and attended meetings, and we believe that our efforts have their support and confidence. But the support and confidence have not traveled down to those of us in the trenches; rather, the senior administrators gave their cautious imprimaturs at the beginning, and then allowed faculty and mid-level administrators to build up the vital networks of trust. These networks have allowed us to conduct such activities as:

- Summer Chinese language instruction at SCU. UW has teamed with Arizona State to send approximately 20 students from each American university for intensive second, third, and fourth-year Chinese language study at SCU.

- Administrators' workshops at UW. SCU has sent four teams of mid-level administrators (deans, directors, associate deans, etc.) to UW for intensive, three-week workshops.

- Urban planning and earthquake rebuilding research. Professor Li Wei of SCU College of Architecture and Professor Daniel Abramson of UW College of Built Environments have conducted research on sustainable rebuilding and tourism in earthquake-ravaged areas of the Min River Valley north of Chengdu.

- Confucius Institute. Because of our longstanding relationship, Sichuan University proposed that we jointly establish a Confucius Institute, funded by the Chinese Government, to teach Chinese language in other countries. We formed the Confucius Institute of Washington in 2010 as a collaborative effort among Sichuan University, the Chinese National Office for Teaching Chinese as a Foreign Language (Hanban), the Washington State Office of Superintendent of Public Instruction, the Seattle Public Schools, and the University of Washington.

- Health Disparities Summer Institute. The UW Office of Global Affairs is sponsoring its first joint summer institute in China; we chose health disparities because primary care medicine, nursing, and public health are UW's strongest areas, and Huaxi Medical College of Sichuan University is a leader in primary care in China. The institute will involve workshops led by distinguished faculty from UW and SCU, and will take place in Chengdu in August 2011.

Lessons Learned

What began as a grand plan has evolved into a working web. The vision of the founder was brilliant but unsustainable. Through flexible accommodation on both sides, it led to a web of relationships that has continued to expand and to provide mutual benefits to the two universities. A few principles that we have learned over the last 12 years include:

1. Be flexible and adaptive. The original plan lacked realism, but the principle behind its vision—that international collaboration is not only beneficial but necessary—has been vindicated even as we have altered the structure.

2. Develop an appropriate level of asymmetry, while maintaining reciprocity. Different institutions, especially those embedded in different national traditions, have different requirements. What is important is not that the same goods and services travel both directions, but that each side respects the other's needs, accommodates them when possible, and recognizes that the other side is trying to do the same.

3. Work through organic connections. The original plan unintentionally made light of the fact that faculty, students, and administrators at both universities were embedded in institutional cultures that change only slowly, and that faculty are research-driven. Plenty of connections could be established through organic links based on mutual research interests and mutual educational interests, without inventing new structures from the top down.

4. Funding is important, but not everything should be funding driven. Our current activities have little funding of their own, though they do parasitize funding for other projects in creative and productive ways. But we have found out that we can do a lot with a little. Not nothing, but a little.

5. Dream big, but still celebrate what has happened. Recognize that academic conventions exist; don't scorn them, but don't be bound by them. There are many ways to measure success.

Thus two large, regional, comprehensive universities have established a working relationship based on mutual interest, organic connections, and the slow buildup of trust. The various programs that we are now conducting have only a moderate degree of substantive connection between them. The important connection is that we have a connection, and one that we trust will continue.

Chapter Five

IDENTIFYING AND SELECTING APPROPRIATE PARTNER INSTITUTIONS

SABINE C. KLAHR, DIRECTOR OF THE INTERNATIONAL CENTER,
UNIVERSITY OF UTAH IN SALT LAKE CITY

Introduction

Among the most important tasks in developing effective international partnerships is finding the best match for your institution. The question is: What constitutes the best match for your particular institution, and what are the expectations for the partnership? Partnerships are effective only when they achieve the outcomes as outlined in the MOU. Therefore, the first question to consider in evaluating a potential partner university is whether your counterparts at this institution have similar expectations and desire similar outcomes for students and faculty. Also, does the potential partner university place the same importance on the partnership as your institution? Is there potential for developing multidimensional initiatives with the other institution? It is also critical to assess whether you have faculty at your institution who will be engaged in the partnership. Long-term engagement by multiple faculty members is vital to implement and sustain activities.

Assessing the Purpose of a Partnership

Generally, I believe institutions put too much emphasis on finding partners that are similar in type. For example, at my previous institution, a university that is a liberal arts women's college at the undergraduate level, the only partnerships that existed when I arrived were with other small women's universities in Asia. This restricted the institution's potential in Europe and other parts of the world where women's colleges do not exist and where my counterparts may not be aware of the mission and potential of women's colleges or liberal arts colleges in general. I think it is preferable to focus on the feasibility and purpose of specific types of activities, while keeping in mind the value that some universities place on external factors such as international rankings and the desire to partner with institutions of similar or higher ranking.

In my experience, it is most important to select partner institutions that can accommodate your institution's needs and view potential activities with your institution as critical to accomplishing specific goals. For the purposes of this chapter, I will use Spain as an example of a country where your institution may see the need to develop a partnership for a bilateral student exchange. Students at your institution may have the need to study courses in their major in English while improving their Spanish language skills.

Therefore, it would be critical to find a partner university that 1) offers courses in similar academic disciplines in English, 2) offers a Spanish language and culture program for international students, and 3) sees demand from their Spanish students for exchange programs in the U.S. In addition, it would be important to determine if the Spanish students' English language skills are sufficient to study in the U.S. Most critical is determining whether the potential partner institution has a need to partner with your institution. It has to be a mutually and equally beneficial partnership; otherwise, activities may never be implemented or may fizzle out due to a lack of urgency in making the partnership work.

The Process of Selecting a Partner University

As mentioned earlier, faculty engagement is vital; therefore, a first step would be to consult with faculty who teach Spanish language courses as well as those in academic disciplines whose students would be most likely to study abroad in Spain. Faculty members may know of universities of interest in Spain and may even have colleagues at Spanish institutions who could be helpful in moving the partnership along. I would also consult with colleagues at other universities who have established partnerships in the desired location.

Once a shortlist of institutions has been created, I would establish contact with my counterparts at these institutions to assess interest, support services for exchange students, existing partnerships the institution may have in the U.S., courses offered in English, details of the Spanish language and culture program for international students, and any other relevant information. Once interest is expressed, it is helpful to meet colleagues from potential partner universities face-to-face to discuss all details. This can be done at a conference or as part of a site visit. Since site visits to multiple potential partner universities may not be affordable, a meeting at a conference is often the best option.

Ultimately, prior to implementing activities, a site visit is necessary. It is best for a small delegation to conduct the visit, including the head of international programs or education abroad and several faculty members. It may also be beneficial for the Chief Academic Officer or President of your institution to participate in a site visit as the partnership is being developed, especially if an agreement-signing ceremony is important to the partnering institutions. A visit from the top administration signals the importance and value an institution places on the cooperation, thus making it a powerful driver for implementation.

International partnerships often develop from existing faculty contacts rather than through the strategic process described above. In this case, it is important to evaluate whether the partnership could be expanded beyond the faculty members' interactions with a colleague and beyond the research project on which they may be collaborating. The initial research collaboration itself may be long-term and sustainable, and potentially evolve to include graduate student research exchanges, joint grant and publication development, capacity building, international development projects, technology transfer, etc. The next step would be to assess whether the potential partner university could be suitable for student and faculty exchanges, joint/dual degree development, collaborative teaching, hosting of faculty-led short-term programs, and other initiatives of broader scope.

If faculty members' collaboration with colleagues at a university abroad is focused on their own research with scant potential for implementing initiatives that would draw in other faculty and students, there is little reason to establish a partnership. Developing and maintaining partnerships over time requires resources: administrators' time and funding for site visits, hosting colleagues from the partner university, etc. Activities and partnerships based on one faculty member's involvement tend to fizzle out when the research funding and focus shift to other projects or when faculty members who started the partnership leave the university. Also, single purpose partnerships tend to not be conducive to transformative initiatives for the institution and offer little potential to advance the internationalization strategy.

Potential Challenges to Identifying a Partner

Economic and financial inequality can be a significant barrier to developing a partnership and should be carefully evaluated from the perspective of funding or in-kind contributions, especially for students. For example, a student exchange with a partner university in a developing country may not be feasible if your institution cannot provide low-cost or free housing for incoming exchange students. Alternatively, the potential partner university may be in a location that is too expensive for most of your students in terms of airfare and living expenses; therefore, the exchange will never be in balance or never really get off the ground. There are also situations in which your institution may not have sufficient funding for faculty to travel to the partner university to implement a complex initiative, such as a dual degree program, that would require the careful evaluation of curriculum, teaching practices, and student selection at the partner university. These issues should be evaluated as the details of a potential partnership are developed.

Conclusion

Generally, as partnerships are being considered, the opportunities and challenges should be evaluated. Opportunities may constitute overlapping or complementary research expertise and facilities, the capacity for student and faculty exchanges at each institution, an interest and need for a dual-degree program, interest among faculty to co-teach classes via distance technology, and many others. Challenges may include lack of capacity to support student needs, a poor academic match in the disciplines offered at each institution, engagement by one faculty member with little opportunity for expansion, lack of an equal need for the partnership, and funding issues for students and faculty. Each potential partnership should be assessed according to these types of opportunities and challenges as well as the transformative potential and impact on advancing internationalization for the institution. In the end, the success of developing a partnership may simply depend on the personalities of the individuals engaged in the process at both institutions. As in any process involving human interaction, colleagues at the partner institutions may simply "understand each other" and establish a strong bond and communication from the beginning, leading to the development of a solid foundation for the partnership.

Chapter Six

DEFINING YOUR X-FACTOR FOR HEALTHY COMMUNICATION IN TRANSNATIONAL PARTNERSHIPS

ADRIA L. BAKER, ASSOCIATE VICE PROVOST FOR INTERNATIONAL EDUCATION,
RICE UNIVERSITY

International partnerships are relationships that parallel personal friendships and affil-iations, yet on an institutional and cross-cultural level. Both organizational relationships and personal friendships manage complex and dynamic variables that influence communication due to: 1) the distinct personalities of both parties, 2) unique past experiences, 3) the goals and outcomes being sought from the relationship by each partner, and 4) language and cultural implications. On an institutional level, we also must factor in the complexities of each partner's accepted business practices, including communication mores within each establishment.

Healthy relationships are commonly tied to open communication. Given the intricacy of intercultural communication, however, achieving healthy communica-tion between international partners can be challenging. Building communicative clarity in transnational collaborations takes time, energy, flexibility, clarity of purpose, and patience. Moreover, each cross-national partnership must seek and nurture a unique and strategic program factor that sets it apart from every other international exchange program.

International relationships are ever-changing. The partnership can alter as a result of transitions in the personnel managing the programs, institutional priority modifications, financial restraints, or contemporary sociopolitical events around the world, particularly in the countries of the partners. A one-size-fits-all approach for achieving and maintaining strong communication between partners is not feasible due to the complex variables that define alliance relationships. Therefore, a strong foundation in communication must have built-in flexibility passageways to adjust to unexpected changes.

All international collaborations require a great deal of groundwork whereby the stakeholders should clarify their primary goals and motivations. Certain questions to answer within one's institution and then with one's international partner include:

1. What do we seek as our principal outcome? What about our partner? Do the outcomes overlap? Where can we complement each other?

2. What are my institutional limitations in this project? What are my partner's restrictions? How can we work around our limitations in the agreement? Can the partnership counterbalance our limitations?

Key Problems That Can Derail Transnational Communication

Trust is vital in any healthy relationship. Establishing trust with an international partner in the beginning stages depends on: 1) positive recommendations from respected parties, 2) observing your partner's collaborative record with other groups, and 3) participating in focused projects that can lead to larger and more multifaceted ones. Trust builds when expectations are consistently met, and is lost when a partner perceives the opposite has happened.

A perceived lack of efficiency also hinders any institutional partnership. Even if a great amount of work has been accomplished on the partner's side, there may be lack of communication as to what has been done. The impression that the work is unbalanced and unshared will ultimately damage the partnership or lead to a breakdown.

While working on a joint international project, my office faced efficiency issues that impacted our level of trust. In the end, the collaborative project was short-lived. My group felt that we were providing the bulk of the preparation time and program cost on the joint workshop trainings. However, when the workshops were presented, there was little or no time for my office staff to present their ideas. My group had believed we were participating in a project that reflected equal-work and equal-participation time, but our partner's group had envisioned that they were responsible only for giving the presentation of the training, and not for assisting with the administration and organization of the project. Had we defined the unique factor and outcome that both parties sought during the planning stages, a more collaborative product could have resulted.

A further example of how perceived inefficiency affected trust was when our international partner repeatedly changed the terms of our agreement, including the dates of the program, costs, and agreed-on activities. Moreover, our partner negotiated the changes seemingly to benefit their end only. When our institution sought to clarify issues with our collaborators, we learned that our partners would not provide answers to questions that they did not want to say "no" to, since the direct negative seemed too harsh. In spite of these challenges, this program has continued to grow. We have learned to counterweigh our communication and expectation differences. We seek to compensate for their changes, and do what we can to anticipate and address in advance any possible adjustment our partner may pursue.

Key Solutions for Positive Communication in Transnational Relationships

As mentioned earlier, clarifying one's purpose and expected outcomes for the joint venture is crucial. It is also vital to ensure that one's own institution will benefit from the endeavors. Equally important is to communicate to one's international partner that they too should correspondingly benefit from the collaboration.

Further, international partners should seek and communicate the unique factor that defines the project and relationship. In most cases, the factor will be how the partners can develop "community" with the participants. Definitions of "community" vary widely and may include: 1) how the participants create knowledge together, 2) an active academic learning setting, 3) service-learning projects, or 4) openness and friendship between partners.

We found in our international partnerships that if our communication included only facts and efficient program planning, then our international partners were less responsive, which in turn caused the work to move more slowly. However, when we included aspects of developing a relationship and building community between our two groups, the response rate was much higher. We built trust simply by inquiring about our partners' families; as a result, our transnational communication and planning became more efficient. In addition to achieving the expected program outcomes, the collaboration evolved into a shared relationship between the partners.

All colleagues value verbal and written expressions of appreciation. Written expressions of gratitude may include examples of things that a partner has done that have been particularly helpful. One international partner told us that his institution's higher administration places high priority on those organizations that explicate carefully the details of the collaborative program, instead of simply offering a general overview. Their expression of appreciation to our institution for expounding on the programmatic particulars, curriculum goals, and expected outcomes helped to increase the numbers of visitors they send to our short-term educational programs.

In essence, our international partner expressed gratitude in two ways: 1) directly through writing, and 2) indirectly through offering enhanced numbers and more collaborative programs. The latter was the ultimate expression of appreciation from our partner's point of view. Although we were unable to accommodate the increase at that time, our group valued their gesture of appreciation.

Understanding international partners' holidays and celebrations is important for positive transnational communication. When our university closed for our winter break and holiday celebrations, we let our international partners know that there would be a delay in responding to them. However, at one point we nearly expressed concern about our partner's lack of response after we hadn't heard from them, without realizing that it was during one of their significant holidays. Fortunately, we checked the dates of their holidays and refrained from expressing concern. Overall, the timing for communicating certain requests needs to be carefully considered.

Seeking feedback is helpful for positive communication. However, it is often difficult to provide negative feedback to one's international partner. The concern is that the feedback could either become lost in the cultural differences and expression, or result in hurt feelings that could affect the relationship. Offering choices as a means to seek input and answers can be perceived as less confrontational and more objective.

Humor, if used appropriately, can serve as a great tool for bridging communication in international collaborations. However, utilizing humor can be extremely sensitive, and only those who are deeply familiar with the context of the humor, and the nuances of the language, will be able to use it effectively. In a recent collaboration with an international partner, our conversations became tense, which negatively affected the joint project. Once we came up with a friendly nickname that reflected the leader's close association with our community, the difficult communication decreased and we were able to move forward with the project. In essence, our upbeat and humorous nickname became a positive tool for building a closer relationship, creating a greater sense of "community" between our groups.

International partners should believe that their collaborators will defend one another if a question were to arise. Clearly, this reflects trust based on the integrity of the partners. In an international training program, our international partner's integrity had been brought to question in public. When our organization defended our joint decision and expressed our unquestionable support for our international collaborator, not only were they grateful, but the relationship between the two groups intensified, and our commitment to expanding programs has grown.

Expressing kindness is requisite, as it is the universal bridge for all positive relationships. Since international collaborative programs can be threatened by cultural differences, potential misunderstandings, and failed expectations, kindly treatment in all communications will lead to constructive outcomes. My office dealt with a partner whom we considered was pushing their needs beyond what was acceptable or balanced from our standpoint. In one particular situation, we could not provide the services that were being asked of us, and we had to decline the request. Although the partner was disappointed and expressed worries due to pressures from their government to move forward, kindness prevailed throughout the negotiations. In the end, we were able to offer alternatives, and they conceded as well. Overall, despite disagreements about a shared program or policy between international associates, how needs are expressed is generally more important than what those needs are.

Gift-giving is generally a positive cross-cultural communication tool when used properly. However, caution is advised as there are many underlining meanings and rituals associated with giving gifts. Nonetheless, a simple present can go a long way to conveying appreciation. In particular, a souvenir representing one's own region or institution is a strong expression of friendship. The gift is an illustration of thoughtfulness, which can carry partners through tense or awkward moments in transnational program collaborations. It is important that gift-giving represents an expression of appreciation and thoughtfulness, not a manipulation tool to which the partner feels indebted.

Finally, it is important that international collaborators support one another and know that their relationship is supported from the highest levels of their institutions. International partners who clearly communicate their administration's endorsement to their counterpart build in a stronger reinforcement of trust.

Conclusion

With each international partnership, a sense of "community" needs to be created. How the relationship develops varies based on the sought outcomes and objectives that the parties have identified for their joint project. Sometimes we are fortunate and inadvertently discover the factors that create a unique transnational relationship. Leaving the relationship up to fate, however, is not recommended. Therefore, discovering and defining this unique factor should be part of the original planning stages of the collaborative program. The x-factor of any transnational partnership should be the central issue that allows for excellent international and cross-cultural collaboration, communication, and understanding.

REFERENCES

Althen, G., & Bennett, J. (2003). *American ways: A cultural guide to the United States of America* (2nd ed.). Boston, MA: Intercultural Press.

Andrade, M. S., & Evans, N. W. (2009). *International students: Strengthening a critical resource.* Washington, DC: American Council on Education.

Green, M. F., & Hill, B. A. (2005). *Building a strategic framework for comprehensive internationalization.* Washington, DC: American Council on Education.

Hill, B., & Green, M. (2008). *A guide to internationalization for chief academic officers.* Washington, DC: American Council on Education.

Hudzig, J. K. (2011). *Comprehensive internationalization: From concept to action.* E-Publication by NAFSA: Association of International Educators. Retrieved from http://www.nafsa.org/uploadedFiles/NAFSA_Home/Resource_Library_Assets/Publications_Library/2011_Comprehen_Internationalization.pdf

Morrison, T., & Conaway, W. A. (2006). *Kiss, bow, or shake hands: How to do business in sixty countries* (2nd Ed.). Avon, MA: Adams Media, a division of F+W Media, Inc.

Williams, D., Baxton, M., & Watkins, R. (2010). *AACRAO international guide: A resource for international education professionals.* Washington, DC: American Association of Collegiate Registrars and Admissions Officers.

Chapter Seven

USING GLOBAL GATEWAY OFFICES AS A MODEL FOR EXPANDING INTERNATIONAL PARTNERSHIPS

WILLIAM I. BRUSTEIN, VICE PROVOST FOR GLOBAL STRATEGIES AND INTERNATIONAL AFFAIRS, THE OHIO STATE UNIVERSITY

MAUREEN E. MILLER, DIRECTOR OF COMMUNICATIONS, OFFICE OF INTERNATIONAL AFFAIRS, THE OHIO STATE UNIVERSITY

When E. Gordon Gee, President of The Ohio State University, stepped off the plane in Shanghai, China, in June 2010, he knew that a significant transformation was about to take place, one that would require the support of the entire institution. Opening the first Global Gateway office in Shanghai would expand Ohio State's collaborations internationally and forge new partnerships with a multitude of audiences, thus enhancing the university's research, teaching, and engagement mission.

We have entered an era in which internationalizing universities is fast becoming the norm, broadening opportunities for students, faculty teaching and research, and connecting with institutions of higher education and businesses whose strengths complement their own. In order to enhance their relationships across the oceans, U.S. universities have begun opening their doors in other parts of the world, which have included small liaison offices that focus on recruiting international students and others that have invested on a larger scale by developing branch campuses.

As Ohio State methodically planned to expand its global reach, the development of Global Gateways, or smaller, multifunctional offices, proved the best approach, providing the university more flexibility and offering new and unique ways in which to build partnerships with a wide variety of constituencies. The Gateway concept was born out of the need to be more strategic in the university's international engagement. The idea of establishing a physical presence in key locations around the world would enable Ohio State to develop broader and deeper ties. Ohio State looked at a variety of Gateway models, including building "brick and mortar" campuses, but this concept was not a good fit for the mission of a public land grant university. Building a campus would take a significant capital investment and would limit Ohio State's ability to expand to more than one international location. Opening Global Gateway offices proved the most viable and accessible way for Ohio State to build its presence across the globe.

To determine specific locations for the Gateways, Ohio State reviewed its existing international connections, including Memoranda of Agreements and institutional partnerships, its international student populations, locations of study abroad programs and Ohio State alumni, and the presence of Ohio corporations in other countries. It was important to identify locations that already mapped well with the university in terms of existing collaborations, whether it was students, faculty, alumni, or businesses. The final analysis deemed that the Global Gateways concept would advance Ohio State's engagement in a wide variety of international settings and fulfill its strategic partnership goals at many different levels.

The Gateway as a tool to widen the circle of international partnerships must be undertaken with careful thought, knowledge, and understanding of a university's current collaborations and future opportunities. Ohio State's Gateway site locations emerged from a systematic examination of those activities, and took into consideration which countries Ohio-based companies had expanded to globally. Ohio State has opened its China Gateway, and is scouting opportunities in India, Brazil, Turkey, Europe, and sub-Saharan Africa in order to match student and faculty interests.

This chapter will provide the blueprint for how Ohio State increased its international partnerships through its Global Gateways, built alliances, engaged faculty, students, and alumni, and connected its international partnerships with businesses in order to benefit the local economy. As with all new initiatives, there were some growing pains along the way, and lessons learned from the experience will be shared.

Building Partnerships through the Gateways

As with any major institutional goal, there must be buy-in from senior leadership as well as faculty, administrators, and staff. They must perceive the Gateways as adding value to what they do as well as viewing them as one of the foundations of the internationalization process. To help pave the way, Ohio State set up faculty advisory committees for each of the regions in which it planned to open Gateway offices. Additionally, leadership from the colleges as well as senior administrators in the special interest areas of development and communications worked together to build bridges that would attract potential new contacts for the university. The Gateways would have eventually withered on the vine if forced to depend solely on altruistic motivations or top-down enforced compliance.

The role of the university president cannot be overlooked when it comes to opening doors and building relationships in other countries. With the opening of Ohio State's China Gateway, President Gee, along with other senior-level faculty and university administrators, took advantage of the visit to China to establish new relationships. Meetings took place with leadership at universities and key government administrators and community leaders. In addition, a reception was held in Shanghai for students enrolled at Ohio State as a way of welcoming them to the university and providing them with an opportunity to talk one-on-one with President Gee and other university officials. Meetings with community and government leaders helped introduce Ohio State and its Gateway presence to the Shanghai community and paved the way for future partnerships, while the reception held for incoming international students built a level of trust with their parents who were sending their son or daughter thousands of miles away to a country in which they have no connection. As a result, Ohio State's recruitment efforts, coupled with the opening of the Gateway office in Shanghai, resulted in a 52 percent increase in the number of Chinese students attending Ohio State.

Signing on the Dotted Line

International institutional partnerships constitute a major building block of the global university. However, there must be strategic, mutually beneficial reasons to establish a partnership with a foreign institution and they must be agreed on in advance. For the partnership to have a realistic chance of succeeding, each side must see it as adding value to their institution.

The Ohio State Gateway has facilitated several Memoranda of Agreements that will solidify study abroad programs and student exchanges and support collaborative research in food safety and age-related diseases such as Parkinson's. Additionally, Ohio State has made progress in developing dual or joint degree programs with our close partner universities, which include internships with Ohio-based multinational companies.

IIE/AIFS Foundation Global Education Research Reports

DEVELOPING STRATEGIC INTERNATIONAL PARTNERSHIPS: MODELS FOR INITIATING AND SUSTAINING INNOVATIVE INSTITUTIONAL LINKAGES | 41

Whether building partnerships with institutions in developed or developing countries, the reality is that viable and sustainable partnerships typically evolve from collaborations in which both partners believe that they are benefiting from the relationship.

Engaging Faculty

The Gateway office has the ability to engage faculty in partnering with international institutions to further research projects and provide new experiences for students to experience another culture. Several Ohio State colleges and departments partnered to provide funding for grants and scholarships in the Gateway regions that Ohio State had identified. Grants were made available for faculty to:

1. develop course content that could be adapted into collaborative activities between an Ohio State class and one or more international partner institutions;

2. develop discipline-specific study abroad programs at an international institution; and

3. engage in research collaboration with international partners that explore global issues in a regional context that are aligned with Ohio State's five Centers of Excellence: Climate, Energy and the Environment; Health and Well-Being, Human Behavior and Bioinformatics; State, Regional and Urban Development; Food Production and Supply; and Safety Materials, Manufacturing Technologies and Nanotechnology

Incentivizing faculty who have interests in the Gateway countries can deepen the university's international relationships, which benefits both the faculty members and the institution as a whole.

Reconnecting with International Alumni

Ohio State has more than 500,000 living alumni around the world, and the university prides itself on ensuring that their connection to Ohio State remains strong. Having a physical presence in regions around the world can impact the university's ability to reconnect and strengthen relationships with international alumni. Ohio State's China Gateway has recharged our alumni living in Shanghai and the surrounding area. They have formed an Ohio State China Alumni Club, which doubled its membership in 12 months. The group meets monthly for social gatherings, but also helps the university locate additional alumni and connect with businesses in the area with which partnerships may develop.

Opening Doors to the Corporate Community

The Gateways provide an avenue for universities to build rapport with U.S. corporations doing business overseas. A university's international alumni can help facilitate meetings between university officials and corporate executives to determine mutual interests. Furthermore, a university's faculty provides one of the richest resources for international student internships through their collegial networks and contacts with the private and public sectors. Since many of our international and domestic alumni work in multinational corporations and NGOs, they are well positioned to locate and organize international internship opportunities. Our institutions need to take advantage of these rich resources.

Ohio State seeks to connect with Ohio-based businesses operating globally as a way to contribute to the growing local economy. The University plans to offer executive training programs to corporate groups, and Ohio State faculty have begun developing programs based on their expertise in the areas of food safety, supply chain management, intellectual property, and others. This effort will undoubtedly build stronger ties to the business community globally while generating revenue to offset operational costs of the Gateway office.

Lessons Learned

Expanding Ohio State's partnerships through the Global Gateways has been an exciting initiative, and it is important to take a look at some important lessons learned throughout the process.

1. Patience. Know that opening an office in another country is a long-term investment in both time and funding. For example, in China there is much involved in obtaining government permissions and appropriate licenses for the type of work a university plans to conduct in the country. Relationship building is key. Face-to-face contact with Chinese officials takes time, but in the long run, a university can reap the benefits of the trust gained and the time invested.

2. Institutional commitment. A university must have the commitment from leadership to move international initiatives forward. The support needs to be far more than "talking the talk." It needs to be backed by a financial commitment.

3. Engage faculty and students. Faculty and students must be included in the planning process. Tangible examples of the benefits of the Gateways and partnerships abroad must resonate with faculty and students so that they can see how these initiatives have a positive influence on their research and learning.

IIE/AIFS Foundation Global Education Research Reports

DEVELOPING STRATEGIC INTERNATIONAL PARTNERSHIPS: MODELS FOR INITIATING AND SUSTAINING INNOVATIVE INSTITUTIONAL LINKAGES | 43

4. <u>Be true to your university.</u> Know your university's comparative advantages and capitalize on them. Examine the academic expertise at your particular university and identify fields of excellence. Emphasize your strengths and find a niche that sets your university apart from the rest.

Foreseeing the Future

The building blocks (students, faculty, staff, administrators, alumni, surrounding community, foreign universities, private and public sectors) participate in the making of sound international partnerships. The successful universities of tomorrow will not be confined by four walls. The Gateways enable us to develop multifaceted, meaningful partnerships that link back to the central campus. This type of collaboration will allow us to achieve true global competence by comprehensively internationalizing the teaching, discovery, and engagement missions of higher education through effective partnerships.

Chapter Eight

Grits, Greens & Gari: Reflections on the Partnership between North Carolina Agricultural and Technical State University and Kwame Nkrumah University of Science and Technology, Ghana

Samuel Owusu-Ofori, Boeing Professor of Mechanical Engineering, North Carolina Agricultural and Technical State University

Minnie Battle Mayes, Founding Director, Office of International Programs, North Carolina Agricultural and Technical State University

Background

"Grits, Greens and Gari" is the title of a recurring presentation during International Education Week at North Carolina Agricultural and Technical State University (NC A&T), where students participating in the exchange program between NC A&T and Kwame Nkrumah University of Science and Technology in Ghana share their experiences in Ghana and the U.S. The title builds on some of the cultural similarities between North Carolina and Ghana: grits are similar to gari, and in both cultures greens are a highly cherished part of the diet (North Carolina's collard greens are similar to Ghana's cocoyam leaves, *kontomire*). With their academic and social similarities, the road between Greensboro and Kumasi has become a well-blazed trail.

Nearly 20 years ago, NC A&T, located in Greensboro, North Carolina, began a partnership with the University of Science and Technology in Kumasi, Ghana (now called Kwame Nkrumah University of Science and Technology or KNUST). This exchange program was established as part of the Memorandum of Understanding (MOU) between the North Carolina Consortium for International and Intercultural Education (NCCIIE) and the major universities in Ghana, namely, KNUST, the University of Ghana, and the University of Cape Coast. NCCIIE is a consortium of public and private Historically Black Colleges and Universities (HBCUs) in North Carolina.

Founded in 1989, the NCCIIE consortium was created to provide shared opportunities for international/intercultural learning experiences for students and faculty at member institutions. At that time, none of the member institutions had full time international program offices dedicated to study abroad or the infrastructure to maintain international partnerships individually. It was thought that by forming a consortium, the strengths of the member institutions could leverage opportunities for all. The Consortium successfully applied for grants to develop programs to provide international experiences for students in Ghana and several other countries.

The Consortium leadership first headed to Ghana in 1992 to make contacts and establish linkages between its members and universities in Ghana. NC A&T and the University of Science & Technology (UST), Kumasi, were a good match because both had strong engineering schools, technology, agriculture, the arts and sciences. Additionally, there were faculty members on the NC A&T campus who were alumni of UST, Kumasi.

During a 1992 visit to Ghana, the parties agreed to cooperate in a number of endeavors, including the exchange of students for undergraduate/graduate studies, joint research programs, and the exchange of academic, administrative, and technical staff. Discussions on logistics continued at the highest administrative levels after the agreement was signed. The challenges at that time included grade transfer, how tuition for the KNUST students would be handled at NC A&T, and how to provide financial assistance to the Ghanaian students when they arrive at NC A&T, since students at KNUST do not pay for tuition, room, and board.

In 1995, the College of Engineering at NC A&T and the School of Engineering at the University of Science & Technology signed an articulation to implement these exchanges. One year later, a conference on manufacturing technology was jointly organized and held in Ghana to enable the parties to meet and exchange ideas as part of the agreement. In 1998, the first round of student exchanges began with two undergraduate mechanical engineering students from NC A&T. In a reciprocal manner, KNUST sent two undergraduate mechanical engineering students to NC A&T. However, KNUST found it challenging to send undergraduate students to NC A&T: the grading schemes and the number of credit/contact hours were different. They also did not have an international office.

Given these challenges, it occurred to KNUST that there was a greater need for junior faculty to be involved with the exchange than undergraduates, as many of their junior faculty members did not have master's and doctorate degrees. Thus, it was agreed that junior faculty would come to NC A&T to work on research projects, and master's or doctoral degrees for one year periods in exchange for undergraduate exchange opportunities for NC A&T students at KNUST. The program was institutionalized to include all disciplines of both universities in 2001, after NC A&T established a university-wide Office of International Programs. This has led to participation by students from various disciplines, faculty members, and administrators.

North Carolina A&T State University Campus Plan

North Carolina A&T State University acknowledges that students with diverse and international experiences tend to be better prepared to face the challenges of a globally interdependent world. Central to this direction is the development of visionary and distinctive academic studies, research, and service, which include global collaborations and partnerships as part of the learning experience. The NC A&T campus plan consists of three interrelated subprograms centered on the university-wide Global Studies Certificate Program: 1) International Exchange Programs, 2) International Student Projects, and 3) Scholarship Program. The program is illustrated by Figure 8.1.

FIGURE 8.1: MODEL OF THE NORTH CAROLINA A&T STATE UNIVERSITY CAMPUS PLAN

Ghana International Exchange Program

This program is designed to allow students to experience other systems of education, improve their understanding of other cultures, allow them to know their potential customers and collaborators, and simply "break the ice" for international travel and cooperation. Students follow the academic program and complete the degree requirements of the home institution. Courses taken abroad are approved by the respective departments, and the credits are transferable. Although the exchange program was initiated with undergraduate students in mechanical engineering, the program is now institutionalized and students from all applicable disciplines are eligible to participate in the program.

The first two exchange participants from KNUST were senior mechanical engineering students. However, to better meet the needs of KNUST, NC A&T undergraduates were exchanged with junior faculty, usually in their second year of teaching at KNUST, who could work on research and graduate level study. NC A&T faculty members serve as seminar speakers, workshop instructors, and visiting professors at KNUST. This provides faculty development at KNUST in the respective disciplines to improve the programs/courses in which our students will be studying.

Joint International Projects

Developing engineers with international teamwork experience who have knowledge of international standards and codes for design and manufacturing is our primary goal. An example is NC A&T's involvement in the Society of Automotive Engineers (SAE) mini-Baja student design competitions. In this competition, students design and fabricate a single-seat, off-road, 10-horsepower vehicle that must be extremely rugged and lightweight. These basic requirements make aluminum an important material choice with which students must learn how to properly design. Bauxite is a major natural resource in Ghana, and it is desirable for the engineers to know how to design parts with aluminum.

The initial phase of this collaborative effort involved the participation of KNUST students as guests during the mini-Baja competitions. Soon, KNUST students began developing their own vehicles as senior design projects. The NC A&T faculty advisor for the motor sports program continues to travel to Ghana to assist in the development of the specifications of this vehicle. KNUST students and their faculty advisor travel to the United States to work with the NC A&T team and to participate in the mini-Baja competition. In 2002, the KNUST students unveiled their first vehicle at a Ghana Auto Show.

Scholarship Program

In 1999, the Alcoa Foundation began supporting the partnership between NC A&T and KNUST. Alcoa operates the largest bauxite facility in Ghana. The Alcoa Scholarships provide NC A&T students support for round-trip airfare. KNUST students (junior faculty) are given a teaching assistantship to study at NC A&T for a maximum of two semesters as part of the exchange program. Currently, NC A&T students may use financial aid for their study in Ghana. Additionally, NC A&T now has its own scholarship program that will assist students with their airfare, thereby reducing dependency on outside funding to sustain the program. The NC A&T Study Abroad Travel Grant comes from a fund created by the recently implemented (2010) student fee of $10 per year, per student.

The Global Studies Certificate Program

Students participating in the Ghana Exchange Program typically earn a Global Studies Certificate. They enroll in the Introduction to Global Studies course during the semester before they go to Ghana. This prepares them for study abroad through learning about global and cultural issues. They can focus their independent research paper and other assignments on Ghana. Upon their return to the U.S., they also take the capstone seminar in Global Studies, in which they use the knowledge they gained from their coursework (they also take two global courses in their major) and their experience abroad to interpret and analyze current global issues and events.

Challenges and Opportunities

With all the obvious successes of this partnership, there have been some major challenges on both sides. The first challenge involved the death of an NC A&T student, in Spring 2004, due to a rare form of malaria. This frightened students, faculty, and administrators alike. While given the option to return to NC A&T, the three remaining students made the difficult decision, with the support of the International Office at NC A&T, to complete their semester at KNUST. However, it was three semesters before an NC A&T student would go to Ghana again.

As a result of this experience, we implemented procedures requiring students traveling anywhere abroad to complete a confidential health questionnaire, which is reviewed by the Director of International Programs to ensure any health issues or concerns are proactively addressed before the students leave the U.S. Students are also advised to use a health insurance company to identify a participating doctor and give him/her their medical records upon arrival so that they already know whom to go to if they have any chronic health issues or become ill.

The inclusion of the joint project experience into the partnership has provided technical expertise that can be adapted to community benefits, such as the development of a simple vehicle to cart goods from the farm to the market in an inexpensive way. The challenge is the availability of parts needed to build this vehicle on a consistent basis.

Sustainability

The 20-year partnership with KNUST has established NC A&T as a viable and strategic partner in building capacity at KNUST as well as at NC A&T. Many faculty who had never been out of the country before participated in various ways with KNUST. We have worked hard to build the partnership around programs and projects rather than individuals, because individuals come and go. However, this too is challenging because behind every sustainable linkage are people who drive the programs. Even with the many changes in administrations at both universities, this linkage has remained a priority.

Other ways the partnership has expanded include a Sister Library Program between the university libraries of both institutions. Visits by the head librarians of the campuses led NC A&T's Bluford Library to donate a container of reference books to the KNUST Library. The KNUST library provides copies of publications from the KNUST University Press for Bluford Library. The NC A&T School of Nursing set up a summer program for nursing students to gain preceptorship experience in Ghanaian hospitals and visits nursing schools. The Honor's Program organizes a spring break faculty-led study tour to Ghana, and the Department of Visual and Performing Arts takes dance majors to KNUST for a required international experience in dance and culture.

Undergraduate students at both universities are pressing for undergraduate student exchanges. Our students return from their semester at KNUST and want to know why their classmates from Ghana cannot come to NC A&T. We are currently working on a strategy to raise funds to provide travel scholarships for undergraduates from KNUST to come to NC A&T. The earlier problems with credit transfer and equivalencies are no longer issues.

Conclusions

As we enter our fourth renewal of the partnership agreement, the effects of our collaboration are clear. Twelve KNUST faculty members have been trained at NC A&T and many NC A&T students have studied at least one semester in Ghana. Dozens of students, faculty, and staff have participated in the Ghana study tours.

Equally important are the experiences afforded students at NC A&T to work with student teams from Ghana on the mini-Baja competition; the experience of the faculty members who have taught modules in Ghana; the sister libraries and the wealth of materials available on both campuses.

Dr. Owusu-Ofori serves as a member of the KNUST College of Engineering Advisory Board and moderator for the mechanical engineering program, performing periodic reviews of the curriculum and examination questions. Three NC A&T faculty members have been appointed as adjunct faculty members supervising graduate theses and dissertations at KNUST. Additionally, with a grant from Alcoa Foundation, eight KNUST engineering faculty members are currently enrolled in doctoral programs at NC A&T and will return to Ghana upon earning their degrees in 2012/13. Two junior faculty members from KNUST, in the sandwich doctoral program in mechanical engineering, have already returned to KNUST and have completed the degree requirements.

This collaboration has helped to forge a bond between North Carolina Agricultural and Technical State University, and indeed the state of North Carolina, and Kwame Nkrumah University of Science and Technology in Ghana.

Community Partnerships and Capacity Building

Chapter Nine

SOCIAL JUSTICE AND CAPACITY BUILDING: A NEW MODEL FOR STRATEGIC INTERNATIONAL PARTNERSHIPS AT LIBERAL ARTS COLLEGES

KIRAN CUNNINGHAM, PROFESSOR OF ANTHROPOLOGY, KALAMAZOO COLLEGE

NITA KUMAR, BROWN FAMILY PROFESSOR OF SOUTH ASIAN HISTORY, CLAREMONT MCKENNA COLLEGE, AND NIRMAN

JONAS REDWOOD-SAWYERR, VICE-CHANCELLOR AND PRINCIPAL, UNIVERSITY OF SIERRA LEONE

ABU SESAY, VICE-CHANCELLOR AND PRINCIPAL, NJALA UNIVERSITY (SIERRA LEONE)

JOSEPH L. BROCKINGTON, ASSOCIATE PROVOST FOR INTERNATIONAL PROGRAMS, KALAMAZOO COLLEGE

Introduction

For most liberal arts institutions, international partnerships are formed in the context of international education, which has typically meant study abroad in one form or another. Kalamazoo College has been a leader in study abroad for decades, sending

IIE/AIFS Foundation Global Education Research Reports

DEVELOPING STRATEGIC INTERNATIONAL PARTNERSHIPS: MODELS FOR INITIATING AND SUSTAINING INNOVATIVE INSTITUTIONAL LINKAGES   53 roughly 85 percent of its graduates abroad for three, six, or nine months every year. With the birth of the new Arcus Center for Social Justice Leadership, Kalamazoo College is attempting to reframe international education and partnerships around mutuality, collaboration, and capacity building.

Heretofore, the goals for strategic international partnerships at Kalamazoo College have been two-fold. First, a new international partnership must fit within the College's mission of preparing "its graduates to better understand, live successfully within, and provide enlightened leadership to a richly diverse and increasingly complex world" (2010-2011 College Catalogue). Secondly, for over 15 years the Kalamazoo College Center for International Programs (CIP) has striven to identify new partnerships that offer not only international opportunities for students in the area of study abroad, but also independent research opportunities. More recently, the criteria for new international partnerships also includes the ability of partner institutions to offer interesting opportunities for Kalamazoo administrators, faculty, and staff. On the whole, these arrangements tended to be one-sided.

A New Direction for Strategic International Partnerships

With the opening of the Arcus Center for Social Justice Leadership (ACSJL) in 2009-2010, Kalamazoo College is looking at potential international partnerships that contribute to the mission of the ACSJL: supporting "the pursuit of human rights and social justice by developing emerging leaders and sustaining existing leaders in the field of human rights and social justice, creating a pivotal role for liberal arts education in engendering a more just world."[1] While not every new international partnership will serve the mission of the ACSJL equally, a new *strategic* international partnership will fit both the College mission as well as that of the ACSJL.

Kalamazoo College is embarking on an experiment in pursuing international partnerships with the University of Sierra Leone, Njala University (Sierra Leone), and NIRMAN (India). Rather than approaching partners with ideas of how "they" can serve "our" needs and how "we" can help "them," the partnerships began with discussions of each institution's goals and desired outcomes for the partnerships and how the partnerships can contribute to meeting those goals for both sides.

In the case of the College's partnership with NIRMAN, which is supported by a grant from the U.S. Department of State's Bureau of Educational and Cultural Affairs, as well as the College's study abroad program, the grant proposal was developed collaboratively, ensuring that the grant-funded activities would meet the goals of both NIRMAN and Kalamazoo College. The goal of this collaborative project is to build capacity to host a larger and more consistent number of U.S. students through increased staff, staff development, and program development. The program emphasizes an Indian Studies curriculum that challenges U.S. students to consider their assumptions and prior knowledge of India through rigorous academic coursework on Indian history, religion, economics, fine arts, and culture; intensive Hindi language study; and opportunities for cultural immersion.

Kalamazoo College has also enjoyed partnerships with both Njala University (NU) and Fourah Bay College (FBC) since 1962. Up until they were suspended in 1994 due to Sierra Leone's civil war, Kalamazoo's partnerships with both universities were grounded in a study abroad program that involved many Kalamazoo College students studying at NU and FBC and a few NU and FBC students studying at Kalamazoo College. There were also occasional exchanges of faculty.

Today, in the wake of a brutal and destructive 10-year civil war that ended in 2001, the nation of Sierra Leone is in the process of rebuilding and strengthening its governmental and educational infrastructure. Both of the public universities, for example, have expanded their scope of offerings and are serving increasing numbers of students. Within this context, the partnerships between Kalamazoo College, Njala University and the University of Sierra Leone (USL) are now being re-established, but this time all are working together to ground them in true collaboration and mutual capacity building. The foundation for these partnerships is being laid though the development of inter-institutional collaborative capacity building projects. Faculty and staff at Kalamazoo are working with peers at Njala University and at USL to define and implement capacity building projects in such priority areas as pedagogy, faculty research, student research, information technology, and strategic planning.

All three institutions hope that these capacity building projects will be a new model for inter-university collaboration with a dynamic framework of activities that can have several pathways for further partnerships.

Njala University's Goals and Priorities for the Partnership

Njala University, one of the two public universities in Sierra Leone, is a rural university, operating on two campuses in the Southern Province of the country. It attained university status in August 2005 through the Universities Act of 2005, which restructured the old University of Sierra Leone into two universities: Njala University and the new University of Sierra Leone. Njala University College, the predecessor institution of Njala University, established in 1964, and which until 2005 was a constituent College of the former University of Sierra Leone, was a vibrant institution, attracting students from across the African continent. During the civil war (1991-2002), the institution suffered massive damage, losing 70-80 percent of its residential, teaching, and research facilities. Experienced staff members were either killed or scattered to locations within and outside the country; the campus was abandoned for 15 years.

Today, the major priorities confronting Njala University are:

- Improvement of the quality and efficiency of teaching and learning;
- Rehabilitation and rebuilding of its Njala campus;
- Production of a highly trained human resource base for national development;
- Facilitation of increased information and communication technology use;
- Enhancement of research performance, through research collaboration;
- Exposure to best practices in higher education leadership/ administration; and
- Overall efficiency in Njala University operation.

Central to the achievement of most of these priorities is the strengthening of Administrative and Education Information Systems and availability of ample and reliable Internet accessibility. Thus the re-establishment of the partnership with Kalamazoo College, with the agreed-on areas of cooperation in pedagogy, management information systems, staff and student research collaboration, and strategic planning, comes at an opportune time for Njala University.

University of Sierra Leone's Goals and Priorities for the Partnership

The University of Sierra Leone was reconstituted in 2005 as one of two public universities in Sierra Leone. It comprises three constituent colleges. The oldest is Fourah Bay College, a traditional college founded in 1827 with faculties of Arts, Engineering and Architecture, Social Science and Law, and Pure and Applied Sciences. The other two colleges are the Institute of Public Administration and Management, the business school, and the College of Medicine and Allied Health Sciences. The total student population of the University of Sierra Leone is about 9,000.

The partnership with Kalamazoo College will focus on key priority areas for the University:

- Facilitation of computer literacy for all students;
- Development of a computer science degree program;
- Enhancement of research performance, through research collaboration;
- Pedagogical development and training of lecturers to enhance faculty competencies in teaching; and
- Overall efficiency in University of Sierra Leone's registrar function.

Moreover, through the partnership new and innovative avenues for students' collaborative study research will be developed that foster friendship, academic discourse, and the sharing of cultural experiences.

NIRMAN's Goals and Priorities for the Partnership

New Initiatives in Research, Management and the Arts (NIRMAN) is an NGO in Varanasi, Uttar Pradesh, India, established in 1988. The mission of the organization is to work for the creation of a new India and a new world through a focus on youth and education and through innovative programs in the arts and international exchange. NIRMAN has three units: Vidyashram – The Southpoint School for children ages four through seventeen; The Centre for Postcolonial Education, a research center devoted to sponsoring intellectual and change-oriented activity on the subjects of children, education, women, and civic and environmental values; and The Resource Centre with a variety of arts studios. Since 1990 NIRMAN has been working to understand the problems that make inequality and injustice entrenched in an otherwise humane society such as India's. NIRMAN works to achieve results through practice—service as well as advocacy—by experimenting with a wide variety of possible solutions.

NIRMAN's aim is to nurture young leaders through teaching and mentoring, and through planned study of and exposure to the challenges of development in India, an ancient, rich, but hierarchical society. This complements Kalamazoo College's mission to prepare its students for leadership in an "increasingly complex world." NIRMAN's goals and priorities for the partnership include:

- Increase capacity for American undergraduates to study in Varanasi, India;
- Develop a Hindi language instruction model;
- Increase opportunities for internship positions; and
- Create faculty exchange to enhance Indian Studies at Kalamazoo College.

Kalamazoo College's Goals and Priorities for the Partnership

For its part, Kalamazoo College has entered the conversations with its partners in Sierra Leone and India with specific goals in mind, including:

- Develop opportunities for students and alumni to engage in joint projects with counterparts in Sierra Leone and India;
- Increase the College's capacity for social justice work;
- Enhance the capacity of faculty to engage in collaborative research and curriculum development with international counterparts; and
- Develop a partnership model grounded in principles of social justice.

However, Kalamazoo College has not let these goals determine the outcomes of these conversations. In particular, the College is interested in partnerships that will offer study abroad, internship, and senior project opportunities with social justice leadership as the focus, along with opportunities for students and alumni interested in the areas of health, peace and justice, sustainability, and business to engage in joint projects with counterparts in Sierra Leone and India. The College also hopes to be able to offer opportunities for faculty to engage with Sierra Leonean and Indian colleagues through research and social justice curriculum development, and for faculty and staff to engage with their Sierra Leonean and Indian faculty and administrative peers in institutional capacity building work. Lastly, the College hopes for heightened recognition and reputational enhancement through the development of a partnership model grounded in principles of collaboration, mutual capacity building and social justice, and increased capacity for collaborative, intercultural, social justice work at the College.

Conclusion

By grounding the development and institutionalization of these international partnerships in a framework of social justice, Kalamazoo College, NIRMAN, the University of Sierra Leone, and Njala University hope to stimulate and facilitate the development of collaborative and mutually beneficial programs that enhance the intellectual life, cultural development, and capacity for peace building and social justice work for all institutions involved. Through the collaborative, peer-to-peer projects that are central to these partnerships, involving students, faculty, staff, and administration, we are already building a broad and deep set of inter-institutional relationships that will provide the mortar for meaningful, multifaceted, sustained cooperation well into the future.

---

[1] For more information, please visit: https://reason.kzoo.edu/csjl/mission/

Chapter Ten

MANAGING PARTNERSHIPS FOR SUCCESS AND SUSTAINABILITY: THE DAEGU GYEONGBUK ENGLISH VILLAGE PARTNERSHIP

ANTHONY J. SHULL, DIRECTOR OF GLOBAL PROGRAMS, COLLEGE OF EDUCATION, UNIVERSITY OF COLORADO, COLORADO SPRINGS

Introduction

In early 2006, The University of Colorado at Colorado Springs (UCCS) was approached by Yeungjin College YJC of Daegu, South Korea, to partner on an English immersion village to be constructed in the mountains outside of Daegu, South Korea. The village was developed with the goal of providing families in the region an economic way of offering their children English-language instruction in a simulated immersion environment. An agreement was signed in September 2007, and the doors were opened to the village in October 2007. The fact that this particular form of partnership had not been developed before suggested that no benchmarks existed and that a lot of trial and error would take place.

In this chapter, I will attempt to explain a few of the challenges the partnership faced and how we were able to move beyond them to create a healthy, sustainable project and partnership.

Overcoming Challenges and Differences

Private vs. Public

One challenge stemmed from the fact that UCCS is a public (not-for-profit) university and YJC is a private (for-profit) university. As such, this complicated, large-scale project was developed by two different institutional cultures. Our YJC partners offered academic courses and packaging programs in such a way that would bring profit, which was a different approach than UCCS. This prompted many conversations for review of objectives and goals between the partners. An important strategy in overcoming this dilemma involved defining the roles and responsibilities for each partner. It was decided that YJC would be responsible for the funding and construction/maintenance of the village along with promotion of programs, facility operations, and enrollment management. UCCS, in contrast, would be responsible for contracting qualified ESL instructors, managing and training instructors, and developing curriculum. Through the careful definition of roles and responsibilities, the profit/not-for-profit issue was resolved. The careful definition of roles and responsibilities is key to any international partnership and should be agreed on before an agreement is signed.

Building Trust through Open Communication

A specific challenge for the teachers that were recruited involved the way that the village is operated. Teachers asked many questions about operations and especially the implementation of their contracts. This was a new experience for many of our Korean partners, as we have found that it is fairly uncommon for employees to ask questions about contracts. At first the questions led some to believe that instructors were not trusting of administrators, but with more communication and open dialogue this challenge was overcome.

In addition, the situation allowed for enhanced clarification of contractual language, which has resulted in a contract that is easily understood by all stakeholders. Through this experience, it is now understood by all stakeholders that questions about contracts are normal and that trust is built on good communication. Open communication is key and leads to trust and shared goals and governance.

Hierarchical Organizational Approach

We have observed that management in South Korea is often top-down and that it is fairly uncommon for management to solicit ideas and strategy from subordinates. However, in countries such as the United States, empowerment leads. Managers expect to hear from their subordinates, as professional development is seen as the lifeblood of organizations.

When the village first opened, instructors were handed lesson plans and syllabi and were not asked to be involved in the development and improvement of courses. This scenario elicited a flood of complaints from instructors, who felt that their experience and credentials were being underutilized. Many of our Korean partners were perplexed. After further conversation we discovered that our Korean partners believed that they were doing a favor to the instructors by preparing lesson plans and syllabi, as they were more familiar with Korean students than the Western instructors.

What started as a small pilot program that allowed instructors to get involved in lesson planning and syllabi creation for a Daegu teacher program later led to the involvement by teachers in developing curriculum and devising a Teaching English program for local public school teachers of Daegu. Through this experience we learned to never to assume anything and always communicate everything. Misunderstandings are easily overcome with sufficient conversation. Creating an environment of trust that allows for open, respectful communication will allow for inclusion and the ability to overcome seemingly insurmountable obstacles.

Reactive vs. Proactive

Another difficult challenge that we faced was the difference in the way that each partner school planned. In the United States, being proactive is generally positive. It is often suggested that having to react to issues sheds light on problems. However, in South Korea, we have sometimes found that planning too far ahead may be seen as creating problems that do not exist rather than attempting to avoid future problems. However, since our Korean partners would be working with up to 50 Western ESL instructors, we knew that we would have to be proactive in order to avoid potentially problematic developments in the future.

We also knew that over time there would most likely be complaints from instructors about their quality of life, specifically housing and food options. Though there were many advantages to having instructors live in a dorm at the village and having them eat in the cafeteria, we noticed that the demeanor and attitudes of many teachers would change for the worse after about the six-month mark of their twelve-month contract. However, in many cases, instructors did not complain to administrators about these issues. As a result, when we brought up the idea of giving teachers the opportunity to live outside the village in the nearby city, it was received with skepticism. The same response was given to suggestions for adding more fresh vegetables and some Western-style food to the cafeteria selections. The question from our partner was: Why change if instructors are not complaining?

We suggested a round of meetings with instructors where they were provided the opportunity to speak openly about housing and food. The situation was direr than we had suspected. Several teachers were considering leaving before their contracts were up. However, communication prevailed and out of these candid, respectful conversations came pilot programs where food was adjusted and some teachers with seniority were allowed to live in the city. The strategy has evolved into policy, and now second-year instructors are given the option of living in apartments in the city. In addition, instructors have access to an organic vegetable garden. With a few minor adjustments, we were able to retain instructors and create a situation where 12 instructors, practically one-third of the teaching staff, now live in the city.

Conclusion

The Daegu Gyeongbuk English Village partnership continues to flourish. The village was home to 20 ESL instructors and about 2,000 students in 2007, and currently has 42 ESL instructors and was visited by more than 21,000 students. It has eight academic programs and instructors continue to work closely with both YJC and UCCS administrators to create new programs and improve current ones. The partnership remains strong and further inter-institutional programs have developed, including student-teaching practicums in Daegu and visits by YJC undergraduate and middle-school students to UCCS. Given the many achievements of the partnership between Yeungjin College and the University of Colorado at Colorado Springs in a short amount of time, it would be prudent to suggest that this partnership is on the path to even more sustainable success in the future.

I would like to conclude with a few tips regarding the establishment of a partnership such as this one.

- Proper research and preparation is a must. Know yourself and your partner.
- Put everything in writing and make sure that the language used is understood by all stakeholders.
- Define everything, never assume.
- Be respectful and patient. The partnership/project is more important than any one person or group.

Chapter Eleven

Building Institutional Capacity for Establishing Successful Higher Education Partnerships: An Ethiopian Case Study

By Cheryl Francisconi, Director, Institute of International Education Sub-Saharan Africa

The Growing Demand for Quality Higher Education in Africa

The demand for quality higher education in sub-Saharan Africa is growing at a rapid pace. Since 41 percent of the region's population is under the age of 15, the population is projected to grow much more rapidly than in developed countries where the populations are aging. By 2050, the population of sub-Saharan Africa is projected to be over one-fifth of the world's population, the majority of whom will be youth, and the future leaders of their countries.[1] Thus, improving the access to and quality of higher education for millions of young people is an increasingly important item on the development agenda.

Ethiopia, the second most populous country in sub-Saharan Africa, has made a strong commitment to expanding access to higher education. Thirteen new

IIE/AIFS Foundation Global Education Research Reports | 63

Developing Strategic International Partnerships: Models for Initiating and Sustaining Innovative Institutional Linkages universities have been established in recent years with more projected to be built. This visionary commitment is based on the Ethiopian government's understanding that poverty cannot be addressed and the development of the country cannot move forward unless there is an educated and skilled workforce.

This rapid expansion of higher education, however, comes with its own set of challenges. Ensuring that there are sufficiently qualified faculty, access to high quality academic resources, adequate housing, and strong administrative leadership are some issues that Ethiopian policymakers and educators currently face. These challenges bring opportunities for U.S. higher education institutions interested in partnering with their counterparts in Ethiopia. And the opportunities for partnerships are not limited to Ethiopia alone. Many countries in sub-Saharan Africa are facing these challenges and offer similar opportunities for partnerships.

Unfortunately, several barriers hinder the development of sustainable partnerships between institutions across borders, including:

- the ability to effectively communicate joint expectations needed to establish and maintain a partnership;
- unequal access to funding;
- logistical challenges such as differences in academic calendars and curricula; and
- insufficient housing and working facilities needed for African universities to host students and faculty from abroad.

In addition, while access to technology is improving in many countries, the challenge of maintaining regular Internet communication is still cumbersome, especially for universities in more remote regions.

Hosting a Capacity Building Conference

To address some of these barriers and to assist U.S. and Ethiopian universities with practical tools for establishing and maintaining effective short- and long-term partnerships, the Institute of International Education and the United States Embassy in Ethiopia organized a two-day conference, "Building Sustainable U.S.-Ethiopian University Partnerships," in December 2010. The purpose of the conference was to:

1. present models of successful university partnerships;
2. provide tools to better manage partnerships once they are established; and
3. give exposure to existing institutions and initiatives that support higher education development globally and in the region.

More than 100 participants attended the conference, including representatives from all of the Ethiopian public universities and selected private universities, faculty from some U.S. higher learning institutions, and members of the Ministry of Education in Ethiopia.

A pre-conference survey was given to participants from Ethiopian universities to help conference organizers better understand the challenges and opportunities for partnership building. Survey results indicated that while all Ethiopian universities surveyed would like to partner with U.S. universities, and that many have made some attempt to do so, most Ethiopian universities lack a clear and comprehensive strategy for building and sustaining effective partnerships with U.S. institutions. In addition, respondents indicated that they lack information about how to establish partnerships with U.S. universities, and they believe that there is little interest on the part of U.S. universities to collaborate with Ethiopian institutions.

All Ethiopian institutions surveyed indicated a strong desire to increase both the quality and quantity of their partnerships with U.S. universities. Their primary reasons for wanting to establish partnerships include: 1) increasing mutually beneficial joint research and collaborative projects, 2) promoting cultural and knowledge exchange through staff and student exchange programs, and 3) increasing the international profile and competitiveness of their institutions.

However, survey respondents indicated that their institutions experienced difficulty establishing partnerships due to a lack of a clear and comprehensive strategy for engaging with U.S. universities, a shortage of connections with U.S. universities from which to build partnerships, and worries over the costs of partnering (including salary demands from U.S. scholars, potential project costs, and perceived lack of scholarships and funding opportunities). Ethiopian institutions suggested that the following factors could support their capacity to build effective partnerships: more linkages with U.S. universities, strategic planning regarding how partnerships can be mutually beneficial, more scholarship and funding opportunities, and raising the visibility and reputation of their country's programs.

Based on the information gathered in the survey, and on the advice from a design team made up of representatives from various higher learning institutions in Ethiopia and the Ministry of Education, the conference was designed to give participants practical tools for building and sustaining effective partnerships. Academic conferences at which participants read or listen to academic papers do not frequently have the kind of targeted impact as workshops and seminars with more interactive content and a stated objective. Thus, the conference incorporated meeting methodologies so that universities would be able to initiate new partnerships once the conference was over. The meeting design included experience-sharing of best practices and successful models by both U.S. and Ethiopian counterparts, and concurrent workshops on such topics as "Developing a Strategic Partnership Program for the 21st Century," "Steps to

Designing a Research Partnership," "Managing International Partnerships for Success and Sustainability," and "Establishing Mutually Beneficial Exchange Programs."

The Importance of Dialogue

When forming partnerships in contexts where there is an inequity of resources, it is important to create space for participants to freely exchange ideas. On the first day of the conference, a World Café dialogue session was hosted in which participants discussed the following topic: "What does my university offer that would be beneficial to an international partnership?" Participants had the chance to move around the room during the three hour session in order to cross-fertilize ideas with many different colleagues. The importance of creating space for discussion cannot be overemphasized. It is easy for institutions in resource-poor countries to become more focused on what they need and less reflective on what they can offer. Conferences like this are successful when they encourage the development of mutually beneficial partnerships with both sides bringing their strengths to the table. Participants from developing country contexts will benefit from opportunities to look at the strengths and advantages that they bring to a partnership. This levels the playing field so that partnerships can be built on a stronger foundation, helping to ensure that they succeed.

In the Ethiopian context, participants reflected on the comparative advantages that Ethiopian universities could offer to U.S. institutions, especially in terms of their unique research strengths. These areas of comparative research strengths include:

- Ecotourism
- Health (e.g., traditional medicine, tropical diseases; some universities have well-established longitudinal health research centers)
- Anthropology and culture (e.g., pastoralist communities, indigenous knowledge, ethnic groups, cultural diversity, cross-border activities and movements)
- Ecology (e.g., climate diversity, climate change, solar energy)
- Agriculture (e.g., organic coffee and fruits)
- Livestock
- Flora and Fauna
- Geology
- Archaeology (e.g., paleontology finds such as Lucy)

In addition, the dialogue created space for participants to reflect on the advantages of living and working in Ethiopia, as well as some of the challenges and strategies to overcome them.

Key Lessons Learned

The two-day conference gave participants opportunities to engage with each other and to hear from resource persons from the U.S. and Ethiopia who have had success in establishing mutually beneficial partnerships. They departed with tools and resources to aid them in strengthening existing partnerships or establishing new ones. Some of the key learnings and recommendations from the conference include:

- Look for ways to build upon existing relationships with faculty and administrators in other countries.

- Develop a clear institutional strategy for the type of partnership your institution wants to create (e.g., faculty/scholar exchange, collaborative research and projects, etc.) and identify potential international partners that are compatible with your strengths/needs and mission.

- Once you have identified a potential international partner, hold discussions about how partnership projects and activities can be mutually beneficial and can involve the sharing of expertise, faculty, and students between universities.

- In negotiating partnership agreements, set out clear expectations and assign responsibilities for each partner.

- Ensure that both institutions have resources and structures in place to sustain the partnership over time, including mechanisms for addressing conflicts.

In order to sustain the gains of the conference, a list-serve was established for all participants so that they could communicate with each other and stay informed about opportunities for future partnership-building. The Institute of International Education offered to assist in helping participants identify potential partners for future activities.

Seed Grant Competition

At the conclusion of the conference, the U.S. Ambassador to Ethiopia announced a small grant competition for "seed money" to start innovative partnerships between U.S. and Ethiopian universities. The objectives of the grant competition were: 1) to grow mutually beneficial and sustainable partnerships between U.S. and Ethiopian universities and colleges; 2) to introduce new higher education institutions to U.S. and Ethiopian partnerships; and 3) to strengthen the skills and experience of faculty and administrators in both countries in developing and implementing partnerships.

In March 2011, the U.S. Embassy announced five grants of $15,000 each for new partnerships. The projects ranged from research collaborations to faculty training and capacity building. The participating universities represent many different regions in both countries, and three grants were given to partnerships that focused on newly established universities in Ethiopia. The project topics also reflected the wide range of interests between the U.S. and Ethiopia—from agriculture cultivation to alternative energy to cultural heritage. The Embassy hopes to publish the experiences and lessons learned from the seed grant competition partnerships in the future.

Conclusion

Donors and their implementing partners make important contributions in building the capacity of higher learning institutions from both the developed and developing world to establish successful partnerships. Partnerships often fail because parties do not have the necessary practical tools or enough knowledge or experience in making their goals a reality. Conferences like the one described in this chapter not only address these challenges but also help partners to identify cultural differences that may contribute to differences in expectations and communications. With only a modest investment, along with some technical assistance and follow-up, the quality of higher education in sub-Saharan Africa, and indeed other regions of the world, will continue to improve, ensuring that educators can meet the growing demand for quality higher education in the developing world.

NOTES

[1] For more information on the "Building Sustainable U.S.-Ethiopian University Partnerships" conference, please download the IIE White Paper on the subject available at www.iie.org/publications.

Chapter Twelve

BUILDING INTERNATIONAL PARTNERSHIPS BASED ON COMMON GOALS AND MISSION: FOUR CASE STUDIES FROM THE UNIVERSITY OF CALIFORNIA, DAVIS

WILLIAM B. LACY, VICE PROVOST–UNIVERSITY OUTREACH AND INTERNATIONAL PROGRAMS, UNIVERSITY OF CALIFORNIA, DAVIS

JENNIFER N. WADE, DEVELOPMENT ANALYST, UNIVERSITY OUTREACH AND INTERNATIONAL PROGRAMS, UNIVERSITY OF CALIFORNIA, DAVIS

Building strategic international partnerships is a central component of internationalizing the campus and core to pursuing research, education, and outreach. As Dr. William Bosher, former Dean of the School of Education at Virginia Commonwealth University, succinctly stated a few years ago: "The focus of the university should not be location, location, location, but relation, relation, relation. A central ingredient to strong international programs is the establishment of meaningful relationships based on common values and goals and a sense of trust between partners. In today's globalized world this reality has never been more important" (2006: 32).[1]

Opportunities and obstacles are inherent parts of developing international university partnerships. Establishing the strategic plan for building these partnerships can take many forms. While no one path can guarantee a successful outcome, there are many steps that, when taken together, will increase the probability of building long-lasting and productive partnerships.

At the University of California, Davis, we have developed numerous long-term relationships throughout our 100-year history. We have evaluated and refined our processes and procedures for building collaborations and successful partnerships, and have created useful guidelines. Before entering a partnership, we review the potential benefits and strategically assess these relative to the goals of our campus. Partnerships can strengthen students' education and prepare them to work and live in a global economy and a multicultural world. They may also enhance the quality of research; generate new revenues through areas such as tuition and research funding; enable the extension and application of knowledge to address global needs; encourage mutual understanding, tolerance, and respect among students, faculty, and staff of partner institutions; and promote peaceful solutions for international issues and conflicts.

The context in which international partnerships are developed is another critical element that requires evaluation. A relationship will be impacted by the context within the region (e.g. Southeast Asia, Middle East, north Africa), within the country (e.g. Myanmar, Vietnam, Iran, Egypt), and within an area in a single country (e.g. northern Japan, U.S.-Mexican border, southern Philippines). Each partner should evaluate the culture, politics, and economy of their potential partner. Are there cultural, political, or economic issues that may threaten the formation or conduct of the partnership? At the same time, the organization and structure of higher education in partner countries, states, prefectures, or provinces need to be assessed. To what extent are policies determined at the federal, state or providence, or institutional level? How will this strengthen or weaken the partnership? Finally, the institutional context of each partner—including its mission, vision and goals, academic quality, strengths and weaknesses, value placed on internationalization, existing partnerships, and language requirements—should be reviewed in order to determine the degree of compatibility and areas of possible collaboration.[2]

Potential partners may be identified in many ways. A key place to begin is with existing international connections of faculty, students, postdoctoral scholars, alumni, and local business leaders. Partners may also surface through international professional meetings in high-priority disciplines and regions, through international visiting delegations, or through careful assessment of institutions with comparable strengths.

Once a partner is identified, certain steps are essential to building a strong international partnership. First, each partner should: 1) specify their rationale for developing the partnership (e.g. goals, strategy, priorities, regions of world, subject matter); 2) share their policies and procedures; 3) identify appropriate leadership (e.g. faculty, administrators); and 4) determine the degree of institutional commitment to the partnership. Then, the parties should commit to a standardized general agreement of cooperation or Memorandum of Understanding, where appropriate, and develop active working agreements that delineate the specific goals, activities, responsibilities, resource implications, and budget at the unit level. Finally, it is valuable to require regular progress reports and establish procedures for the renewal or sunset of these agreements.

The type of partnership may take many forms. Frequent components include student and faculty exchanges, joint or dual degrees, collaborative research, faculty development activities (e.g. workshops, conferences), faculty affiliate status, local and national development cooperation, administrative exchange, branch campuses, or international multi-institutional networks.[3]

No partnership is devoid of challenging issues and costs. It is useful to anticipate as many of these as possible, which may include: differences in education quality and standards; unrealistic student and faculty expectations; incompatible customs, language, and cultural practices; level of commitment by the parties; and differing resource allocations. Other challenges may include issues of academic freedom; health and safety issues; legal issues (e.g. legal liability, intellectual property, employment issues); and changes in priorities and goals over time.

Using four case studies, we illustrate our processes for developing international relationships—from identifying the underlying rationale for developing a partnership to selecting the best type of partnership, while remaining aware of the obstacles that may arise and determining the best way to resolve them.

Zhejiang University

UC Davis's relationship with Zhejiang University is a multifaceted partnership with several different components, all of which began informally several decades ago and were formalized as a single institutional agreement of cooperation in 1998. As one of the top research universities in China, Zhejiang University was selected for its academic quality, leadership in Chinese higher education, and strengths in disciplines compatible with UC Davis. Moreover, Zhejiang University is located in a country that is becoming an increasingly important partner with UC Davis.

Involving senior leadership was essential to launching this collaboration. In 2000, then Chancellor Larry Vanderhoef visited Zhejiang University. An agricultural biotechnology workshop, conferences, and new research projects followed in the next five years, funded in part by seed funding from UC Davis's office of University Outreach and International Programs. UC Davis Extension has offered current students from Zhejiang University the opportunity to attend an Honors College program entitled, "American University Academic and Cultural Orientation." In the last decade, over 450 students from Zhejiang University have participated in this program and other research and study abroad programs. Recently, the Global Study Program at UC Davis Extension began a full immersion program for undergraduate students for up to a year. In 2005, seven committees co-chaired by faculty from both institutions created a UC Davis-Zhejiang University Center for Academic Partnerships in Agriculture, Food and the Environment. In spring 2011, the Chancellor and President of the two institutions met in Beijing to discuss strengthening and expanding this research and educational collaboration. The UC Davis Provost and Vice Provost for International Programs visited the Zhejiang University campus to plan expansion of our agricultural and environmental partnership and proposal preparations.

Last year, a new 3+X program (bachelor's and master's degrees) was initiated, which shortened the time for completion of undergraduate and master's degrees for Zhejiang University undergraduates. Selected undergraduate students, who have completed at least three years of their coursework at Zhejiang University, may apply for a non-thesis master's degree program at UC Davis. Accepted students spend a quarter of their senior year with UC Davis Extension's Global Study Program. Following successful completion of this program and upon receipt of their bachelor's degree from Zhejiang University, they enroll in the master's program at UC Davis to which they were conditionally accepted. In 2010-11, students were hosted by four UC Davis graduate groups, including Horticulture and Agronomy; Hydrologic Sciences; Transportation Technology and Policy; and Biological Systems Engineering. In 2011-12, up to 14 graduate groups will host students.

Partnering with Zhejiang University required that UC Davis address many issues. To begin, UC Davis sought a strong research partner in the agricultural, environmental, and life sciences. Zhejiang University was the only comprehensive university considered among the top ten Chinese universities with disciplinary strength and excellence in these fields. In addition, since Zhejiang University students complete their final undergraduate courses at UC Davis in the 3+X Program, finding a partner with equal educational quality and standards was essential to Zhejiang University, the degree-awarding institution. Since UC Davis offers conditional admission to these Zhejiang undergraduates, it is important that they are able to compete with other highly qualified applicants and earn their place in a graduate group. Thus UC Davis needed to ensure that intensive English courses and support services were available to foster the success of these students. UC Davis's partnership with Zhejiang University is an example of how the institutional context of one's own university plays an important role in the formation of partnerships.

Kyoto University

Kyoto University and UC Davis have a longstanding partnership. However, even when partnerships are carefully considered and successfully developed, tragedies can occur that may threaten or terminate the relationship. In 2000, several UC Davis and Kyoto University environmental scientists and graduate students were on a research expedition on the Sea of Cortez in Mexico when their boat capsized. Five people perished (three Kyoto researchers and two UC Davis researchers). The accident greatly affected both institutions. The respective university President/Chancellor traveled to its partner institution. The UC Davis Chancellor met with the families in UC Davis and Kyoto, a memorial service for the five individuals was held, and a garden to honor them was established in the UC Davis Arboretum.

Since then, rather than declining, this partnership has grown even stronger. One unique example is the Kyoto University-UC Davis Administrative Staff Exchange Program established in 2005. While the typical agreement of cooperation between universities involves faculty and student exchanges, this program offers an opportunity for a staff exchange between our two institutions on an annual alternating basis. Staff from each university participate in a practicum at either the International Affairs Division of Kyoto University or the Office of University Outreach and International Programs at UC Davis, and give presentations about their respective culture and institution. This staff partnership encourages mutual understanding, tolerance, and respect among students, faculty, and staff of partner institutions and strengthens our overall relationship.

Chile–California Partnership

One of UC Davis's most productive, as well as one of its oldest, partnerships involves multiple institutions and campuses. In 1963, Chile and California developed an agreement for technical cooperation that led to several bilateral UC Davis/Chilean university agreements. More than 50 Chilean students attended UC Davis in the 1960s and 1970s for graduate training in agricultural sciences. These students, known in Chile as the "Davis Boys," helped to develop their country as one of the leading exporters of fresh fruit. In 1980, the University of California campuses began an Education Abroad program that enabled numerous UC Davis students to study at the University of Chile and La Pontificia Universidad Católica de Chile.

In 2008 and 2009, during a visit by President Michelle Bachelet, previous agreements with Chile were confirmed and expanded, particularly with the University of California campuses. The goals of these agreements included 500 scholarships for graduate education per year and 200 faculty scholarships for Chilean and University of California professors. UC Davis has been one of the most active participants in the program. Coinciding with President Bachelet's visit to UC Davis, several specific agreements of cooperation with UC Davis were initiated by our campus and Chilean partners for research collaboration in seed biotechnology, viticulture and enology, water resources management, and food science. This has led to numerous faculty and student exchanges, conferences, and workshops and joint research as well as the development of the Outreach Water Center in south-central Chile in conjunction with the Universidad de Concepción. Recently, PIPRA, a UC Davis-based nonprofit initiative that strives to assist developing countries in accessing genetic resources and new technologies, opened its first international office in Chile in collaboration with the Foundation for Agricultural Innovation.

In the Chile–UC Davis partnership, some of the potential issues to be addressed included shifting priorities and goals and a change in political leadership. While there continues to be a high level of commitment by both parties, with significant resource allocations to education and mutual research, a change in government, a significant economic downturn, and an earthquake in Chile led to a reevaluation of the program's scope and a delay in implementation.

United Kingdom Performing Arts

A final example of unusual international partnerships is that between two UC Davis departments—English and Theatre and Dance—and two British theater and television institutions.

The UC Davis Granada Artists-in-Residence program began over 25 years ago and is unique in American university theater, bringing prominent British theater artists—directors, playwrights, choreographers, and filmmakers—to UC Davis each academic quarter to teach and develop a work for public performance. This program is a special opportunity for graduate and undergraduate students to gain cross-cultural experience with major theater and dance practitioners. These departments have also formed a partnership with Globe Education at Shakespeare's Globe Theatre in London to establish a research institute that studies playhouses and the playing conditions of theaters in early modern England. This research draws on the original practices at Shakespeare's Globe Theatre and includes such areas as music, history, literature, and design to help understand Renaissance drama through the study of acting, stagecraft, and language.

Since these two partners are not higher education institutions, issues of different institutional goals and mission had to be addressed. However, the two programs involve UC Davis faculty, graduate, and undergraduate students and give UC Davis access to some of the world's prominent theater artists, which strengthens our student's education and prepares them to work and live in a global economy and a multicultural world.[3]

Conclusion

These partnerships and the many others that we have formed illustrate the numerous challenges and subsequent commitments of time, energy, and resources required to ensure their success. Moreover, these examples illustrate the essential role that partnerships play in achieving our primary goals and mission. It is important to enter each partnership with a clear understanding of the broad international institutional context, the compatibility of each institution's vision and goals, the appropriate policies to maximize success, and the potential obstacles. Finally, partnerships are about people. Professor Takoi K. Hamrita Tartir expressed it well in a recent *IIENetworker* article: "The most effective international linkages, regardless of their size, scope, goals, and context, begin with people who put the common good before their own and cut across barriers to pull together whatever it takes to form that bridge" (2007: 46).[4]

NOTES

[1] Wood, V. R. (Spring 2006). Globalization and higher education. *IIENetworker Magazine*, 26-34

[2] Van de Water, J., Green, M. F., & Koch, K. (July 2008). U.S. higher education in a global context: Working paper #2, international partnerships: Guidelines for colleges and universities. Washington DC: American Council on Education.

[3] UC Davis Department of Theatre and Dance (2011). Retrieved from theatredance.ucdavis.edu

[4] Tartir, T.K.H. (Spring 2007). A multidisciplinary international linkage. *IIENetworker Magazine*, 46-47.

Chapter Thirteen

ENHANCING GLOBAL ENGINEERING EDUCATION AND RESEARCH: BUILDING INSTITUTIONAL PARTNERSHIPS WITH CHINA

YATING HALLER, ASSISTANT DIRECTOR OF GLOBAL PROFESSIONAL PRACTICE, PURDUE UNIVERSITY

ECKHARD A. GROLL, PROFESSOR OF MECHANICAL ENGINEERING AND DIRECTOR OF THE OFFICE OF PROFESSIONAL PRACTICE, PURDUE UNIVERSITY

Introduction

Globalization brings opportunities along with significant challenges. The resources necessary to advance science and engineering, including facilities, equipment, and support staff, continue to grow, so leveraging global expertise and global infrastructure is necessary. Opportunities that enable students and early career professionals in science, engineering, technology, and mathematics (STEM) to participate in global teams and experience research abroad can have a profound impact on the development of these individuals and on the STEM workforce of the future.

There is urgency for the scientists and engineers of the 21st century to acquire global competency. As a result, many U.S. higher education institutions have not only re-examined their curriculum in STEM disciplines but also pursued international partnerships and collaborations in order to help their students to acquire global competency. The primary motivation for such institutional partnerships derives from the competition between nations for a global STEM workforce. The rationale is often driven by global economics, and the changing landscape of a "flat world."[1]

This chapter focuses on the engineering profession, and examines how engineering schools across the U.S. collaborate and form partnerships with rising economies, mainly China.

The Need for International Partnerships

Economic globalization is transforming the engineering profession. Today, the conceptualization, design, and manufacture of devices and systems involve global market analyses and implementation through distributed work centers and worldwide supply chains. As companies expand their operations across borders, international assignments of U.S. engineers have become a common business practice. Recently, global enterprises have set up engineering as well as research and development centers worldwide, which they have staffed with a combination of national and international engineers and scientists.[2]

To flourish in this environment, future engineers need to be not only proficient in technical subjects, but also informed about international technological trends and business practices and familiar with different languages and cultures. The National Academy of Engineers recently addressed the needs of global engineers in a report entitled *Educating the Engineer of 2020: Adapting Engineering Education to the New Century*, which concludes:

> U.S. engineers must become global engineers. They will have to know how to replenish their knowledge by self-motivated, self-initiated learning. They will have to be aware of socioeconomic changes and appreciate the impact of these changes on the social and economic landscape in the United States and elsewhere. The engineer of 2020 and beyond will need skills to be globally competitive over the length of her or his career.[3]

Partnerships within U.S. Engineering Schools

The changing global landscape necessitates the cultivation of global engineering competency. As noted in the Newport Declaration,[4] "the world is experiencing dramatic geopolitical and technological changes which are continually revolutionizing transportation, communication, commerce, education, and life experience" and "these transformations are intertwined with rapidly increasing human population and resource consumption." For global challenges such as these, engineering is a necessary part of the solution. For that reason, the Newport Declaration closes with: "To this end, we call on engineering educators, engineering administrators, and engineering policy leaders to take deliberate and immediate steps to integrate global education into the engineering curriculum to impact all students, recognizing global competency as one of the highest priorities for their graduates."

The types of strategic institutional partnerships for science and engineering schools are driven more by scientific advances and engineering innovation, and less by cross-cultural exchanges. Nevertheless, it is essential for engineering students as well as faculty members to gain a global perspective and an appreciation of the societal implication of their work. The skills and values gained by students who participate in global engineering programs allow them to be competitive as engineers in the 21st century marketplace.

In 2010, the National Academy of Engineers issued a report that outlines 14 "grand challenges" and calls for engineers to collaborate across the world. Strategic institutional partnerships can be formed among U.S. and international STEM disciplines to solve the following global problems[5]:

1. Make solar energy economical.
2. Provide energy from fusion.
3. Develop carbon sequestration methods.
4. Manage the nitrogen cycle.
5. Provide access to clean water.
6. Restore and improve urban infrastructure.
7. Advance health informatics.
8. Engineer better medicines.
9. Reverse-engineer the brain.
10. Prevent nuclear terror.
11. Secure cyberspace.
12. Enhance virtual reality.
13. Advance personalized learning.
14. Engineer the tools of scientific discovery.

While principle investigators (PI) form partnerships to solve these engineering grand challenges, administrators and international educators often find it difficult to integrate such collaboration into education curriculum and opportunities for students.

We also have substantial obstacles and challenges to the integration of international experience into mainstream engineering programs at academic institutions. Examining 24 U.S engineering colleges and schools across the nation, Parkinson[6] synthesized the following obstacles for participation in international experiences and partnerships:

- Difficulty in scaling;
- Negative impact on time to graduate;
- Negative impact on finances;
- Lack of faculty incentives;
- Unclear outcomes assessment; and
- Rigid curriculum structure.

These obstacles are familiar to international educators. In many cases, the details and unforeseen incidents of international travel become obstacles to a successful experience. Unprepared PIs were surprised by the overwhelming amount of overseas management, e.g., underperformance of students, overconsumption of alcohol, liability and risk management, visa regulations, and housing.

One way to overcome this issue is to engage the on-campus office in charge of study abroad programs and international students. While most PIs found the pre-departure orientations administered by the study abroad office helpful, others found that study abroad orientation sessions may not be applicable to students who travel abroad to conduct research. Therefore, it is important to communicate with the overseas office about the difference between a research internship abroad and study abroad.

International educators and higher education administrators need to understand the delicate balance between collaborative and competitive dynamics of global engineering education. Different types of institutional partnerships provide leverage to internationalization of STEM disciplines and global engineering education.

Types of Institutional Partnerships

The majority of engineering personnel in academia do not possess the "big picture" of partnerships at the institutional level. The partnerships that interest and engage them are research collaborations that advance scientific findings. The underlying rationale for global engineering education is a balance between *collaborative advantage* and *competitive advantage*.

The spectrum of educational activities that can have an impact in this regard include:

- Global engineering content in class examples and homework in traditional coursework;
- Global and cross-cultural content in course projects;
- Distance global design team experiences;
- Traditional study abroad, often with non-engineering courses;
- Engineering coursework and research abroad, including global service learning projects; and
- International internships or other professional practice abroad.

Many U.S. engineering schools have identified countries like India, China, Germany, and Colombia with which to form such educational partnerships. The strategic rationales of choosing to collaborate with these countries are based on their rapid science and engineering developments, as well as on emerging economic growth. The next section of this chapter will focus on some of the best practices for forming institutional partnerships in China.

Why China?

China's significant investment in research will ensure that global engineers develop research global competency skills and partnerships in a country with an increasing impact in the field of engineering. As shown in Table 13.1, China's gross expenditures on research and development have grown by more than 100 percent between 2000 and 2004. This increased research activity is also reflected in the share of science and engineering journal articles published by Chinese researchers. Between 1993 and 2003, the share of all such articles from China increased from 11.08 to 22.3 percent.

TABLE 13.1: GROSS EXPENDITURES ON RESEARCH AND DEVELOPMENT, 2000–2004 (MILLIONS OF CURRENT PURCHASING POWER PARITY DOLLARS)

Year	Asia	China	Japan	Singapore	S. Korea	Taiwan	EU-25	U.S.
2000	174,008	44,771	98,850	1,810	18,395	10,182	182,567	267,768
2001	190,501	52,418	104,161	2,007	21,166	10,749	194,759	277,820
2002	209,936	65,154	108,248	2,202	22,247	12,085	205,263	276,260
2003	229,628	76,891	112,715	2,255	24,274	13,494	210,168	292,437
2004	NA	93,992	NA	2,678	NA	14,951	NA	312,535

Source: National Science Foundation

Obama's 100,000 Strong Initiative

In November 2009, President Barack Obama announced the 100,000 Strong Initiative, a national effort designed to increase the number and diversify the composition of U.S. students studying in China. Carola McGiffert, the director of the 100,000 Strong Initiative, pointed out that the initiative seeks to prepare the next generation of U.S. experts on China who will be charged with managing the growing political, economic, and cultural ties between the U.S. and China.

From a STEM disciplinary perspective, China is a critical partner with which to solve grand challenges because of the country's major outsourcing and global supply chains/production. The U.S. Department of State has echoed this need by stating that

> there is perhaps no more important or complex relationship in the world than that between the United States and China in terms of securing global peace and security. Virtually no major international issue—whether global economic recovery or climate change or nuclear non-proliferation can be solved without the active engagement of both the United States and China, working in concert.[7]

Working with the Chinese

From a strategic partnership perspective, the abundance of human resources in China can be an obstacle when international educators and faculty members try to convince Chinese businesses and trade partners to work together. Therefore, personal and social networking is critical to the success of developing institutional partnerships with China

"Guan Xi" is the Chinese word for mutually beneficial relationships critical to the success of business and interpersonal relationships.[8] It entails the delicate art of building and nurturing such ties. Critics might say that this type of social network has a negative connotation of favoritism and cronyism. However, this chapter argues that if "Guan Xi" is maintained with honest and open communication, then partnerships can be developed without guile.

Study and intern-aboard programs require a substantial amount of "Guan Xi." Institutions need to leverage the personal relationships of its faculty members and community trade partners. Face-to-face interaction and the ability to speak the native language make a difference while placing students in research laboratories and universities. Over the past decades, English language has been incorporated into elementary and secondary education in China. As a result, according to Chinese official media, over 300 million Chinese studied English in 2006—nearly a quarter of the country's population.[9] In contrast, only 50,000 Americans are learning Chinese per year.

U.S students' lack of Chinese language proficiency continues to be an obstacle in building institutional partnerships. However, communication is not the only obstacle for STEM students overseas. Gender roles vary from culture to culture. STEM students should learn that gender roles might be different from what they are used to in their home culture, and that such differences may impact the engineering work environment and practices. Both female and male students should be made aware of such differences, and be open-minded and willing to learn about different cultures and people.

Funding Opportunities

Strategic institutional partnerships are not sustainable without funding and faculty support. Funding mechanisms and programs to support international collaboration are crucial to sustaining productive partnerships.

As STEM education makes advances globally, government agencies—such as the National Science Foundation, USAID, the U.S. Department of Education, the U.S. Department of Defense, and the U.S. Department of State—have supported institutional partnerships that have international components. Currently, requests for proposals for STEM activities are supported predominantly by the Office of International Science and Education (OISE) of the National Science Foundation. Funding opportunities managed by OISE include:

- Developing Global Scientists and Engineers (International Research Experiences for Students (IRES);
- Doctoral Dissertation Enhancement Projects (DDEP);
- East Asia and Pacific Summer Institutes for U.S. Graduate Students (EAPSI);
- International Research and Education: Planning Visits and Workshops;
- International Research Fellowship Program (IRFP);
- Pan-American Advanced Studies Institutes Program (PASI); and
- Partnerships for International Research and Education (PIRE).

Conclusion

STEM faculty members and students are keen on working to solve the grand challenges of this world. Our approaches to strategic institutional partnership, therefore, must support such cause.

While the heart of global engineering education is to compete and collaborate with engineers across nations, it would be a missed opportunity if the partnerships we develop forgo cross-cultural competencies as a learning outcome. As we form partnerships across the world, we must learn to balance the *collaborative advantage* and *competitive advantage* between institutions.

NOTES

[1] Friedman, T. (2005). *The world is flat: A brief history of the twenty-first century.* New York, NY: Farrar, Straus and Giroux.

[2] Chang, Y., & Hirleman, E. D. (2008). Proceeding of NSF IREE 2008 Grantees Conference. Retrieved from https://globalhub.org/resources/nsfiree2008granteesconference

[3] National Academy of Engineering (2005). *Educating the engineer of 2020: Adapting engineering education to the new century.* Washington, DC: The National Academies Press.

[4] The Newport Declaration: To globalize U.S. engineering education (2008). Retrieved from www.globalhub.org/newportdeclaration

[5] The National Academy of Engineering: Grand challenges for global engineers (2010). Retrieved from http://www.engineeringchallenges.org/cms/challenges.aspx

[6] Parkinson, A. (2007). Engineering study abroad programs: Formats, challenges, best practices. *Online Journal for Global Engineering Education.* Retrieved from http://digitalcommons.uri.edu/ojgee/

[7] U.S. Department of State: 100,000 Strong Initiatives (2009). Retrieved from http://www.state.gov/p/eap/regional/100000_strong/index.htm

[8] Buderi, B., & Huang, G. Guanxi (2006). *The art of relationships: Microsoft, China, and Bill Gates's plan to win the road ahead.* New York, NY: Simon and Schuster.

[9] McGiffert, C. (2011). 100,000 strong: Building strategic trust in U.S.–China relations through education. *IIENetworker Magazine,* 21-22.

Chapter Fourteen

Developing Research-Based Partnerships: Florida A&M University's U.S.-Brazil Cross-Cultural Initiative

Clifford Louime, Assistant Professor, College of Engineering Sciences, Technology and Agriculture, Florida A&M University

Joseph V. Jones, Interim Assistant Vice President, Office of International Education and Development, Florida A&M University

Terry-Ann Jones, Associate Professor of Sociology and Anthropology, Fairfield University

Introduction

Brazil has been steadily ascending as one of the world's most economically and politically powerful nations (Karlin, 2011). Its recent economic boom, due mainly to an unprecedented expansion of the energy sector, has made the country one of the shapers of the new world economic landscape (Luxner, 2008). This expansion resulted from an outpouring of investment capital by the Brazilian government and private industries in research and technology (Pinheiro-Machado, 2001). Their most notable accomplishments in the past decades have been in the biofuels and agricultural sectors (Wall, 2010). The Brazilian biofuels initiative has been heralded as an example for governments worldwide that seek to achieve independence from fossil fuels. This novel energy paradigm emerged partly from some of the best academic and research institutions in the nation, such as The Brazilian Agricultural Research Corporation, Empresa Brasileira de Pesquisa Agropecuária (EMBRAPA) and University of São Paulo. These higher education institutions have become magnets for Asian, U.S., and European scholars, who are investigating ways to collaboratively solve their own energy issues.

Consequently, Florida A&M University is seeking to develop and expand its international educational partnerships with Brazilian institutions in the fields of biofuels, language, and cultural acquisition. The goals of such partnerships are to develop our students and faculty research capability and to move the U.S. toward energy sufficiency. In this chapter, we will discuss some of the key aspects of establishing and managing such partnerships with Brazil and how these collaborative programs can be maintained over time. This chapter will highlight: 1) establishing goals, 2) selecting partner institutions, 3) procedures, 4) institutional support, 5) program sustainability, and 6) key challenges.

Establishing Goals

Florida A&M University is committed to advancing research in all fields. The following excerpts from the university's mission statement demonstrate the broad support for research: "FAMU is committed to inspirational teaching, exemplary research and meaningful public and community service through creative partnerships at the local, state, national and global levels. The University is also committed to the resolution of complex issues that will enhance humankind" (FAMU, 2007). Our collaborative partnerships with Brazil in the area of biofuels represent efforts toward "the resolution of complex issues." The benefits derived from these partnerships, including having a positive impact on the U.S. national energy crisis and improving the economy in rural areas, will raise the research profile of Florida A&M University, which will likely lead to greater support to the institution for research and the training of students.

The primary goal of the "U.S.-Brazil Cross-Cultural Initiative: Sustainability and Attractiveness" collaborative research initiative is to provide a globally-focused, immersive, and experiential education to U.S. undergraduate students and faculty in the area of biofuels. Through this biofuels project, participants have been exposed to some of the cross-cultural, ethical, sociopolitical, demographic, and environmental challenges that they will face as tomorrow's leaders. Referring to Jean Piaget's paradigm of learning and cognitive development, Lutterman-Aguilar and Gingerich (2002) argue that "learning takes place as people test concepts and theories in their lived experience and as they develop new concepts and theories based upon their experiences." Educators have long promoted study abroad for the potential benefits on students' personal and academic development. However, the pedagogical utility of study abroad can be augmented when complemented by experiential learning. According to Lutterman-Aguilar and Gingerich (2002), "the intellectual study in experiential education provides students the framework for interpreting what they see and experience." Collaborative research with faculty along with an internship provide the U.S.-Brazil exchange program the structure needed to reinforce the qualities of the study abroad experience.

Furthermore, Dolby (2004) contends that the greatest impact of study abroad on U.S. students is the development of their sense of U.S. identity. She emphasizes that this "encounter with an American self" does not represent a dichotomy between embracing and rejecting this U.S. identity. Rather, the encounter provokes a complex construction and understanding of students' self-awareness as Americans vis-à-vis their host country. Although this perspective is not novel (see Hansel, 1988, for example), it does underscore an additional benefit that transcends learning about the host society.

This biofuels project has provided opportunities for global awareness and leadership by establishing new working relationships among young U.S. researchers and their Brazilian counterparts at different levels. Faculty and students' professional experiences have been enhanced through team building, cross-cultural communication, project planning, proposal writing, and international R&D infrastructures, which were integral parts of the collaborative process.

The objectives of the U.S.-Brazil partnership program are to:

- provide U.S. students two- to six-month internships with a Brazilian university or business organization;

- provide U.S. faculty two-week summer research and training programs at Brazilian partner universities;

- create a core group of research students in renewable energy, natural resources, and the environment by devising research projects, which will contribute to the students' personal development and enhance their concept of scientific research;

- encourage social and cultural awareness by introducing U.S. students and faculty to the social and cultural dimensions of Brazil; and

- promote Portuguese language development in both U.S. students and faculty through formal and informal language training.

Selecting Partner Institutions

We based the selection of partner institutions on several criteria: experience, quality of facilities, facilitators to support students, good communication networks, access to potential students, good infrastructure, sustainability, and accreditation. Furthermore, it is expected that the host institution will provide study and research privileges equivalent to those available to resident faculty members and students at Florida A&M University.

One of our partner universities—Universidade Federal de Viçosa (UFV)—is located in the state of Minas Gerais, which is in the center-south of Brazil, the region where most of the ethanol production is concentrated (Garten, 2007). The State of São Paulo alone accounts for about 60 percent of Brazil's total ethanol production (Hall, 2009). The Southeast and Central regions combined have been producing almost 90 percent of Brazil ethanol since 2005.

Our second partner, Universidade Federal de Ceará (UFC), is located in the Northeast. This region accounts for 15 percent of Brazil's total ethanol production. In addition, 20 percent of the country's sugarcane is produced in the Northeast, as is the majority of the sugar produced for export (Jones 2009). This region illustrates the potentially detrimental effects of poor agricultural practices on the ecosystem. Much of the Northeastern region has faced deforestation and desertification as a consequence of long-term forest removal, as well as overuse and misuse of the soil. Furthermore, its proximity to the Amazon forest makes the Northeast an attractive area of study, especially in terms of greenhouse gas emissions resulting from land-use changes. The selected universities have state-of-the-art research equipment and facilities that will accommodate the level of research that this project fosters. Currently, they are engaged in diverse approaches to create bio-energy using algae and cellulosic materials.

As a major industrial hub, São Paulo has provided the perfect background to explore technologies that are essential for the commercialization of biofuels production activities, such as fuel quality, supply chain, and transportation infrastructure. Future studies at the UFC site will allow us to enhance current methods for economic, life cycle, and sustainability analyses of biofuels production pathways. Finally, by comparing methodologies, sharing germplasm, and identifying best practices at UFV, this project has allowed us to develop criteria for sustainably-produced biofuels. Each of these scenarios has allowed us to gauge the applicability of biofuels production in the U.S. and other regions of the world.

Talks are now in the works to engage the Facultade Zumbi dos Palmares (FZP), a new university founded in 2004. ZPU is Latin America's first institution of higher education designed to serve Afro-Brazilian (black) students. Brazil has the world's second-largest black population after Nigeria: 170 million Afro-Brazilians, almost 50 percent of the entire population in Brazil. However, only two percent of Brazil's three million college students are black. ZPU, located in a working-class neighborhood of São Paulo, seeks to train entrepreneurs to compete in the white-dominated corporate world. This project is aimed at collaborating with business faculty to evaluate the economics and technological issues of biofuels production in Brazil. The location of

São Paulo is instructive in complementing this study in several aspects, such as indus-try, pollution, air quality, and human capacity.

Procedures

FIGURE 14.1: PROCEDURES FOR INITIATING AND DEVELOPING AN INTERNATIONAL PARTNERSHIP

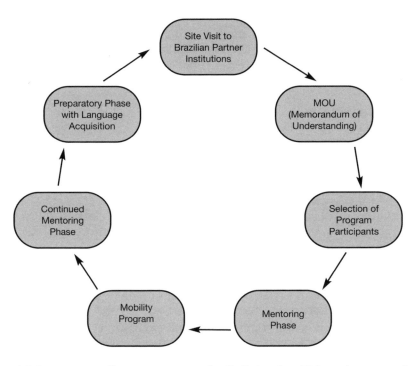

a) The site visit allows us to assess the facilities that U.S. exchange students will use and to address any deficiencies.

b) The MOU sets the legal framework for the partnership.

c) Participants are selected based on set criteria such as GPA, classification, interest in the biofuels area, language aptitude, and attitude toward different cultures.

d) The initial mentoring process includes pairing one U.S. and one Brazilian student, selecting a research project, getting acquainted with the host labora-tory, and disseminating reading materials.

e) In addition to language acquisition, the preparatory phase includes acquiring travel documents (passports and visas) and reading about Brazilian culture from the U.S. Department of State website and literature in the Office of International Education and Development.

f) The mobility phase of the program starts with U.S. students traveling to Brazil several weeks before classes begin to participate in intensive Portuguese language and culture courses, followed by semester-long academic study and participating in biofuels research projects.

g) While in Brazil, the mentoring process continues with professional development workshops, seminars, symposiums, and conferences where student and faculty research findings are presented.

Institutional Support

During his inaugural address, President James Ammons of Florida A&M University expressed a new vision for the university to become recognized for producing graduates with a strong commitment to personal integrity, competence in multicultural understanding, and dedication to professional responsibility. In the following years, the University has encouraged greater engagement from its students in issues that transcend the borders of the United States. Among Florida A&M University's extensive international programs, there has been growing interest in developing relationships with Brazilian institutions. The University's programs in Brazil were, for the most part, initiated by faculty members with research interests in the region, and funded by grants from the United States Department of Education. Student and faculty interest in sustaining these programs has resulted in support from the University. Portuguese language instruction, for example, has grown at Florida A&M University, enabling students to prepare for future study in Brazil. Florida A&M University has also developed courses that students are able to take in the United States while incorporating a research component in Brazil.

As students become aware of the global need for alternative sources of energy, the biofuels project has created an opportunity for them to explore the area of biofuels in a country with extensive experience in ethanol production. The biofuels project has helped us to identify a critical mass of faculty and students whose interests in the area could be sustained through the development of research-based courses that are taught in both countries and that underscore the areas in which U.S. students can learn from their Brazilian counterparts.

The biofuels project is also tightly linked to the University's Strategic Plan for advancing research. Three years ago, the FAMU College of Engineering Sciences, Technology and Agriculture (CESTA) instituted the first FAMU BioEnergy Group.

Plans have been made to continue this research through institutional funds with an annual budget of over $150,000 long after the DOE grant expires. In addition, the U.S.-Brazil research initiative has built upon an existing grant from the U.S. Department of Education (DOE Grant # P116M090009) to develop two online courses and add a cross-cultural perspective to existing courses in environmental sciences, business, agricultural sciences, and language and culture of the host country.

Program Sustainability

According to the Institute of International Education (IIE), between the 1996-1997 and 2006-2007 academic years, the number of U.S. students studying abroad increased by 150 percent (IIE, 2008). Studying abroad can have positive implications on students' personal and professional development. However, IIE also reported that despite these strong numbers, the participation rate remains marginal, especially among underrepresented groups, including minorities. One of the concerns is the demand for relevant programs of high academic quality. The long-term sustainability of our proposed U.S.-Brazil biofuels research program lies in its relevance to contemporary sociopolitical and environmental concerns in the U.S. and elsewhere. This program has proven to be applicable to a wide range of potential career paths for students.

This biofuels project has enabled us to consolidate our relationships through the following channels:

1. The establishment of a Memorandum of Understanding between partner institutions in the United States and Brazil that will promote and sustain research by U.S. students and faculty in Brazil.

2. The development of an internship program in Brazil through which students can receive academic credit working with Brazilian institutions, corporations, and nongovernmental organizations that are connected to the biofuels industry.

3. The development of partnerships between U.S. and Brazilian corporations and organizations for the purpose of furthering student research and increasing potential employment.

4. The establishment of strategic partnerships with organizations that share a common interest.

5. Technology transfer or university-business enterprises with potential for royalty or patent income.

From a resource leveraging perspective, these approaches have proven to be effective in getting partners to engage and commit resources. For example, another

U.S.-Brazil project on sustainability has been funded by the U.S. Department of Education. In addition, a private Petro Chemical Company provided a $300,000 grant to Florida A&M University BioEnergy Group to develop biofuels feedstock of relevance to the Caribbean.

Key Challenges in Developing International Partnerships

While the internationalization of a campus provides unparalleled learning opportunities by expanding participants' perceptions of our inextricably interdependent planet, it also brings significant challenges (Wood, 2006). Drawing from our experiences of jointly funded research initiatives with Brazilian partner institutions, we will point out some of the problems that we encountered when developing research practices across international borders:

- The dubious concept that everything is better in America is often perpetuated in the U.S., making it difficult to generate interest in international exchange programs.

- For a variety of reasons, some parents may not readily support or encourage their children's participation in an international exchange program. Parents who have never been abroad tend to be more opposed to the idea.

- The long-standing notion that the world needs to learn "American English" is still prevalent, resulting in a lack of enthusiasm from our students to acquire a foreign language. The acquisition process was therefore lengthier and more tedious than expected.

- There is a lack of information on the importance of study abroad programs. To the contemporary student, it is not always evident that study abroad program enhance one's career opportunities.

- Educational systems vary from country to country, and one needs to be aware of subtle nuances between and within systems, which can make a big difference in program approach and applicability.

- In the U.S., degrees are granted by the state; therefore, one needs to make sure that students involved in exchange programs meet not only university but also state requirements while taking courses abroad. Courses need to be aligned with students' curricula and approved by appropriate channels to ensure proper grade transfer.

- Students' timely graduation should be a high priority. A semester of study abroad should complement and reinforce participants' course of study, rather than delay their graduation.

- Courses taught in a language that students have not yet mastered can be challenging. Therefore, one has to make sure that U.S. students participating in these exchange programs can keep up with the research and teaching pace of the partner institutions.

- Finally, even if the administration has offered its full support, these international relationships need to be nurtured and institutionalized. In addition, changes of the guards (deans, directors, etc.), budget cuts, and other institutional changes happen constantly and can negatively affect work flow, research outcomes, and the sustainability of partnerships.

In response to these first of the challenges, we maintain that studying abroad not only increases students' interests in other cultures, but also increases their awareness of and concern for international political events. Carlson and Widaman's 1988 study of the effectiveness of study abroad illustrated that students who had studied abroad exhibited greater "international political concern, cross-cultural interest, and cultural cosmopolitanism." Carlson and Widaman also found that students who had studied abroad held attitudes toward their *own* country that were significantly more positive, yet more critical, than students who had not studied abroad. We argue here that the challenge now is to create a more complex study abroad experience, wherein students can move beyond basic cultural exposure and immersion, and develop a deeper understanding of their roles as global citizens. Helping them to integrate these concepts with their career choices is one way in which we intend to confront this challenge.

A Memorandum of Understanding between partners can address the other structural challenges and establish a framework for mutual benefits; however, it cannot capture the details involved in the daily course of a project that ensure a successful partnership. One needs to closely monitor the program's progress based on set evaluation criteria. As such, an external evaluator who can provide an objective assessment of program success based on well-designed and systematic evaluation criteria is an integral part of a program's success, as it was with our U.S.-Brazil Cross-Cultural Initiative. Moreover, evaluation results can provide stakeholders with information regarding the expected effects of adequately implemented exchange programs.

Conclusion

As one of the most rapidly developing countries in the world, and a global leader in energy and biofuels technology, Brazil is a natural choice for educational partnerships with U.S. institutions of higher education that seek to cultivate their expertise in this field. These programs are mutually beneficial to U.S. and Brazilian students and scholars. In addition to energy capabilities that U.S. students acquire through these programs, the study abroad experience also encourages the personal development and cultural knowledge that students will need in an increasingly competitive and internationalized job market. Although numerous international exchange programs exist, our model particularly helps to break patterns of cultural imperialism that can sometimes accompany partnerships between developed and developing countries. This model illustrates the dynamic ways in which the former can learn from the latter. These partnerships teach students one of the fundamental elements of successful twenty-first century scientific research: international and cross-cultural collaboration.

REFERENCES

Batchelder, D. (1993). The drop-off. In T. Gochenour (Ed.), *Beyond experience: An experiential approach to cross-cultural education*, 2nd ed. (pp. 135-141). Yarmouth, ME: Intercultural Press.

Carlson, J. S., & Widaman, K. F. (1988). The effects of study abroad during college on attitudes toward other cultures. *International Journal of Intercultural Relations*, 12, 1-17.

Dolby, N. (2004). Encountering an American self: Study abroad and national identity. *Comparative Education Review*, 48(2), 150-173.

FAMU–Division of Research (2007). 2006 Annual Report on Research. Retrieved from http://www.famu.edu/DOR_division_of_research/FAMU07-web.pdf

Hansel, B. (1988). Developing an international perspective in youth through exchange programs. *Education and urban society*, 20(2), 177-195.

Institute of International Education (November 17, 2008). Open Doors 2008: U.S. Students Studying Abroad Briefing: Washington, DC.

Jones, T. (2009). Migration theory in the domestic context: North-South labor movement in Brazil. *Human Architecture: Journal of the Sociology of Self-Knowledge*. VII(4), 5-14.

Karlin, A. (2011). Top 10 most powerful countries in 2011. Retrieved from http://www.sublimeoblivion.com/2011/01/16/top-10-powerful-countries-2011/

Lutterman-Aguillar, A., & Gingerich, O. (2002). Experiential pedagogy for study abroad: Educating for global citizenship. *Frontiers: The Interdisciplinary Journal of Study Abroad*, 8, 42-82.

Luxner, L. (November 18, 2010). Brazil basks in newfound energy, economic boom. *The Washington Diplomat*. Retrieved from http://washdiplomat.com/index.php?option=com_content&view=article&id=6536:brazil-basks-in-newfound-energy-economic-boom-&catid=987:march-2008&Itemid=270

Pinheiro-Machado, R., & de Oliveira, P. L. (December 2001). The Brazilian investment in science and technology. *Brazilian Journal of Medical and Biological Research*, 34(12), 1521-1530.

Rothkopf, G. (2007). *A blueprint for green energy in the Americas*. Washington, DC: Inter-American Development Bank.

Wall, S. (August 27, 2010). Brazil: Fast becoming a global powerhouse. Retrieved from http://xszene.com/brazil-fast-becoming-a-global-powerhouse/2256/

Wood, V. R. (2006). Globalization and higher education: Eight common perceptions from university leaders. Retrieved from http://www.iienetwork.org/page/84658/

Chapter Fifteen

BUILDING NETWORKS FOR TECHNOLOGY-BASED STUDENT ENGAGEMENT: EAST CAROLINA UNIVERSITY'S GLOBAL UNDERSTANDING MODEL

ROSINA C. CHIA, ASSISTANT VICE CHANCELLOR FOR GLOBAL ACADEMIC INITIATIVES, EAST CAROLINA UNIVERSITY

ELMER C. POE, ASSISTANT VICE CHANCELLOR FOR EMERGING ACADEMIC INITIATIVES, EAST CAROLINA UNIVERSITY

BIWU YANG, PROFESSOR, DEPARTMENT OF TECHNOLOGY SYSTEMS, EAST CAROLINA UNIVERSITY

In this chapter, we describe a successful Global Understanding course that we developed at East Carolina University (ECU) in 2003. It now includes 36 partner institutions in 23 countries across 5 continents. In spring 2011, ECU is offering 9 sections of this course and in the fall, with additional partners, we will expand to 11 sections. We will then explore the steps leading to the development and maintenance of the partnership.

Description of the East Carolina University Global Understanding Model

The ECU Global Understanding course features faculty and students from four diverse global institutions who learn from each other through interaction in a video-based common classroom. The sixteen-week semester is divided into three five-week sessions and a closing week. During each five-week session, we video-link with students from another country to learn about each other's culture. A typical five-week session consists of the following components:

- The faculty briefly describes the partner country with which they will link.

- In the second class, all participants introduce themselves. There are 16 students from each country and they form one-to-one partners. Each set of partners will complete a collaborative project over the five weeks.

- In the third class, faculty members from each side give short lectures, followed by questions from students of both sides.

- In the remaining classes, the students engage in discussions on: family, college life, cultural traditions and customs, the meaning of life, and prejudice and stereotyping. During each class, students are divided in half; one half participates in a live video discussion of the day's topic with half of the students on the other side. The remaining students participate in a private chat session with their partners at the other university. Halfway through the class, the students switch activities so that each student has the experience of both group and individual interaction. Both experiences are important: group discussions highlight social norms as well as the diversity of opinions within each culture, while individual chat sessions offer individuals the opportunity to express their feelings even if they do not follow the social norms.

- Discussions begin with familiar and safe topics so that students can develop a sense of trust. Then they progress to more sensitive and difficult topics.

- Students are required to maintain a daily journal of their experiences, what topic was discussed, what was consistent with their view before class, what aspects of the interactions surprised them, etc.

- The two student partners must complete a teacher-approved, collaborative project based on a topic discussed in class. Students work outside of class using a variety of synchronous and asynchronous tools. During this time the students get to know each other and in many cases develop personal friendships that may last beyond the course.

- In the last five-week period, the teachers help their students to integrate and synthesize their knowledge and impressions about the other culture using their daily journals.

- This same five-week process is repeated for a second and then a third partner institution.

All common readings are available on a website, including English-language versions of newspapers in all participating countries. Students are required to read the headlines to learn about the current situation of their partners.

Objectives of the Global Understanding Project

One important aspect of our model is the administrative independence of all partner institutions. The objective of the Global Understanding project is to provide opportunities for students from all over the world to interact and collaborate on joint projects. Therefore, students enroll in and receive academic credits from their local institutions and pay local tuition. No tuition dollars or academic credit change hands. Each faculty assigns tests, examinations, and papers at the local level. This enables all partners to maintain their own academic standards and meet their own accreditation criteria. It also takes into account the academic calendar differences among partnering institutions.

From the beginning, we chose technologies that would be feasible for partners in different parts of the world, including in developing countries. We chose H.323-based videoconferencing since it is a stable, widespread, bandwidth-tolerant, and standards-based communication protocol. For those partners who do not have video equipment, help is provided to acquire a webcam and the PVX H.323 software, at a total cost of less than USD $300. If faulty Internet connections impact the video/audio, we have created several levels of fallback or what we call "plans to fail." Faculties are prepared to lead a discussion or provide a lecture if the connection fails. In this way, we ensure the continuity of instruction throughout the course.

To make Global Understanding affordable, we selected minimum hardware requirements that should be available in most institutions worldwide. At the minimum, each site needs 10 PCs to make connections. In a few institutions, Internet bandwidth is the biggest challenge although only 256Kbps is needed for a reasonable quality DVC connection. Gaining permission from the the Chief Executive Officer (CEO), the Chief Administrative Officer (CAO), and the Chief Information Officer (CIO) to safely open the firewall is another requirement.

Our success in developing new partners for this project stems from its cost and time effectiveness, its self-sustainability, and its ability to conduct continual classes even in cases of political unrest or epidemics of contagious diseases. Since 2003 we have developed 32 partner institutions in more than 20 countries. In May 2008, partner institutions from 13 countries joined together either in person or virtually at East

IIE/AIFS Foundation Global Education Research Reports

DEVELOPING STRATEGIC INTERNATIONAL PARTNERSHIPS: MODELS FOR INITIATING AND SUSTAINING INNOVATIVE INSTITUTIONAL LINKAGES | 97

Carolina University in Greenville, North Carolina, to form the Global Partners in Education (GPE), an organization that promotes the partnership and expands the partner activities beyond the Global Understanding course. GPE has since held annual conferences at partner institutions in Beijing and Peru. Partner collaborations have broadened to include exchange lectures, joint module classes, co-taught classes in several disciplines, and several multi-national research projects. The Global Understanding project has won several awards for innovative international education and continues to grow.

Steps and Key Components for the Global Understanding Project

1. <u>Why we need a Global Understanding course</u>
   We live in an interconnected environment; major problems facing the earth such as climate change, terrorism, and contagious diseases can be solved only with a global effort. Less than four percent of U.S. students participate in study abroad programs, so there is a need for new experiences that complement traditional programs.

2. <u>How to align the global partnership with your institutional mission</u>
   It is essential that your program supports the mission and vision of your institution and aligns with that mission. This will help to acquire the support and resources needed to operate a successful program.

3. <u>How to mobilize support from a team of key players in your institution</u>
   The project will have long-term success only if it is supported by a community within your campus. The CEO/CAO, deans, chairs, and department faculty must understand that this kind of project will not only open students' minds, but also prepare them for global careers. The CIO should understand the technology requirements and be amenable to supporting the project.

4. <u>What criteria to use for selecting a global partner</u>
   You should start with institutions with which you already have active and successful partnerships through your International Affairs Office. If your institution has specific countries in which it is particularly interested, you might focus your selection in that region. You may have foreign colleagues who might be interested in working with you on such a venture. Once you have identified the initial partners, you can begin to discuss possibilities. We usually send them a one-page description and one-page minimum sheet. In our experience, it takes three to six months to develop a workable partner, and 60 to 70 percent of partners we started to work with never make it to the stage of establishing a full partnership. But persistence pays off as long-term partners yield many activities for your students.

5. How to convince a foreign institution to join the global partnership

It is important to be able to "sell" your project to potential foreign partners. For our Global Understanding course, we not only have ECU students meeting with students from three other countries, we also provide three diverse foreign partners for each of our partner institutions. In this way we offer the opportunity for our partners' students to work with students from three different countries. In addition, the course is administratively independent with no additional cost, and it fits into their regular curriculum and meets their own accreditation guidelines. These reasons make it an easily sellable project.

6. Key points in setting up an itinerary for a successful site visit

You will need a letter from the CEO/CAO of the partner institution stating that they understand and meet the minimum requirements and would like to establish the partnership. The purpose of the site visit is to establish a good working relationship with them as well as ensuring their readiness to join the project. We always have two faculty members in the visiting team. One takes care of the technology issues while the other takes care of the pedagogical issues. The visit includes an evaluation of possible classrooms to determine the arrangement of the camera, speakers, lighting, and seats, as well as a discussion of the value of the project and the course activities. It is essential to see the CAO/CEO early in the visit to secure administrative support for the program. Presentations of the project to groups of interested faculty and students help create interest on the campus. While on campus it is essential to test the technologies at the time that the class will actually meet through connections back to your home university.

7. What needs to be done before the partnership begins

Between the time of the visit and actual class time, you need to be in frequent communication with the teaching faculty and the technology support person. Video-link tests are essential to make sure that all equipment works smoothly.

8. How to manage partnerships for long-term success and sustainability

After the visit, emails should be sent to the CAO/CEO and the CIO that thank them and request their continuous support for this project. At the end of each semester, it is always good practice to write another letter about the success of the global partnership. Always keep in touch with the teachers and technology support persons at all partner institutions. When partner institutions have misunderstandings, it is your job as the "host" institution to help resolve them. Often there may be technological challenges that you will also have to help resolve. The importance of being hands-on while maintaining a global partnership cannot be stressed enough.

IIE/AIFS Foundation Global Education Research Reports

DEVELOPING STRATEGIC INTERNATIONAL PARTNERSHIPS: MODELS FOR INITIATING AND SUSTAINING INNOVATIVE INSTITUTIONAL LINKAGES | 99

This is a brief outline of our project and the steps that we have taken to make it a success. We have helped several institutions in using technology to enhance global experiences for their students. We welcome you to join us in setting up more global partnerships so we can all function better in the global community.

REFERENCES

Abbot, L., Livingston, R., & Robinson, A. (1993). *Videoconferencing ad distance education learning.* University of Ulster Press.

Andrews, T., & Klease, G. (2002). Expanding learning opportunities through a virtual faculty: The video conference option. *Journal of Education Technology.*

Austin A., Abbott, L., Mulkeen, A., & Metcalfe, N. (2003). Dissolving boundaries: Cross-national cooperation through technology in education. *The Curriculum Journal.*

Bradsher, M. (1996). Making friends in the global village: Tips on international collaboration. *The Journal of Learning and Leading with Technology.*

Chia, R. C., & Poe, E. (March 2007). *Bringing international experience to your campus.* Indianapolis: The Center for Interactive Leaning and Collaboration.

Chia, R. C., & Poe, E (Spring 2004). Innovations in International Education. *International Psychology Reporter.*

Chia, R. C., & Poe, E. (April 2004). *Learning in a virtual collaborative environment-discovery, exploration and engagement between cultures.* Chicago: The American Association of Colleges and Universities Annual Conference.

Chia, R. C., & Poe, E. (August 2004). A pioneering international virtual cultural course. Xian, China: The XVII International Congress of the International Association for Cross-Cultural psychology.

Chia, R. C., Poe, E., Meng, F., Benhallam, A., Olivos, M., & Nazarenko, A. (February 2007). *Virtual global partnership: Bringing real life international partners to your institution.* Washington, DC: The Association of International Education Administrators.

Chia, R. C., Poe, E., & Manhas, P. S. (2008). An interactive virtual global cultural course: Building a real time cost effective global collaborative learning environment. *International Journal of Emerging Technologies in Learning, 3,* 187.

Chia, R. C., Poe, E., & Wuensch, K. L. (2009). Attitude change after taking a virtual global understanding course. *International Journal of Social Sciences, 4.* 75-79.

Chia, R. C., & Poe, E. (February 2010). Global partner in education: Bringing universities around the world together through technology. Washington, DC: Association of International Education Administrators Conference.

Chia, R. C., Poe, E., & Yang, B. (March 2010). Technology infused global understanding for generation Y. Washington, DC: Intercultural Management Institute Annual Conference.

Chia, R. C., Poe, E., & Austin, B. (June 2010). Education excellence in the digital age: Initiatives in education, science and culture toward enhanced collaboration. Alexandria, Egypt: Invited presentation at the New Beginning: From Discourse to Action—Moving Forward Together Conference.

Chia, R. C., Poe, E., Yang, B., Chen, J., Irias, L., Ullrich, K., & Manhas, P. S. (February 2011). Global climate change: Student collaboration from 5 countries. San Francisco: Association of International Education Administrators Annual Conference.

Edmundson, A. (2007). *Globalized e-learning cultural challenges*. Hershey, PA: Information Science Publishing.

Feenberg. A. (1993). Building a global network: The WBSI executive education experience. In L. Harasim (Ed.) *Global network: Computers and international communication*. Cambridge: MIT Press.

Glen, F. (2001). *The changing faces of virtual education*. Vancouver, Canada: The Commonwealth of Learning Press.

Hall, C., Chia, R. C., & Smith, K. (April 2005). Using virtual communication technology to enhance international experience. Las Vegas: The National Social Science Association Annual Convention.

Harasim, L. (1991). Designs and tools to augment collaboration in computerized conferencing systems. Hawaii: Hawaii International Conference on Systems.

Heath M. J., & Holznagel, D. (2002). Interactive videoconferencing: A literature review. *NECC*

Hiltz, R. (1994). *The virtual classroom: Learning without limits via computer networks*. Norwood, N.J.: Ablex Publishing.

Kankanhalli, A., Tan, B. C., & Wei, K. K. (2006). Conflict and performance in global virtual training. *Journal of Management Information Systems*.

Kragel, P. J., & Chia, R. C. (November 2004). Innovations in medical education using a global classroom to study culture and health care in other countries. Boston: Association of American medical Colleges Annual Convention.

Laws, E. M. (2005). *Promoting understanding using a virtual learning environment*. Gilwice, Poland: ICEE.

Massey, A. P., Montoya-Weiss, M. M., & Hung, Y. T. (2003). Because time matters: Temporal coordination in global virtual project teams. *Journal of Management Information Systems*.

Nieto-Ferreira, R., Curtis, S., Poe, E., Chia, R. C., Yang, B., Herdman, A., Thompson, R., Margolis, J., Chen, J., Irias, L., Maiochi, C., & Manhas, P. S. (August 2010) A multi-national course on Global Climate Change. Foz do Iguaçu, Brazil: American Geophysical Union Meeting of the Americas

Pauleen, D. J. (2003). Leadership in a global virtual team: An action learning approach. *Leadership & Organization Development Journal*.

Piccoli, G., Ahmad, R., & Ives, B. (2001). Web-based virtual learning environments. *Journal of Management Information Systems Quarterly*.

Vogel, D. R., Davison, R. M., & Shroff, R. H. (2001). Sociocultural Learning: A perspective on GSS-enabled global education. *Communications of the association for information systems*.

TABLE 15.1: CURRENT PARTNERS IN THE GLOBAL UNDERSTANDING PROJECT

Africa	
Algeria	Université Aboubekr Belkaid Tlemcen
Egypt	Pharos University in Alexandria The Gambia University of The Gambia
Morocco	Institute for Leadership and Communication Studies
Asia	
China	China Agricultural University Henan Polytech University Shandong University Shaanxi Normal University
India	Jay Hind College MATS University St. Aloysius College St. Xavier Institute of Education The Maharaja Sayajirao University of Baroda University of Jammu
Japan	Ryukoku University University of Shimane
Malaysia	University of Malaysia Terengganu
Pakistan	Azad Jammu & Kashmir University Fatima Jinah Women's University
Russian Federation	Lomonosov Moscow State University Maritime State University Tomsk State Pedagogical University Vladivostok State University
Taiwan	Fu Jen Catholic University
Turkey	Istanbul University
Europe	
Macedonia	University American College Skopje
Moldova	Moldova Medical University
Netherlands	HAN University
Poland	Krosno State College
United Kingdom	University of Central Lancaster
North America	
Mexico	Universidad Regiomontana
United States	East Carolina University
Oceania	
Samoa	National University of Samoa
South America	
Brazil	Faculdade de Jaguariuna
Ecuador	Universidad Del Pacifico
Peru	Universidad ESAN, Universidad San Ignacio de Loyola

Chapter Sixteen

THE STORY OF A NETWORK FROM THE BEGINNING: THE DORICH HOUSE GROUP OF EUROPEAN UNIVERSITIES

JOAN-ANTON CARBONELL, MANAGER, EUROPEAN AND STUDY ABROAD OFFICE, KINGSTON UNIVERSITY, AND COORDINATOR OF THE DORICH HOUSE GROUP

European institutions have multiple opportunities for cooperation, which creates a dispersion of efforts with a large number of partners involved in only one or two activities. Given the difficulties of managing such large partnerships, Kingston University believed that creating a network of higher education institutions would help to build on strategic and existing collaborations. Contemplating ways to improve international partnerships and the European and Study Abroad Office (then European Office) prompted an internal debate that resulted in the approval of a proposal by the Academic Directorate in 2007. Thus, the Dorich House Group was initiated and immediately attempted to answer a number of questions.

What Are the Goals?

The primary goal in setting up a new structure was to benefit from a better use of resources and to increase joint activities with our European partners. International activities in Europe engage a large number of partners. The majority of these relationships do not go further than exchanging emails and documents at specified times of the year. As such, we endeavored to create a network where partnerships could represent a good value and not simply a document signed by high-level individuals.

Knowing partners better helps to create a better atmosphere and increase confidence among institutions. I was fortunate to be able to interest my senior colleagues in Kingston in the initiative. Little money was needed and the results would depend on us and not on external suppliers. As a result, we were granted a green light for the second step.

Who Are the Best Partners to Invite?

Our list of partners showed great diversity; accordingly, we needed specific criteria to make an initial selection. Geographical location was the first. In reality, there were more opportunities for funding with European countries. That limited the list to only 120 institutions. Further criteria included: successful exchanges, good reports from students, geographical spread, one institution per country, potential complementarities, similar size to Kingston and similar type of institution, not too old, not created last year and, possibly the most important, did we know anyone at the given institution?

Once a short list was produced, we used a European conference (the European Association for International Education) to meet potential members and introduce the possibility of creating a network. Unsurprisingly, all those approached responded enthusiastically. I received initial approval from six institutions: Carl von Ossietzky Universität Oldenburg (Germany), Istanbul Bilgi University (Turkey), Mykolo Romerio Universitetas (Lithuania), Universidad de Cádiz (Spain), and Université Jean Moulin Lyon 3 and Université Lumière Lyon 2 (France). My institution invited their representatives to Kingston. In addition to giving a presentation about their universities to our staff, we had the opportunity to agree on the best ways to proceed.

How Do We Organize Our Activities?

The representatives that met in June 2007 came from university offices that dealt with European and/or international issues. From the beginning, it was clear that we did not want to be the only ones involved in the activities. We discussed ways to engage the rest of the institutions, and decided that a Memorandum of Understanding was a good tool to measure progress. But more than having a document full of nice (but empty) words, we wanted an Action Plan that included the possibility of creating a network.

Once the Action Plan was signed by the heads of the institutions, the second and the third challenges were immediate: linking and involving the institutions beyond a signature in a document. Negotiations for bilateral agreements started in parallel to prepare for what was supposed to be the defining point: a meeting of the rectors, presidents, and vice-chancellors to name and define the network and its objectives. In November 2008, Kingston hosted the delegations, and the outcome of the meeting was the official birth of the Dorich House Group of European Universities, named after the museum owned by the University where the meeting was held.

A new Action Plan for the following year included all types of mobility for students and staff and the development of other activities in the months to come. Special attention was given to the promotion of joint research and the development of double degrees as elements for the consolidation of the network. It was also decided that: a) a Steering committee would meet every November to monitor the results and make decisions on future developments, and b) an Operational Group would coordinate the activities with one representative from each member.

The Operational Group is in contact via email to keep the communication updated. Several other colleagues are involved in different processes to avoid concentrating all the efforts in a small number of colleagues. An intranet is being developed to improve the processes.

Getting Results

The need for improving the results of the collaboration every year and adding new activities to the list is of great importance. Because joint research is a priority, three groups were established to put together colleagues from all institutions for collaborative work. Bilateral agreements are signed among all members and the Dorich House Group has become a reference for potential partnerships.

An important element to consider is the flexibility of the Group in allowing member institutions to join activities. The philosophy behind the network stresses that a project with four partners is better than the inexistence of projects due to a lack of agreement between colleagues from different backgrounds. This makes things work smoothly and increases the commitment level among the colleagues involved.

Some figures from 2009-2010: five research or collaborative projects were submitted with all members involved in at least one of them; a book was published on sustainability; 98 student exchanges took place (an increase of 20 percent from the previous year); 18 staff members (academic and administrative) visited other member institutions to explore cooperation or to share experiences; and 34 researchers met to discuss joint projects (not including the hosts of the meetings). These are promising figures for a network that only started in 2009.

The Immediate Future

The Dorich House Group now has eight members. Malmö University (Sweden) joined last November and brings new initiatives to the Group. Few members are expected to join in the future. The network prefers a small group of institutions to make activities easier to promote and implement. We are still considering opening the network to non-European institutions. This would have clear advantages, but also would change some of the foundations grounded in European funding and origins.

In addition, 2011 brought new developments in research. Five new groups are at the initial stages of discussing potential collaboration. This means that eight groups will be working in fields such as migration, aging population, sustainability, new media and communication, urban studies, justice and human rights, art and design, and employment and human resources. The Group benefits from the wide variety of degrees offered by its members, and their different areas of interest and approaches to research activities.

Conclusion

In conclusion, there are two important issues to mention: the challenges in the near future and how to embed the activities of the Group in the ordinary life of our institutions.

The need for growth is a constant worry for those who manage the Group. How we can run more activities and enlarge the population involved are recurrent topics for discussion. However, it is important to stress the practical approach taken from the very beginning. Some activities have proven to be less successful than expected and have been abandoned if there was not a clear plan for improvement. The Group has always preferred to start new activities than to maintain those with little chance for survival.

The involvement of our colleagues at home has been one of the more challenging issues and still has a long way to go. But it is also fair to say that the mention of the Dorich House Group is common in many of the activities run in our institutions. After giving priority to the Group for mobility or allocating small amounts of money to facilitate an incipient possibility, the Dorich House Group is seen as a positive venture for our institutions, and the initial reaction to proposals for collaboration is better received. And that is exactly what the objective was.

Chapter Seventeen

Establishing International Linkages at Historically Black Colleges and Universities: The Case of Winston-Salem State University

Peggy Valentine, Dean, School of Health Sciences, Winston-Salem State University

Jessica Bailey, Dean, School of Business and Economics, Winston-Salem State University

Joti Sekhon, Director of International Programs, Winston-Salem State University

Introduction

Higher educational institutions prepare students to serve and compete in a global society. For Historically Black Colleges and Universities (HBCUs), this has been challenging. Many of these campuses harbor concerns about limited resources, lack of an international focus, and heavy teaching loads of the faculty.

HBCUs often have had limited resources with which to establish international linkages (Haines, 2010; Ezzell and Schexnider, 2010). Further, many students attending HBCUs have not had the opportunity to develop proficiency in a second language, and have insufficient resources to travel abroad and experience foreign cultures (Blum, 2011). As a result, African-American participation in international linkages has remained relatively low in comparison to the general population. This is confirmed by a report on current trends in U.S. study abroad (2007), where African-Americans represent four percent of U.S. study abroad programs, even though they make up twelve percent of the U.S. population.

Because of limited resources, HBCUs have often placed other commitments and priorities over institutionalizing international education. As a result, few faculty members on these campuses are sufficiently immersed in international research or teaching (Akomolafe, 2000). When faculty members lack these experiences, they are unable to share accurate information on international opportunities to students. Nevertheless, there are opportunities to increase the involvement of HBCUs in international education through diversity initiatives that encourage partnership and collaboration with minority-serving institutions.

Background on Winston-Salem State University

Certain larger HBCUs, such as Howard University, Florida A&M University, and Southern University, have longstanding global presences. Smaller HBCUs, such as Winston-Salem State University, whose primary mission is teaching may be more challenged to provide these opportunities to its faculty and students. This chapter highlights the efforts of Winston-Salem State University to increase its international education efforts for faculty and students.

Winston-Salem State University (WSSU) is a historically black university that traces its history to September 1892. Much has changed since the first class of 25 aspiring teachers were educated by one faculty member in a one-room building. The university now enrolls 6,400 students and has a faculty of about 500 members. As a constituent institution of the University of North Carolina, its participation in international programs developed slowly over time, as the original focus was on teaching. The primary reason for becoming involved was to meet the University of North Carolina's strategic goal of promoting "an international perspective throughout the University community to prepare citizens to become leaders in a multi-ethnic and global society."

It is estimated that fewer than 100 students at WSSU have participated in study abroad programs during its 119-year history. During the past decade, however, the university has expanded its international education efforts based on changing demographics and the need to prepare students to compete globally.

The establishment of an Office of International Programs in September 2000 was a key factor in expanding international linkages at WSSU. This office coordinates and executes programs that prepare students for a wholesome life of responsive citizenship, leadership, and service in the global society. It further allows the university to promote global readiness through increased international partnerships for global awareness of faculty and students. Through this office, there has been an increased focus on international education, including study abroad, curriculum infusion, and faculty and student exchanges.

International Efforts

Study abroad experiences typically range from one to sixteen weeks. These include faculty-led study abroad programs, such as the Ghana and Benin program, designed to expose students to the political, economic, social, and cultural realities of contemporary Africa. It focuses on the historical legacy of the trans-Atlantic slave trade and of British (Ghana) and French (Benin) colonialism in Africa. The program is interdisciplinary in nature and open to sophomore, junior, and senior WSSU students from all schools and departments, with a particular emphasis on the social sciences, humanities, education, and health sciences. This program is part of a comprehensive partnership for student and faculty exchanges as well as for research collaboration with the University of Cape Coast in Ghana. Students also participate in summer or semester-long study abroad through the University of North Carolina Exchange Program, the partnership with three Brazilian universities through a grant from the U.S. Department of Education's Fund for the Improvement of Postsecondary Education (FIPSE) program, as well as through other study abroad providers. Through a partnership with Johns Hopkins University, Minority Health Infrastructure Research Training, WSSU students in the health sciences have served on research teams in Europe and Africa.

Numerous examples can be cited for the provision of faculty and student service, including a partnership with Santa Paula University in San Jose, Costa Rica, for an international fieldwork practice. This experience enables occupational therapy students to function in a global society by developing and advancing culturally competent skills that result in improved client-centered care. During this same period, the curriculum content has been expanded to include courses in global understanding, global health, Portuguese, and Swahili. There is a Bachelor of Arts program in African and African-American Studies, designed to help students acquire a comprehensive and critical knowledge of Africa and the African Diaspora.

Various international courses have been developed, including one where nursing students enrolled in a global understanding course communicate real time through the Internet with physical therapy students in Costa Rica. Even after several years, several of these students have stayed in contact and some have visited each other. Through technological linkages, instructors from France have taught business classes that allow for cross-cultural interaction among students from both countries. The School of Business has added a course entitled, Fundamentals of International Business, to its core curriculum; an important dimension of the course is the module concerning cross-cultural communication and understanding. This affords students the opportunity to appreciate the richness and diversity of doing business in international locations and prepares them for upper-division international courses, such as Global and Ethical Issues in Accounting, International Trade and Financial Institutions, International Finance, Global Issues in Management, Global Electronic Commerce, and International Marketing. The university also hired the former ambassador from Lesotho to the U.S. to serve as diplomat in residence in 2009 to increase faculty and student understanding of global issues facing the African continent.

Partnerships have been developed in Wuhan, China, to expand a nursing program for Chinese students desiring a U.S. education. Student exchanges are being explored in other parts of China and India. In 2010, the University was selected as one of ten universities to participate in the International Academic Partnership Program (IAPP) for India developed by the Institute of International Education (IIE), and funded by the U.S. Department of Education. An India Task Force was developed and a strategic planning process was completed that identified strengths and challenges for developing India partnerships. IIE appointed a mentor to assist WSSU with the program. Discussions are continuing on developing this program and identifying resources.

One important factor in increasing student involvement in WSSU's international education efforts was participation in the Ralph Bunche Society (RBS). This student organization, sponsored by Phelps Stokes Inc., seeks to stimulate racial and ethnic minority student interest in international studies and careers in international leadership. As a fitting tribute to the legacy of Dr. Ralph Bunche and his attributes of perseverance, self-reliance, leadership, service, and the pursuit of academic excellence, WSSU was the first HBCU to be selected to participate in the program in 2006.

Conclusion

Because participation in international education is often challenging for many HBCUs, Winston-Salem State University has sought to increase its involvement by adhering to the following key factors:

- Recognizing the importance of internationalization in the curricula of the university and lives of the students;

- Establishing an International Programs Office to coordinate student and faculty opportunities; and

- Establishing partnerships with key institutions and organizations to increase international involvement.

Significant challenges remain, particularly with regard to resources for internationalization in the midst of sharp cuts in the University's budget. A key step toward meeting these challenges is the establishment of the Globalization Task Force by the Provost in Fall 2009 to develop a strategic plan for internationalization in keeping with the strategic goals of the WSSU Strategic Plan.

REFERENCES

Akomolafe, O. (2000). Africanizing HBCU: Problems and prospects of international education in historically black institutions. *African Issues,* 28(1/2).

Blum, J. (April 27, 2010). Regents eliminate more academic programs. *Capitol News Bureau.*

Ezzell Jr., J. L., & Schexnider, A. J. (May-June 2010). Leadership, governance, and sustainability of black colleges and universities. *Trusteeship,* 18(3), 25-28.

Haines, E. (April 5, 2010). Georgia NAACP sues state for underfunding public HBCUs. *Associated Press.*

Obst, D., Bhandari, R., & Witherell, S. (May 2007). Current trends in U.S. study abroad & the impact of strategic diversity initiatives. Institute of International Education, 1.

Chapter Eighteen

Success Factors in Developing a U.S.-Brazilian Educational Partnership Program

Nader Asgary, Professor of Management and Economics, Bentley University

Hans Thamhain, Professor of Management, Bentley University[1]

Introduction

"Brazil was unlike anything I have ever experienced. It opened my eyes to different cultures and personal beliefs. Between the places we visited, the companies we saw…these valuable experiences will help me succeed with all of my future endeavors."

Student comments like this reflect the educational value of institutional partnerships. However, developing these partnerships is no simple task, and outcomes are not always predictable (Altbach & Knight, 2007). They are highly dynamic and intricate processes that require great effort and leadership on both sides. Yet, success is not random. We find that a better understanding of institutional cultures and active engagement among all key stakeholders help build and sustain the mutual trust and interest crucial to such a collaborative venture. To be successful, the leadership team must be capable of more than just executing a partnership plan. They must understand the complex social, technical, and economic issues that determine the culture and value system of their partner institutions. We learned this lesson early in our partnership venture.

Developing the current joint program among four institutions—Bentley University, University of São Paulo (USP), the Universidade Federal do Paraná (UFPR), and University of Texas-Pan American (UTPA)—has required effort, curiosity, optimism, and financial support via a grant from the U.S. Department of Education's (DOE) Fund for the Improvement of Postsecondary Education (FIPSE). This chapter discusses the results and lessons learned from this program, focusing on the critical success factors for such a collaborative venture.

Building Upon Existing Relations

Bentley University and the USP had maintained institutional ties for many years, collaborating on student exchanges, faculty visits, and joint research. A call for grant proposals by the DOE sparked our interest in expanding on these activities. Supported by FIPSE and its Brazilian counterpart, *Fundação Coordenação de Aperfeiçoamento de Pessoal de Nível Superior* (CAPES), the grant aimed to enhance the quality and effectiveness of business education via curriculum development and Brazil-U.S. student exchanges. Realizing the benefits of such grant sponsorship, we organized a team of four institutions to develop a proposal: Bentley University, USP, UTPA, and the UFPR. The existing institutional ties and collaborative relations among faculty proved to be an important condition for developing program details and gaining the commitments necessary for implementation.

The initial objective of this grant program was to strengthen and expand the existing institutional ties by establishing sustainable, long-term, curriculum-based, and student-centered programs in international/global business education at the undergraduate and graduate levels. The consortium program aimed to integrate formal coursework and teaching methods with bi-national classroom learning, global service learning, cross-cultural business knowledge, and the tools and skills needed to solve real-world business problems. Our activities were focused primarily in two areas: student mobility and outreach to the broader community.

In 2007, our consortium won the grant, which provided four years of financial support for the program. An important element of our success was the ten-year relationship among our partners, both bilaterally and intra-nationally. Faculties and administrators from the USP and Bentley University had a longstanding working relationship, including scholarly collaboration, faculty-led student visits, and joint research programs. Similar collaboration existed on joint research and professional networking between Bentley and UTPA, including the organizational framework for study abroad and transferring credits, supported by formal cross-institutional agreements and AACSB accreditation. At the graduate level, three USP doctoral students participated in Bentley's Visiting Fellows Program. This established partnership formed an important basis for further cooperation, thus facilitating grant development and program implementation.

What We Have Accomplished

Student Mobility

The administrative coordination among the participating institutions, such as enrollment, student support, travel logistics, and credit transfer, was organized relatively quickly and executed effectively. All participating students receive a financial stipend to defray the cost of study abroad. Enrolling students in the program requires significant promotion, negotiations, and additional financial incentives (Doyle et al., 2010). Despite this, student recruitment numbers have fallen short of our original plan for reasons discussed throughout this chapter. However, with some innovative curriculum design, onsite support, and student financing, we have been able to complete 35 student exchanges in the following forms.

- Full-semester mobility: We have sent five students to Brazil for a full semester abroad. Competency in Portuguese is critical (Zhang & Mi, 2010). While in Brazil, students took 12-15 credit-hour courses taught in Portuguese at our partner institutions. Although Bentley and UTPA offer Introductory Portuguese I and II each year, many U.S. students are not interested in studying the language and even those who do rarely achieve enough competency to enroll in courses taught in Portuguese. The result has been a lower than expected mobility number. An additional challenge is cost. It is interesting to note that more Brazilian students wish to study at the U.S. partner institutions than U.S. students desiring Brazilian study opportunities. So far, 12 Brazilian students have studied at Bentley and UTPA.

- International internship: This is a three-credit course conducted throughout one month in Rio de Janeiro, Brazil. Before and during their business internship, students engage in Portuguese language training. So far, nine students have participated in this internship course with successful results (Walsh, 2010).

- Two week global business education: For this three-credit course, students are required to study the Portuguese language and the business and cultural environment of Brazil before and during their visit. Sixteen MBA and undergraduate students from Bentley and UTPA have participated in this program to date.

As noted in our surveys conducted at the end of each program, all students were very satisfied with their experience and reported that they acquired significant business and cultural knowledge through the program. The following section describes the courses that have been developed.

Course Development

The partnership program has led to four new course developments that have enriched the business curriculum and enhanced student exchanges between the U.S. and Brazil. The following four courses and short programs have been developed and delivered during the past two years: *Contemporary Practices of Managing Effectively in Technology-Based Business Environments; Enhancing Afro Brazilian Incubator Business Performance; Internship in International Business;* and *Brazil in the Global Economy, Culture, and Commerce.* They are offered at both the graduate and undergraduate level at Bentley and UTPA. Students who enroll in any of these classes are required to engage in Portuguese language training. All courses provide three academic credits.[2]

Service Learning

All student participants of our partnership program engage in dedicated service learning as part of their Brazilian academic and cultural experience. Undergraduate and graduate students work with the Afro Brazilian Incubator (ABI), a not-for-profit organization based in Rio de Janeiro dedicated to supporting minority entrepreneurs. Students' involvement with the Incubator varies depending on their particular program. The minimum level of activity includes meetings and observations with the ABI management team and its clients, but many students immerse themselves more deeply in the Incubator's mission by working intensively with clients, developing business plans, and tying the work directly to their academic experience when they return to Bentley, using the ABI as a case study and making it the topic of research papers and presentations.

Outreach and Program Promotion

In order to promote student exchanges and other multinational business education opportunities within the Brazil-U.S. consortium, Bentley and its partners have developed and disseminated a wide range of information showcasing the components and activities of the program. Our institutional websites and internationally distributed publications, such as *Bentley Global Perspectives* and the *Universidade Federal Do Paraná,* help to inform students and the larger community about the academic program and multicultural events. All students who participate in the International Internship course are required to share their experiences via a formal presentation with the Bentley community. These students must write case studies about SMEs that they visit and develop recommendations to be shared with businesses. Students also develop an awareness of the cultural diversity and collaboration required for managers to succeed in contemporary global business.

Program participants, including faculty, staff, and students, have developed brochures, posters, and events. For instance, we organized campus-wide information sessions and cultural celebrations with the active participation of our international students from Brazil, and hosted a graduate student reception for those visiting from the University of São Paulo. Such grant components create program awareness, expose students to specific academic offerings, and demonstrate the challenges and opportunities of studying abroad (i.e., Dwyer and Courtney, 2004; Ingraham and Peterson, 2004, Doyle et al., 2010).

Challenges and Lessons Learned

Student Mobility

The greatest challenges have been in the area of student mobility, specifically in meeting the promised quota of qualified U.S. students willing to study in Brazil. Based on discussions with prospective students and our own analysis, we have identified five primary challenges:

1. Language barriers and cultural differences appear to be more intimidating with extended visits abroad;

2. Because of the language barrier some students are concerned that taking courses in Brazil will negatively impact their GPA;

3. Students have choices among other study-abroad programs and most are offered in English;

4. The financial support needed from students for full-semester programs often exceeds their capacity to pay; and

5. Students are often unwilling or unable to leave their primary areas of residence for longer periods of time (Asgary and Foster, 2008).

These challenges speak primarily to the need for program flexibility in duration and content. Intensive short-term programs of a one- to four-week duration that also offer the opportunity for extra credit (i.e. double course credit for extra field research, directed study back home, or service learning credit) enhance the attractiveness of the study-abroad module and make it more feasible for students. Furthermore, while our program design originally focused on undergraduate students, we found that such programs are more attractive to graduate students, whose maturity and knowledge enable them to gain more from the experience. They are also more likely to collaborate on scholarly activities with faculty members. The graduate students who have studied in Brazil unanimously praise the program, emphasizing the value of experiential learning and the unique cultural experience. They also contribute effectively to their host organizations, which provide opportunities for internships and field research.

Four-way Partnership Model

Despite the numerous benefits of the consortium, this four-way model has complicated administrative procedures and reduced flexibility and agility compared to a two-way partnership. The lessons learned from these challenges are the need for setting up administrative procedures and operational guidelines early in the partnership that make the subsequent student exchanges and collaborations more autonomous for each partner, yet transparent to all partners, to assure synergism from all partnership activities.

Portuguese Language Proficiency

Ideally, students should possess a basic proficiency in Portuguese before traveling to Brazil. However, this requirement presents a substantial barrier to student recruitment. We observed two factors that mitigate the language challenge. First, in the Brazilian organizations we have dealt with, a sufficient number of personnel speak English. Second, students seem to learn the native language onsite in a natural way, being able to communicate on a basic level relatively quickly. Following academic classroom instructions in Brazil, where most courses are conducted in Portuguese, presents different challenges. To follow these instructions and to participate in discussions requires extensive language training, an investment few students are willing to make. A suggestion for future joint-academic programs is to seek courses at Brazilian universities that are taught in English or even Spanish, which is more commonly spoken among U.S. students.

Critical Success Factors

The ultimate goal of our program is for U.S. students to understand the business and cultural environment of Brazil. Therefore, we as educators have to explore methods that appeal to students' curiosity, intelligence, and sense of adventure. By highlighting academic benefits and minimizing anxiety and financial costs, larger numbers of students will choose to travel to Brazil. Our experience has shown that short-term courses that contain cultural components are far more appealing to students, who wish to explore their host country. Students report that Brazil's open and welcoming culture combined with its rapidly emerging economy make the country an attractive destination. Based on our assessments, all students who visit Brazil for the first time via one of our partnership programs state that they hope to travel there again. It is rewarding that several student participants are currently exploring employment opportunities in Brazil. A few Brazilian partnership success factors are highlighted below.

- Emphasize benefits beyond academic credit. At each partner institution, faculty and staff must make the study abroad program attractive to students beyond academic credit, emphasizing the multicultural benefits and exposure to multinational business practices essential to succeeding in today's global business environment. This requires establishing effective websites, brochures, and information sessions.

- Utilize short programs to attract additional students. Because of the limitations of attracting students for full semester exchanges, we developed several short-term programs that run during semester breaks (Allen, 2010). We expanded already existing academic models for study abroad, including: 1) short term intensive courses, 2) field studies, 3) internships, and 4) community and enterprise outreach that included seminars, workshops, and study tours in cooperation with non-academic partners, local businesses, trade associations, and community organizations (Asgary and Foster, 2008; Anderson et al, 2009).

- Provide financial support to students. Many qualified students who are interested in taking advantage of these study-abroad opportunities cannot afford the full cost of such programs (Doyle et al., 2010). Yet, with some creativity, students' costs can be reduced. We have reduced costs by relying on our partners to assist in planning and guiding us on cultural excursions, plant tours, access to academic facilities, courses and seminars, and accommodations. In addition, group discounts and corporate/educational rates, especially for travel and accommodations, should be fully utilized. All of this requires extra effort by administrators and faculty on both sides of the border. Institutional support for overhead and operational risks is also necessary.

- Support language proficiency. Ideally, institutions with a focus on Brazil need to support and encourage Portuguese language training (Zhang and Mi, 2010). Unfortunately, Portuguese language is not among those considered "common languages" (i.e., Spanish, Chinese), highly demanded by students; therefore, the likelihood that an institution will allocate funding support is low, especially given the financial constraints currently impacting higher education institutions. Sustainable funding for language instruction would have to come from an outside agency (i.e., FIPSE). Other countries such as France are taking the approach of having Brazilian institutions offer a greater number of courses taught in English. It is clear that there are significant challenges in the area of learning Portuguese. Perhaps a larger number of students need to gain exposure to Brazilian business and culture through these short-term programs, which might lead them to learn the language independently via customized language training.

Program Sustainability

It has been gratifying to observe how the FIPSE grant has deepened existing institutional ties among the partner institutions. We have expanded student mobility, curriculum development, and language and cultural knowledge, understanding, and appreciation. Sustaining this momentum in the coming years is our final program objective, which we intend to pursue primarily through service learning, expansion of the MBA program component, and extended outreach.

Service Learning

Bentley University's commitment to service learning is well established. The Bentley Service-Learning Center (BSLC) challenges its students through critical thinking and self-examination to become socially responsible, engaged, and aware leaders. By encouraging students to become co-learners, co-educators, and co-facilitators with faculty and community partners, BSLC seeks to develop a base of educated and philanthropically aware professionals who take the initiative to address the needs of their community. In the long-term, successful service learning should empower students to use the skills and lessons developed in their curriculum- and service-based education to become civic leaders and advocates for change.

We believe it is critical to amplify the Brazil program's current service learning components by increasing the quality and frequency of such opportunities in Brazil and the U.S. The work our students have undertaken with the Afro-Brazilian Incubator serves as an excellent example of how to integrate service learning into an academic offering.

MBA

Expansion of the MBA program component is integral to our sustainability plans. Bentley and USP have an MBA course that allows students from Brazil and Bentley, jointly, to visit U.S. corporations and attend business presentations. Our plans include inviting Brazilian SMEs served by the Afro Brazilian Incubator to participate in this course.

Outreach

We plan to continue to enhance joint faculty research, presentations, and attendance at conferences. Bentley and its partners will continue to conduct scholarly research, involving students as well as faculty. We will broadly disseminate information related to the program through reports, monographs, colloquia at universities and professional organizations, and international conferences. Additionally, there are scholarly collaborations (i.e. case studies) between Bentley faculty and research division of the ABI.

Conclusions

Our proposal contained three primary activity areas: student exchanges, curriculum development, and research. The greatest challenges involved student recruitment with regards to Portuguese language skills and the ability for students to perform well at Brazilian partner institutions where courses are taught in Portuguese. In response, we have initiated a combination of innovative short-term programs that fit students' interests and needs and recruit significant numbers of students to participate in the program. Participating students acquire business and cultural knowledge of Brazil, experience service learning, and develop some degree of Portuguese language competence. Students who participate in these programs rate them highly and state that they acquired a significant degree of cultural awareness and business knowledge through such programs. Some of these students state that they will return to Brazil to explore employment or career opportunities.

It has been challenging to operate efficiently with four partner institutions. Yet, after overcoming the start-up difficulties, we have been able to collaborate with all partners and have had significant success in terms of student mobility and scholarly activities. After operating for four years, faculty and administrators have gained a good understanding of the challenges involved in such a bi-national joint program, and have learned the lessons critical for success. We also learned to direct our energy and resources toward components that are most likely to be successful. Faculty commitment is a key factor in the success or failure of these programs. Incentives such as recognition and intellectual and financial benefits established by educational institutions and grantee organizations can provide strong motivators for attracting faculty to participate in these important partnership programs.

NOTES

[1] Patricia Foster's contribution toward the development of this manuscript is greatly acknowledged.

[2] A more detailed description of these courses is available on the Bentley University website: www.bentley.edu.

REFERENCES

Asgary, N., & Foster, P. (2008). Bentley-Brazil partnership flourishes. *Bentley Global Perspectives,* 2, 5-6.

Allen, H. (November 2010). What shapes short-term study abroad experiences? A comparative case study of students' motives and goals. *Journal of Studies in International Education,* 14, 452-470.

Altbach, P., & Knight, J. (Fall/Winter 2007). The internationalization of higher education: Motivations and realities. *Journal of Studies in International Education,* 11, 290-305.

Anderson, P., Lawton, L., Rexeisen, R., & Hubbard, A. (July 2009). Short-term study abroad and intercultural sensitivity: A pilot study. *International Journal of Intercultural Relations,* 30(4), 457-469.

Doyle, S., Gendall, P., Meyer, L., Hoek, J., Tait, C., McKenzie, L., & Loorparg, A. (November 2010). An investigation of factors associated with student participation in study abroad. *Journal of Studies in International Education,* 14, 471-490.

Dwyer, M., & Peters, C. (2004). The benefits of study abroad. *Transitions Abroad Magazine,* 37(5), 56-60.

Ingraham, E., & Peterson, D. (Fall 2004). Assessing the impact of study abroad on student learning at Michigan State University. *Frontiers: The Interdisciplinary Journal of Study Abroad,* 10, 83-100.

Walsh, K. (2011). Afro-Brazilian business incubator: Students offer small-business consulting overseas. *Bentley Global Perspectives,* 3, 24-26.

Waters, J. (January 24, 2010). Study abroad—pricy and priceless. *Wall Street Journal.*

Zhang, Y., & Mi, Y. (September 2010). Another look at the language difficulties of international students. *Journal of Studies in International Education,* 14, 371-388.

Chapter Nineteen

PERSPECTIVES ON THE SUCCESSFUL START-UP OF STUDY ABROAD PROGRAMS IN HIGHER EDUCATION: THE FACULTY PERSPECTIVE

K. PETER KUCHINKE, PROFESSOR, EDUCATION POLICY, ORGANIZATION AND LEADERSHIP, UNIVERSITY OF ILLINOIS AT URBANA-CHAMPAIGN

This chapter will describe some important aspects of the early phases of international partnerships in higher education, specifically those with a primary objective of exchanging students between universities in the United States and abroad. The perspective is that of a faculty member at a large research university and with a scholarly focus on international and cross-cultural research in workforce and human resource development. Using my experience over the past decade, the chapter will discuss lessons learned, insights gained, and challenges faced. Case examples, drawn from two long-term programs that I developed and direct, will illustrate the different themes and issues.

A point of reference for this chapter is my role as director of two student exchange programs: the first between the University of Illinois and Duisburg-Essen University in Germany established in 2002 and titled BEST (Business and Economics Summer Term), the second as a four-way partnership between University of Illinois, University of Minnesota, University of Sao Paulo, and the Federal University of Brasilia. The latter project started in 2008 and is funded by the U.S. Department of Education's Fund for the Improvement of Postsecondary Education (FIPSE) and its Brazilian government's counterpart, CAPES. Targeted primarily toward undergraduate students, both programs are campus-wide initiatives that attract students from diverse majors and involve tuition and fee reciprocity for outgoing and incoming students. Both programs attract between 10 and 15 students per year, which is comparable in size to other programs on our campus. The following pages address several start-up aspects of these programs, including initiating international partnerships, navigating institutional environments, and motivation and rewards for developing new programs.

Initiating International Partnerships

Contemporary international connections occur in many forms, including meetings at conferences, speaking engagements and short-term lecture visits, writing projects, and research collaborations. These informal network ties, which are central to the research and scholarship of individual faculty, are often the primary means by which formal partnerships begin. Each of the two programs under my leadership, for example, developed from personal connections with colleagues abroad, and almost as an afterthought to ongoing research and teaching collaborations that had existed prior to the start of the exchange program. In the case of BEST, a summer term as visiting professor in the School of Business and Economics at Duisburg-Essen involved an informal meeting with a group of U.S. students who were participating in the summer program. This, in turn, led to an invitation to join the consortium of U.S. universities already involved in BEST. Similarly, the Brazilian FIPSE program came about after I became acquainted with an accounting professor at the University of São Paulo (USP) who had enrolled in my home department to earn a second doctorate. Upon his return, he became head of the department and now serves as the Brazilian project director at USP.

Each new partnership was motivated by a personal commitment to international work, the promise of strengthening and broadening existing relationships, and the recognition that students at my home institution would gain value from a new international program. My own motivation was enhanced by a university environment in which internationalization and the provision of study-abroad experiences of undergraduates are strategic priorities. The institutional receptivity for new programs at Illinois, however, has not translated into tangible support for those interested in establishing new programs. Much of the burden involved in navigating the administrative requirements for forging the partnership for the (not externally-funded) BEST program fell on my own shoulders. The FIPSE project, initiated several years after BEST, was externally funded, and a modest amount of support (equivalent to one course buy-out for one semester during the four-year length of the project) was given during the first year for the drafting and signing of a collaborative agreement. As with many such projects, the work required exceeded the support provided, and the program leadership beyond the initial year was carried out without additional support from the funder or the institution.

These short examples suggest three lessons for institutions desiring to increase international programs: 1) enable faculty to create, maintain, and nurture informal international connections as these often evolve into formal arrangements; 2) create institutional support and training to assist in developing new programs; and 3) build recognition and rewards for program development into the tenure/promotion and annual review processes.

Navigating Institutional Environments for International Agreements

Faculty members planning to implement a new program must navigate an institutional environment of approval and oversight that can be complex and time consuming. Whereas smaller universities seem to have greater degrees of flexibility and unit-level autonomy, large public universities often require extensive administrative and legal review and approval loops before an agreement can be signed and the program can begin. In my experience, the faculty member is often responsible for moving the agreement through the administrative structure, a process that can take several months.

In the case of BEST, much time was spent in negotiation with academic units outside of my own that would send and receive exchange students under this program, each of which had different admission requirements for exchange students, different course prerequisites, and admission quotas. These had to be communicated clearly to the German partner university. A second hurdle came from the fact that incoming German students, for whom the first academic degree tends to be the equivalent of a master's degree (*Diplom*), were classified as undergraduates even though they might be in their fifth or sixth year of study. Without being able to uniformly reclassify them as master's students, enrollment override permits were required for every graduate level course. This hurdle will decrease as German universities, in conformance to the European Union Bologna agreement, have begun to transition to a degree structure similar to the Anglo-Saxon model.

The scope of the FIPSE program was narrower, involving primarily a single college at each university, although the program is open to students from other majors as well. What was gained in ease of negotiation by involving a smaller number of units, however, was lost by the complexities of forging contract language that would pass muster in four large public universities. Numerous drafts were circulated, edited, revised, and reviewed before a version was reached that met the requirements of all four institutions. Review cycles involved multiple levels, including the department, college, campus, and subsequent legal review at each institution. Every change by one institution required a new round of review by the other three, and more than a year was spent on contractual matters, including the translation of the English versions and amendments into Portuguese.

No matter how motivated individual faculty members are to develop the partnership, the project is not official until all the details involved in an international exchange program have been addressed. Much persistence, clear communication, and, sometimes, hard negotiation and compromise are required to bring a program to life. It is mandatory to share a high degree of commitment to the project among faculty leaders at each partner university, for whom the work on the contractual aspects of the program usually comes on top of the regular work responsibilities of research, teaching, and service. Where the intrinsic interest in the program is not present, the attention to detail required for success can suffer. This was illustrated in one partnership in which the original faculty sponsor left the university during the planning period. The substitute, appointed by the Dean, moved the contractual agreement forward but failed to promote the program and subsequently received far fewer student applications.

The development of an international collaboration requires good will, extra effort, diligence, and patience from the faculty sponsors; it also calls for explanations of the often complicated and idiosyncratic administrative requirements to those working within different bureaucratic systems. Funding agencies can provide critical assistance in this respect, in part because of the detailed mandatory administrative arrangements communicated in the request for proposals for specific programs, in part because of the ongoing support for existing grantees. In the case of FIPSE, the U.S. Department of Education has established a basic administrative framework for the program that the Brazilian counterparts agree on and all potential partner universities understand. Equally important are the annual project director conferences where much helpful advice and recommendations are available from agency staff and experienced program directors. A case in point in my project was the suggestion that a series of similar bilateral agreements could take the place of a single four-way agreement so that individual requirements of specific pairs of university partners could be accommodated more effectively.

Rewards and Motivation

Given the substantial effort and workload required to initiate, develop, and maintain an international program, and the formal incentives for faculty members who are assessed based on research, teaching, and service, what explains the relative high level of faculty motivation and initiative for these projects? I suggest three factors: 1) synergy with one's research and scholarship, 2) dedication to enriching student learning, and 3) increased opportunities to network and collaborate with colleagues abroad.

As described earlier, opportunities for institutional collaboration often arise out of existing research and teaching projects of individual faculty members, who when visiting abroad can scan the institutional environment and detect or create collaborative endeavors. While teaching a faculty development workshop in Brazil several years ago, for example, I had the opportunity to meet with the dean of the college, and our conversation turned to exploring opportunities to collaborate at the college and university levels. This conversation, in turn, launched the planning phase for the current project and the decision to apply for funding. While some professors assume this wider role of a representative of their home institution on their own, colleges and universities can emphasize this citizenship role to new members of faculty as part of the expected behavior when working abroad. In annual reviews, program development efforts, such as setting up a new international program, should be recognized and rewarded. A second motivating factor is the commitment of faculty to share with their students their own joy and passion for the enriching process of working and living in other cultures. Higher education has much to gain through the process of a global exchange of ideas; many education researchers concur that solutions to global issues cannot be found in a single country or cultural context. Universities are committed to preparing students for their future role as global citizens, which includes the opportunity to study abroad and experience cultural contexts other than their own. The international connections that faculty members forge as part of their own work can serve as a valuable conduit for enriching the educational experience of our students.

Finally, an important benefit for faculty members developing and directing international student exchange programs is the increased visibility in the home and foreign institutions, and also the increased range of their professional network. Exchange programs often attract students from a range of majors; subsequently, program directors become known to a range of faculty advisors wider than immediate colleagues in the faculty members' area of research specialization. This expansion of the professional network increases the potential for cross-disciplinary work, collaborative projects across professional fields, and enhanced reputation of the researcher and her or his home university. At research intensive universities, specifically, the service and teaching aspect of an international exchange program can and should be enhanced through publications and research projects.

Chapter Twenty

Breaking the Boundaries across Nations through International Partnership Programs: Lessons from a Student Exchange Consortia Program

Luis O. Tedeschi, Associate Professor, Department of Animal Science, Texas A&M University

Cathryn Clement, Coordinator for International Academic Programs, College of Agricultural and Life Sciences, Texas A&M University

Kim E. Dooley, Professor, Department of Agricultural Leadership, Education, and Communications, Texas A&M University

Introduction

In January 2011, at the Association of American Colleges and Universities (AAC&U) annual meeting in San Francisco, the U.S. Department of Education's assistant secretary for postsecondary education, Dr. Eduardo Ochoa, emphasized the importance of establishing international partnership programs (e.g. exchange student programs and study abroad courses) so that the U.S. can become more competitive with other countries when seeking jobs and advanced studies. Currently, U.S. students are more limited in postsecondary education options than students from other countries, specifically European countries (Lum, 2011).

Considerable changes in the teaching and the curriculum of agriculture, especially animal agriculture, have occurred in the U.S. since 1915 (Buchanan, 2008), but few modifications have been made regarding internationalization and globalization of the curriculum. At the end of the 20th century, females were still underrepresented, although gender discrepancies have been decreasing mainly because of an increase in women receiving doctorate degrees (Pell, 1996). More recently, women were reported to be 50 percent of the undergraduate population in animal science (Beck and Swanson, 2003). Gender and race issues are important factors to be brought into this discussion because females have consistently comprised the majority of enrolled students in international education (Shirley, 2006), and because 81.8 percent of the U.S. students that studied abroad in 2007/2008 were Caucasian (American Insitute For Foreign Study, 2010). In addition, from 1999–2009, agriculture students represented less than two percent of students studying abroad (Institute of International Education, 2010).[1] Upcoming challenges we will have to face in the next decades are global in nature. Modifications in the curriculum have to take into account this data and these student profile changes if we are to position our students in the world market.

Brazil and the U.S. have different ruminant (e.g. cattle, sheep, and goats) production systems, but together they have the largest commercial herd of ruminant animals in the world (http://www.fao.org). A production alliance between these two countries is desirable not only to secure commodity trades worldwide, but also to train our students for future market needs. Therefore, a student exchange program between the U.S. and Brazil was designed to increase the awareness of undergraduate and graduate students to differences and similarities of ruminant production and related industries between these two countries. Funding from the U.S. Department of Education through the Fund for the Improvement of Postsecondary Education (FIPSE) in the U.S. and the *Fundação Coordenação de Aperfeiçoamento de Pessoal de Nível Superior* (CAPES) in Brazil provided financial and logistical support for the exchange of students studying ruminant production, nutrition, and related fields. The key steps in developing a successful transnational partnership program will be discussed based on our experiences with this international academic program.

Planning for Meaningful Goals

Clear and attainable goals represent the first step in developing successful transnational exchange programs. Usually one to three goals are ideal, and they can be a mixture of short-, intermediate-, and long-term goals. The goals of our specific exchange project under the FIPSE/CAPES program included: 1) increasing the international competency of animal science students, 2) developing an electronic-mediated course on ruminant production, and 3) promoting collaborative research, education, and outreach projects.

The objectives of the first goal were two-fold: 1) for U.S. students to become proficient in Portuguese, and 2) for U.S. students to become competent in ruminant production scenarios and understand their environmental impact in different regions of production in a tropical region (i.e. Brazil). Accomplishing these objectives would increase the competitiveness and readiness of our students to secure jobs around the world by broadening their areas of performance, scope of knowledge, communication skills, and professional network.

The first goal was met as soon as the exchange students returned to their home institutions. The second goal was to develop a web-based course that would allow students around the world to attend and receive academic credits. The third goal was to encourage faculty exchange among the institutions to develop new collaborative research, educational, and outreach projects. These were designed to be intermediate to long-term goals.

Developing a web-based course presented several challenges, including weaving together the Brazilian and North American approaches to the subject matter, dealing with differences in technology and equipment as well as differences in academic terms and course accreditation. It is necessary for the partners to delineate responsibilities in course preparation, provide clear deadlines, and have frequent communications about the project's progress.

To encourage faculty collaboration among the partner institutions, the dissemination of results, site visits by project personnel to their partner institutions, and frequent communication among the partners are crucial. The dissemination of results was accomplished through seminars given by visiting partners, classroom visits by project directors, sharing project reports, and publishing articles about the project. Annual directors meetings have been used as a starting point for site visits by the participating directors, and email is integral for sharing program-related information, updates, and pending possibilities.

Documenting the Achievement of the Goals

Transnational exchange programs require continuous monitoring of their goals and objectives. Proper documentation of the program's achievements is crucial to measure its success, including changes in the core program; immediate and long-term educational impacts; academic or professional awards; dissemination and publication of effects of training students and faculty; impacts at the local, regional, and national levels; and special activities such as internships and events. One rewarding strategy we used to ensure the practical training of our students after the exchange period was a paid-internship of at least two months at the JBS Five Rivers Cattle Feeding Company in the U.S.

The Internet has provided us with several online tools that can quickly document the evolution of exchange student programs. It has also allowed students and faculty travelling abroad to maintain their connection with their friends and family through social media such as Facebook and Twitter, among others. In our exchange program, we require students to maintain an active blog/journal of their activities while abroad, using eLearning technologies such as Blackboard, Moodle, and a Facebook-based, project specific group.

Journaling provides multiple benefits to the program. The Blackboard and Moodle venues are exchanged only between the student, the project directors, and the evaluator. These allow: 1) students to analyze their experiences and assimilate their lessons through written expression of their activities and their emotional and cognitive responses, and 2) project directors to review the acculturation process the students are going through and provide input when necessary. The Facebook venue allows students to share their experiences and has the additional benefits of: 1) serving as a recruiting tool for new exchange students, and 2) helping prepare prospective students for some of the challenges and rewards they can expect. These journal entries are also a means by which the project evaluator can gauge how successful the program is in developing more culturally competent students.

Procedures Needed to Achieve the Goals

The first procedure is the development of a Memorandum of Understanding (MOU) or Memorandum of Agreement (MOA) that details processes and policies for the transference of academic credits and the facilitation of student exchange. Since most institutions have pre-established models for MOU/MOA, it is necessary to blend each partner's requirements related to institutional, state, or national laws and policies into a document that is acceptable by all parties. Utilizing reciprocal exchange agreements (REEP) provides mechanisms for transferring credits for academic work at the partner institution to the home institution. Students make arrangements for individual course credit equivalencies, and their unit head and/or dean approve them prior to the student leaving their home institution. REEP allow students to pay tuition and fees only to their home institution, so that they maintain continuous enrollment and remain eligible for financial aid. REEP students pay only nominal fees at the host institution, such as ID fees, sport passes, etc. Most institutions require that the numbers of students exchanged be equal over a certain period of time, usually five years, which is commonly the length of MOU/MOA.

Student recruitment is the next stumbling block in a successful student exchange program. We highlight four areas in the recruitment. First, frequent motivational messages are necessary because students are usually the first individuals who need to show initiative to participate in an international program. Particularly useful are informal meetings between interested students and past program participants, as being able to talk to someone who has been through the experience will often help students to make a decision. Second, parents need to be supportive of the international program, and it needs to be made clear to students that their parents are welcome to contact project directors with questions. The third component is partial or full scholarship support. Fourth, creating awareness among academic advisors and other faculty is necessary so that they know to direct students interested in an international academic experience to your program.

The harmony between these components is essential to maintaining a continuous (bilateral) flow of students. In our program, we conducted frequent classroom presentations and group informational meetings about the international program; developed informational flyers for regular and electronic mails to faculty, staff, and students as well as web page slides; and arranged presentations by students who had previously participated in exchange programs at informational gatherings and in classrooms. Other recommendations as suggested by the American Insitute For Foreign Study (2010) include workshops on financial aid and study abroad scholarships, encouraging faculty and staff participation, and creating study abroad job descriptions promoting study abroad scholarships.

Summary

It is urgent to change our core curriculum in agriculture, more specifically animal agriculture, to respond to the needs of contemporary students and the global economy. This can be accomplished by explicitly including internationalization and globalization topics via international partnership programs. The successful organization of international programs requires extra work and time, and a coordinated effort among different institutions around the globe.

NOTES

[1] For more information, please visit: www.iie.org/en/Who-We-Are/News-and-Events/Press-Center/Press-Releases/2010/2010-11-15-Open-Doors-US-Study-Abroad

REFERENCES

American Insitute For Foreign Study. (2010). Diversity in international education—A hands-on workshop: summary report. Washington, DC.: American Institute For Foreign Study. Retrived from http://www.aifsabroad.com/advisors/publications.asp.

Beck, M. M., & Swanson, J. C. (2003). Value-added animal agriculture: Inclusion of race and gender in the professional formula. *Journal of Animal Science*, 81, 2895-2903.

Buchanan, D. S. (2008). ASAS Centennial Paper: Animal science teaching: A century of excellence. *Journal of Animal Science,* 86, 3640-3646.

Chow, P., & Bhandari, R. (2010). *Open Doors 2010: Report on international educational exchange*. New York, NY: Institute of International Education.

Lum, L. (2011). Federal postsecondary education leader urges unit on college completion message. Retrieved from http://diverseeducation.com/article/14693/. Accessed on March 11, 2011.

Pell, A. N. (1996). Fixing the leaky pipeline: Women scientists in academia. *Journal of Animal Science,* 74, 2843-2848.

Shirley, S. W. (2006). The gender gap in post-secondary study abroad: Understanding and marketing to male students. Dissertation, University of North Dakota, Grand Forks, ND.

Chapter Twenty-one

HOW TO DEVELOP INTERNATIONAL PARTNERSHIPS WITH U.S. INSTITUTIONS: MOVING FROM FEEL-GOOD AGREEMENTS TO REAL AGREEMENTS

FANTA AW, ASSISTANT VICE PRESIDENT OF CAMPUS LIFE AND DIRECTOR OF INTERNATIONAL STUDENT AND SCHOLAR SERVICES, AMERICAN UNIVERSITY

LEEANNE DUNSMORE, ASSOCIATE DEAN FOR PROGRAM DEVELOPMENT AND GRADUATE ADMISSIONS, AMERICAN UNIVERSITY

International partners often view the process of developing partnerships with institutions in the United States as a daunting task, given the number, types, and range of potential partnership options. International partners, faced with the sheer number of U.S. institutions and the decentralized structure of higher education, must determine which institutions to partner with and understand the process for developing sustainable partnerships.

As senior international educators we have fielded questions over the years from hundreds of international institutions from around the globe that have expressed an interest in developing linkages and international partnerships, including student and faculty exchange programs, institutional capacity building, curriculum development, dual/joint degree programs, and research collaboration. As a result, we have developed mechanisms for determining potential suitable academic partnerships. This article provides a framework for understanding how to develop partnerships with institutions in the United States and outlines key questions that need to be answered to move forward.

Three Key Dimensions for Developing Institutional Partnerships

Developing institutional partnerships requires the consideration of a number of factors best illustrated by the following wheel:

FIGURE 21.1: FACTORS FOR DEVELOPING INTERNATIONAL PARTNERSHIPS

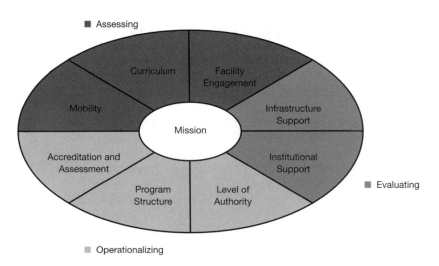

Each spoke of the wheel represents a central element in developing successful partnerships with U.S. institutions.

Core to the partnership is a common mission. Mission and values are what define and differentiate institutions. In selecting a partner, one must have a clear understanding of the mission, values, and culture of one's own institution, and how those are aligned with the mission, values, and culture of the institution with which one wishes to establish linkages/partnerships. It is important to evaluate whether the institution you have identified for a possible partnership is an appropriate partner based on shared mission and values.

Developing institutional partnerships with U.S. institutions involves three key dimensions. The dimensions are as follows: assessing a partnership; evaluating the feasibility of the partnership; operationalizing the partnership.

Assessing Partnerships: Evaluating the Core Mission and Values

In order to determine the feasibility of a potential partnership, institutions in the United States look for and assess "institutional fit." By institutional fit, we mean compatibility of institution, shared vision and mission, faculty interest and engagement, and curriculum "fit." Therefore, international partners must be able to answer the following questions:

- Is the international partner institution of comparable rank or reputation?
- Could the partnership garner sufficient faculty interest and involvement?
- Who are existing faculty with content knowledge and expertise to involve?
- Is the existing curriculum aligned with stated outcome or will the partnership call for enhancements to the curriculum or a new curriculum?
- What would be gained by the partnership (reputation, curriculum enhancements, increased mobility, capacity building)?
- What other institutional partners exist in this region, and how will new institutional partners differentiate themselves in the market?

The issue of institutional "fit" involves tangible and intangible measures. It is therefore helpful for international partners to provide both information about institutional profile and clarity regarding the purpose and mission of partnering. It is our experience that solicitations from international partners often lack clarity of purpose and do not denote an awareness and knowledge of U.S. institutions. Many times requests for partnerships are viewed by U.S. institutions as fishing expeditions, unlikely to yield much result. The standard request for partnering is unlikely to garner a response from U.S. institutions unless it is carefully crafted and specific. The international partner must be able to articulate how the relationship will benefit both parties.

Evaluating the Feasibility of the Partnership

Assuming that "institutional fit" is established, it is important for international institutions to understand and successfully navigate organizational culture and structure. Partnerships with U.S. institutions often involve numerous key stakeholders, each with defined roles and responsibilities and varying levels of authority. Faculty or senior leadership (the president, chancellor, or provost, chief academic officers) are often the drivers in identifying institutional partnerships; however, rarely are they responsible for executing, let alone working out the details of a partnership. It is therefore important for international partners to accurately identify and understand:

- Who the various stakeholders are;
- Who has authority to negotiate on behalf of the U.S. institution;
- Whether negotiation is with the institution writ large or with an individual school or college;
- The level of institutional support for partnerships (who are the institutional champions?);
- Balancing mechanisms—how the partnerships will be supported over time;
- Barriers and challenges to partnerships; and
- A verbal agreement does not constitute an agreement in the U.S. context. An agreement must be written and signed to be binding in the U.S. cultural context.

It is easy to negotiate "feel-good agreements" with U.S. institutions, whereby the senior leadership of an American institution during an international visit is presented with a potential partnership opportunity, and a verbal agreement or handshake takes place only to never fully materialize. A general Memorandum of Agreement may be signed but with no terms and conditions. These "feel-good agreements" are negotiated by a provost, president, or dean, but they have not been vetted by all stakeholders and details have not been worked out in a supplement to the general Memorandum of Understanding or a detailed Memorandum of Agreement. Many institutions in the United States are aware that "feel-good agreements" rarely yield results beyond polite gestures.

Sustainable agreements involve an evaluation of infrastructure support. International partners should look for institutions with multiple and highly developed offices committed to supporting international engagement. Examples of demonstrated commitment include a comprehensive international student and scholar services office; robust study abroad programs and services; an expansive international curriculum; faculty that are highly engaged in international research and collaboration; an interculturally competent staff and faculty; and active international student organizations.

An institution with a high level of infrastructure support for international partners demonstrates its commitment through funding a number of key internationalization efforts. These efforts include funding international student scholarships, faculty travel funds, research grants for international scholars, and funding collaborative research among faculty and students from both the home and host institution.

Operationalizing the Partnership

International partners must answer key questions in order to move from a "feel-good agreement" to a sustainable agreement. Agreements among institutions are generally designed to encourage mobility among students and scholars, develop and enhance curriculum offerings, or build capacity at the home or host institution. These involve multiple factors. For example, to operationalize a partnership involving the mobility of students, institutions need to consider the following:

Admissions Requirements

- What is a typical student profile and are the admissions requirements compatible with those of the home institution?

- Do students in the program(s) have the language skills needed to ensure successful completion of the program?

- How will the application process be coordinated and who is involved in making the admissions' decision? What documents are required for admission (test scores, transcripts, letters of recommendation), and how will students in this program be evaluated for admission?

- Will the deadlines be different for program students, and what type of documentation will be required for acquiring a visa?

Degree Programs/Accreditation

- Which degree programs are covered under this partnership?

- Is the program/university accredited? By whom? Does the sequencing of coursework and the transfer of credits conform with the accreditation standards of the home and host institutions?

Curriculum

- What are the required courses for each program? Is there flexibility in course offerings and electives? Are the courses needed for completion offered during the time a student is at the host institution?

- How are other requirements for the program completed, such as research and language requirements?

- Are sample syllabi available for review and to articulate transfer credits?

Program Structure

- What are the dates for the academic year, per semester?

- How many credits are required to complete the program(s)? How many semesters does it take to complete the degree?

- How are credits awarded? How many credits does a full-time student typically take per semester? How many credits is each class worth? How is the GPA calculated?
- What is the grading scale?
- What is the language of instruction? Is coursework offered in English?
- What would be the payment structure for the program? Can we exchange students for a tuition neutral partnership or must students pay the host institution for their enrollment. What does the fee structure look like and who is responsible for the payment of fees, including health insurance?

Levels of Authority

At U.S. institutions it is essential to understand the various levels of authority, given the decentralized structure of academic activities. Schools and colleges operate with a level of autonomy and often negotiate their own agreements. Therefore, it is necessary to collaborate with several key stakeholders. The individual with the authority to sign on behalf of the university may be different from the person who negotiates the terms of subsequent agreements. A general Memoranda of Understanding or MOU is typically between two universities and may need to be approved at the highest level of authority. Supplements to the General Agreements are often between individual schools and colleges.

Generally both the home and the host institution have a framework for an MOU, and compromises need to be made on language. When negotiating specific terms it is important to include information gathered during the evaluation process. For example, with the exchange of students it is vital to include admissions criteria, the articulation of credits, and reporting and payment requirements. It is essential to agree on who has the authority to resolve disputes and negotiate consensus. In order to ensure that agreements remain active and partners stay engaged, periodic assessment is necessary. All agreements should have a specific sunset/end date so that partners have an opportunity to evaluate the relationship and negotiate future terms and conditions.

Conclusion

To engage in successful partnerships with U.S. institutions, it is imperative to understand the cultural, structural, and communicative contexts at play. Each dimension outlined above can be understood in terms of stages. Stages to institutional partnerships and related activities can best be summarized in Table 21.1.

TABLE 21.1: STAGES OF INSTITUTIONAL PARTNERSHIPS/LINKAGES

Stages	Activities
Exploration	Information exchange
	Explore common goals/mission
	Conduct Needs Assessment
	Determine benefits and challenges
Establishing Trust	Discuss values and mission
	Identify cultural differences
	Ensure transparency
	Agree on terms and details
Coordination	Determine key stakeholders
	Establish working groups
	Agree on communication and protocols
	Set timetable
	Work out all aspects of agreement
Signed Partnership/Contract	Memorandum of Agreement (MOA)
	Memorandum of Understanding (MOU)
	A living document
Assessment/Evaluation	Evaluate outcome
	Make necessary changes/amendments
	Determine continuation/renewal

Chapter Twenty-two

How Institutions in Developing Countries Can Form Sustainable International Partnerships: Experiences from India

P. J. Lavakare, Member, Board of Management,
Symbiosis International University, Pune (India)

Introduction

The internationalization of higher education at the institutional level is a relatively new concept in many developing countries. In the past, individual researchers have worked with their foreign counterparts in more or less stand-alone mode. Now, student demands for exposure to global opportunities through higher education are rapidly increasing, and institutions in turn are seeking to develop strategic international partnerships. Often they do not know how to systematically initiate and sustain partnerships at the institutional level. Based on my experiences in India, I would like to offer some measures that institutions in developing countries should take to develop successful international partnership programs.

Understanding the Need for International Partnerships

For strategic international partnerships to be successful, educational institutions in developing countries must understand their necessity. The boards of management, academic councils, and the various institutional committees should organize debates among their faculties and administrators to highlight the necessity of international partnerships in the changing global educational environment. The open debate should identify the benefits of international partnerships for the students, teachers, and education community as a whole. The implications of international partnerships—additional costs that arise from the internationalization of the campus, the need for improved infrastructure for international students and faculty, and social, health, and security concerns—should be clearly communicated and addressed.

Individual departments should provide opportunities for faculty members to meet counterparts at foreign universities and form collaborative relationships based on similar academic interests. All international exercises involve expenses for traveling abroad and hosting international partners. If a sense of jealousy arises among other faculty members who have not had the opportunity to travel abroad, the departmental head should prioritize the budget to provide opportunities for everyone.

Potential partners can grow frustrated when they receive no response from their counterparts on individual initiatives. It is therefore necessary that institutes as a whole make adequate provisions for projected activities before engaging foreign partners. In reaching out to international partners, not only should you identify benefits to the host institution, but you should also explain the possible benefits that the partners can expect from your institute. Partnerships are likely to be successful only when they provide mutual benefits to both sides.

I have tried to build partnerships for my institution by carefully choosing a like-minded or similarly endowed institution as a partner. However, our management often wanted to collaborate only with the best institutions from a foreign country, without realizing that such institutions were not necessarily the most appropriate fit for our institute. It is therefore important to understand the mutual strengths and weaknesses of the partners, and to convincingly convey this information to the management.

Setting Up an Office for International Partnerships

Once institutional commitment is confirmed, it is necessary to assign the task of administering this partnership to an Office for International Partnerships (OIP). These offices are uncommon in many university exchange programs in developing countries. The engaged faculty members are often responsible for handling the administrative and logistic problems associated with academic exchanges. However, faculty members may not have the necessary infrastructure to address all the administrative and financial issues that are critical to the success of international partnerships. Ideally, the engaged faculty members should be focused on the academic elements of the program, and the OIP should act as a facilitator that oversees the international partnership.

The OIP should also encourage other faculty members by surveying other institutions for partnerships and preparing a database for potential partners based on the policies initiated by the boards of management and the expertise of the faculties. It is important to identify the right personnel for manning an OIP. They should include those who have traveled or studied abroad and are familiar with the global educational scene.

Communication channels should be mainly based on electronic mail. People-to-people contact should precede an extensive e-survey of the available opportunities. The staff of the OIP should be aware of international conferences like the annual NAFSA Conference that expose the global educational partners to opportunities in international education. Organizations in the U.S. like the Institute of International Education (IIE) also offer opportunities for building international partnerships through institutional membership programs.

In a typical university in a developing country, each academic discipline may vie for international partnerships with its own specialists. This structure does not provide the full benefit of international partnerships to the entire institution. I believe that the role of catalyzing internationalization cannot be left to an individual department, but should be done by an independent "department" that considers the interest of all academic units of the university. It is in this context that the concept of an OIP was born in my university. Every department would then expect the OIP to help them in their interests in international collaboration. As I have learned, the process of internationalization has to cut across various disciplines to provide maximum benefit to the institution as a whole.

Identify the Areas of Partnership

International partnerships are formed at different levels and for different target groups. Often, a university receives a high-level delegation from a foreign institution, and a vague Memorandum of Understanding (MOU) is signed to demonstrate the intent of internationalization. However, there are a large number of MOUs signed by universities on both sides that have not advanced beyond these noble intentions penned down amid photo shoots and press releases. Before such MOUs are signed, there has to be an honest commitment to internationalization by both partners.

A country like India receives many political delegations from various countries. In most cases, the agenda is political with some economic plans added in. To make the collaboration look more comprehensive, many countries include education exchanges in the overall agreement signed between the two countries. The academic community is then asked by their foreign offices to follow up on these agreements; however, many institutions have not done their homework on identifying and selecting the areas of cooperation. This leaves the education part of the collaboration ineffective, and often this part of the MOU is ignored. It is necessary for educational institutions to be proactive and indicate to the foreign affairs ministry their specific interests in areas of collaboration and the names of the institutions with whom they would like to work.

Teaching and Research Exchanges

Certain partnerships could introduce innovative ways of teaching based on the best practices from each culture. One approach would entail searching for institutions known for their excellence in teaching. This is not to say that institutions should ignore faculty who are doing research, for teaching and research cannot be divested in the higher education domain. A partnership based on teaching should focus on how given faculty members use various methods for communicating with their students. If the partnership is for research, the focus should be on areas of research common to the two institutions and whether appropriate infrastructure, including the availability of library resources and research scholars, exists on both sides. If an institution hopes to start a new area of research with the help of the partner institution, this can happen only if the partner institution sees a potential for future collaborations as an equal partner.

Regardless of the teaching or research approach, the partnership protocol should clearly indicate whether the partnership involves both students and teachers with mutual exchanges to each other's institutions. Well-planned visits of students and teachers should incorporate the methodology of joint selection. The financial arrangements need to be cleared, including the duration of the stay at each institution.

The most common approach for funding such exchanges is that the sending side pays for travel while the receiving side bears the hosting costs, which are agreed on in advance. Issues related to health insurance and emergency situations need to be kept in mind, and sufficient time should be allowed for obtaining visas and other travel documents. Once the personnel to be exchanged are identified through careful academic scrutiny, direct communication between the two should be encouraged, without over-involvement from the administrative machinery.

In my experience, institutions in India have faced problems of partnering in teaching areas, because there is lack of understanding of how credits are transferred by partnering institutions. Further, the academic calendar of Indian institutions does not match with that of Western institutions. This creates hurdles in scheduling teaching programs. The teaching methodology also varies between Indian and Western systems. In India, we tend to focus more on delivering lectures than on ensuring that students learn by actively participating in the classroom. Internationalization programs should keep these details in mind when undertaking programs of collaboration.

Partnerships for Joint Degrees

Apart from student and faculty exchanges, a new form of partnership is emerging in which institutions agree on giving joint degrees to students who complete part of their course requirements in one country and the remaining in the partnering institution. This is a more difficult partnership to handle, as academic requirements have to be met on both sides. The students and the faculty have to adjust to learning and teaching under different educational cultures.

Private universities in India have been more flexible in undertaking such joint degree programs with international partners. Government institutions have yet to experiment with this innovative way of promoting student mobility. Unfortunately, some joint degree programs are not accepted by employers in India, particularly if the employment is with a governmental organization. Indian students have been able to use such joint degree programs primarily for seeking admissions in Western universities, but not in their own countries. Students in developing countries have found these joint degree programs useful for enhancing their careers abroad.

Campuses Abroad

With opportunities for providing trans-border education, educational institutions are exploring partnerships that involve setting up their campuses in another country. The student community benefits from these kinds of partnerships, but developing countries are concerned that the increased competition may have an impact on their own institutions.

Indian institutions have ventured abroad in countries like Dubai and Malaysia. The pending legislature in the Indian parliament has provisions that may allow foreign institutions to set up campuses in India. However, there is a feeling that the conditions may be too restrictive and unattractive for foreign education providers to venture on Indian soil. Nevertheless, setting up campuses abroad greatly internationalizes the education system and opens opportunities to local students who would otherwise be deprived of an international education experience.

Study Abroad Partnerships

Developed countries are looking to provide global exposure to their students through study abroad programs in developing countries, like India, where credit-based courses allow their students to experience different cultures. Unfortunately, many developing countries are not geared to offering such multidisciplinary and sociocultural-based courses. If developing countries gain expertise in providing study abroad programs, they could be in a position to develop successful international partnerships.

Over the past decade, I have encouraged several universities in India to develop Study India Programs (SIP) for foreign students to come to India for a period of four to six weeks. Normally, the faculty is reluctant to do the extra work of developing a curriculum that is multidisciplinary and requires innovative ideas. The management has given monetary incentives for the faculty to take up the additional task of planning and executing SIP for foreign students from developed countries. We have used the diversity of India to develop culturally rich study abroad programs to enhance our international experience.

Programming and Budgeting

For any successful partnership initiative, the details of the collaboration should be exchanged in advance and included as part of an addendum to the main MOU. This project document should be as detailed as possible. The necessary financial implications must be spelled out in the overall budgets of the partnering institutions. When the MOUs are signed, often there is no mention of the financial arrangements for partnerships. This becomes a major impediment when institutional budgets are affected by external constraints. The international programs tend to be cut under such situations. If institutions are serious about sustaining international partnerships, the financial plan for the internationalization activities must be reflected in the overall budgets approved by the respective boards. International travel and hospitality to foreign visitors need to be adequately provided for. Transfer/repatriation of funds and the relevant income tax regulations also have to be taken into account when deciding on payments to visiting faculty.

I have found that many Indian universities have not yet fully internationalized their campuses. The concept of internationalization is often misunderstood. I recall one university equating internationalization with "world-class" education. Some Indian universities have not yet seen internationalization programs as a means of enhancing the value of education and producing "global citizens." The fact that internationalization programs also can enhance international recruitment is not planned for. The budgeting exercises in our university systems have not yet provided adequate financial provisions for international exchanges, which are the heart of any internationalization program.

Conclusions

As student mobility increases, developing countries are realizing the importance of international education. Educational and cultural exchanges are considered necessary in today's world without borders. Unfortunately, many educational institutions in developing countries are not aware of the modalities that need to be in place in order to develop sustainable international partnerships. In this brief chapter, I have suggested some areas of mobilization that will help educational institutions, particularly from developing countries, understand the issues involved in developing successful and rewarding international partnerships.

Chapter Twenty-three

EXPORTING THE COMMUNITY COLLEGE MODEL: A LESSON IN THINKING LOCALLY WHILE ACTING GLOBALLY

MARY S. SPANGLER, CHANCELLOR, HOUSTON COMMUNITY COLLEGE

ART TYLER, DEPUTY CHANCELLOR AND CHIEF OPERATING OFFICER, HOUSTON COMMUNITY COLLEGE

It is an unsettling irony that just as many of our states are reducing funding to community colleges—our most efficient deliverers of postsecondary academic transfer education and workforce training—there is an overwhelming increase of interest in this same educational model abroad. The American community college has truly been discovered and is starting to be embraced around the world. Suddenly, the community college mission has expanded once again, not by default or the imposition of a local community, state, or federal agency mandate, but by the recognition of its value and application to the need for a skilled workforce to compete in a global marketplace and a flattened world. Global competition is the driving force for improved skills and knowledgeable workers who can aid in the transformations of nations. On the other side of the equation is the value that international partnerships can bring to U.S. community colleges.

Houston Community College (HCC) is a singly accredited Hispanic and Minority Serving Institution of six colleges with more than 75,000 students in the greater Houston region. As of January 2011, with more than 8,000 students, *Open Doors* ranked HCC first in international students nationally and sixth among all U.S. two- and four-year institutions. A cosmopolitan city, Houston is the fourth largest, ranking second in exports nationwide and serving as the global leader in the oil and gas industry. These assets are thus a natural leverage point for articulating a worldwide perspective as part of the college's strategic plan. A key point in this regard is that an institution interested in moving into this arena should have a coherent rationale for its position.

For example, HCC believes in building and leveraging diverse partnerships to prepare for the future. As U.S. Secretary of State Hillary Clinton aptly stated in her welcome remarks (1/22/09) in Washington D.C.: "… [D]iplomacy and development are essential tools in achieving the long-term objectives of the United States." Combining words with actions are essential as institutions such as HCC take seriously the charge to train and prepare students to be citizens and workers in and for a global economy. In terms of diplomacy, the community college model expands institutional ties to help meet the workforce needs of host countries that result in economic development for both the home and host countries. HCC has a commitment to a broader context where many points of view from diverse communities are welcomed and honored. There is a growing recognition that the exportation of the community college model of education is a strategy for transforming sovereign nations. There are economic and social results that have reciprocal benefits to the students' home countries and for the U.S. communities that the college partner supports. The connection must be built into the college's strategic plan. This will provide a coherent basis and structural framework from which to operate.

Many people in the U.S. question the tangible and intangible benefits from international joint ventures like the exportation of an educational model. HCC believes that by working with partners from other countries and expanding these relationships, the college and its partners are reaping both immediate short-term monetary gains and will reap longer-term economic returns in the U.S. So far, HCC has netted $5.8 million from its international endeavors. However, the financial benefits must be leveraged to allow the college to maximize the value of each entrepreneurial engagement. Financial gain is not the sole motive to engage in international activities.

The College (HCC) takes each relationship as an independent experience from which learning occurs, and then translates that new knowledge into greater expertise on which to build new opportunities that lead to expanded development and new challenges. However, the reality is that each project and program has its own integrity and must fit with the College's mission and vision. The goal is not to accept all proposals presented. It pays to be selective. For us, selectivity is built on the recognition that HCC's brand is what has attracted international institutions to approach the college and seek its expertise, partnership, and resources for mutual benefit and opportunity. There must be a benefit to the local community and the students for the College to consider entering into the relationship. For example, Houston is an international city with four pillars of its economy that connect to the global marketplace: energy, health and medical research, finance and banking, and transportation. Locally, HCC provides workforce training in all of these critical areas for Houston's growth and stability. Thus, these are the same areas we have explored in finding joint venture partners around the globe.

Some generalizations about community colleges abroad are based on Houston Community College's experiences locally and connect in the four countries where we have exported our model and services: Vietnam, Brazil, Saudi Arabia, and Qatar. These examples illustrate the range of possibilities that might inform other institutions as they consider global partnerships from a local perspective.

Vietnam

HCC began its global efforts in 2001 with the opening of Saigon Institute of Technology (ST) in Vietnam. It was financed with private capital from Vietnam by an entrepreneur who introduced the American two-year community college model to his country. By re-creating a replicable accreditation process that allows students in Vietnam to earn a U.S. degree there, this configuration lifted the education level, quality assurance, employee credibility, employer confidence, competitiveness, and job placement for ST graduates.

Over the last ten years, almost 1,000 associate degree students have graduated and gone on to full employment. Many other Vietnamese students have also gained workforce skills that have allowed them to enter into the workplace at a higher level of skill and confidence. In addition, this partnership has greatly benefited Vietnamese and U.S. relations, helping Houstonians in normalizing relationships, passing an annexation election in Houston, and improving degree completion. In 2010, the Prime Minister of Vietnam came to Houston as part of a 15-year celebration of normalized relations with the U.S. and lauded the contributions HCC had made in helping to develop, maintain, and strengthen these relations.

Brazil

In 2008, with the support of the U.S. Embassy and USAID, HCC created a partnership with technical schools in Brazil to facilitate a connection for economic development in energy safety and security. The goal was to lay the foundation for shared understanding and mutually-beneficial exchange with other community colleges and technical schools. U.S.-Brazil relationships were formed, curriculum projects and online learning communities were implemented, and faculty exchanges were established. Currently, HCC is collaboratively conducting training in the U.S. and Brazil using traditional classroom and distance education approaches to strengthen the bi-national ties between Brazilian and American industries.

An area of particular interest that has developed from the work done over the last several years appears ready for further development through the leveraging of HCC's local assets that address workforce development needs in key industry sectors in Brazil and can develop mission-driven, income-generating projects. Core areas of opportunity include vocational English as a second language/English for special purposes workforce development; customized training capacity; and international student enrollments. Key sectors focus on oil/gas, renewable energy, and construction/building trades. These have potential for development through corporate partnerships that exist both locally and globally.

The critical factors for success are relationships that already exist and can be further expanded, and community college expertise that can be applied in an international setting. Less obvious but no less important success factors include patience, the willingness to let the project develop on its timetable, and the foresight to not force the partners to adhere to a predetermined or rigid set of expectations.

Saudi Arabia

In 2009, HCC shifted its entrepreneurial focus to the Middle East, serving as a consultant to Riyadh Community College (RCC), part of King Saud University in Saudi Arabia, to identify how to educate its own general population instead of importing workers. Accreditation was necessary to satisfy Saudi parents and students, and HCC adapted the value of the American community college model to fit the Saudi culture. Moreover, HCC used its knowledge of the American accreditation process and requirements to help RCC understand the evidentiary requirements of this process.

HCC worked with the faculty and administration of RCC to develop and implement a plan. RCC was successful in securing its first American accreditation—Council on Occupational Education (COE)—on its first attempt. Subsequently, HCC has been retained to aid in RCC's process to secure a second accreditation with the National Commission for Academic Accreditation and Assessment (NCAAA), which is a Saudi Arabian national accreditation. To date, one of the first of the five major disciplines taught at RCC has been accredited by NCAAA, thanks to HCC assistance. Thus, the international experiences in Vietnam and Brazil provided the opportunity to leverage an expanded portfolio of skills and expertise as the institution's reputation abroad has increased.

Qatar

In April 2010, HCC was selected to provide all of the services and support needed to open the Community College of Qatar (CCQ) in Doha, Qatar. This was a major step in implementing the Qatari educational strategic plan created by Her Highness Sheikha Moza bint Nasser. Despite the challenges of distance, time zones, and culture, HCC was able to create a plan, recruit and hire staff and faculty, design and retrofit a building, recruit and test students, and transfer the HCC model to Qatar for the opening of that nation's first community college. On September 26, 2010, CCQ opened its doors to 304 students, who began an academic equivalent of the HCC educational process. In only four months from the signing of a $45 million five-year contract, HCC had delivered its curriculum to aid the people of Qatar in a new chapter of their educational development. A second facility was completed in January 2011, adding another 150 students with the advent of evening classes to the schedule. By the end of the spring semester, CCQ boasted more than an 80 percent success rate of student achievement and a 95 percent retention rate.

CCQ was designed in accordance with the government's educational reform strategy to reduce the percentage of foreign workers, support access to educational opportunities for Qataris, and recognize the limitation of natural gas as a resource. Qatar was in need of a "feeder pattern" as a pathway from high school to four-year universities or skilled employment and recognized the value of the American community college model adapted to their culture as a vehicle to deliver the educational access and pathway necessary for the country to be competitive into the future. Through an invitational RFP, HCC won the partnership services agreement over seven other community colleges to provide faculty, staff, and administration; curriculum, IT, and consulting services to open a community college. HCC's proven track record and deep resources were significant in demonstrating the ability to deliver within the expected timeframe despite the 9,000 miles separating the two locations. The benefits to both the local and global partners include cross-fertilization of faculty when "expat" faculty return to HCC and greater cross-cultural awareness and exposure for students and faculty as the relationship between the two cities—Doha and Houston—and two countries deepens.

Lessons Learned

HCC follows the principle of finding the "right" fit when selecting an international opportunity. The closer this relationship is, the easier it is to understand the workforce needs of the local community and ensure students are equipped with the skills required to obtain a job with companies in that area. For example, some industries that the partnerships focus on are already partnering with industries in Houston. They focus on their workforce community and developing opportunities for their students.

Dedicated oversight and integrated visions can advance a shared, collaborative agenda to deepen the benefits of working across borders. Generally, it is not difficult to convince those in positions of influence of the value and importance of education to the broad population. More so than ever, other countries are recognizing that to invest in education is to invest in their future. The goal is achieving an educated workforce that can compete in the global marketplace. Further, these same people of influence are also recognizing that the community college can deliver that workforce quickly, affordably, and flexibly. HCC has been able to demonstrate satisfactorily its depth, resources, knowledge, expertise, experience, and willingness to listen and let the culture of the country be a significant part of the relationship. These are critical reasons for the College's success in the international arena.

However, it is sometimes more challenging to convince local constituents that going global has value for them. For the decision to engage on a project with an international partner to have lasting success, the project must be based on more than just the money that the college might make. The opportunities for faculty, staff, and administrators to broaden their global competencies can provide an impetus for these entrepreneurial engagements. The connection through local business and industry to support their needs and create jobs both at home and abroad is critical to responding to calls for isolationism. Add to those ingredients the need for a Board of Trustees that is willing to support international efforts. For this to happen, partnerships must be structured to ensure they are not at taxpayer expense. The administration must be sophisticated in recognizing the opportunities flowing into and out of the college and in being able to create transparency for the public and the Board. With the growing importance of being entrepreneurial, these value-added partnerships must provide benefits to the students, local constituency, and faculty. Successful investments in the global dimension of educational model transfers can enhance the reputation of the college. Perhaps the most lasting effect of these types of creative growth options is the opportunity to impact the culture of the college globally by capitalizing on its natural assets.

Collaborations with an educational entity, a private partner, and the governmental agency are a strong three-way force to support willing exchanges, transform nations and our relationships, and move international agendas forward at the macro level. The question for many community colleges is: Where do opportunities lie and how does an institution capitalize on this foreign enterprise? Does one have to be in an urban environment to have assets that might be beneficial in the global marketplace? Each community college environment is unique, and it is this difference that has value. One must search out the matches in this universe of opportunities to find the right fit.

But time, patience, expertise, and experience are also essential ingredients when working across borders to develop shared opportunities. The American community college has 100 years of experience working from a community-based direction with minimal resources and delivering the needed workforce. Community colleges have their own challenges at home that can limit their ability to export their best practices and share their resources. There must be something of value and benefit for them to bring home in a measurable way. The most limiting flaws in capturing opportunity are lack of vision and lack of understanding about the assets of the institution. If these are recognized and understood, then it is a matter of exercising the institutional will and having the necessary courage to attempt something foreign.

Chapter Twenty-four

THE BRITISH COUNCIL'S UK–U.S. NEW PARTNERSHIP FUND

ELIZABETH SHEPHERD, EDUCATION INTELLIGENCE RESEARCH MANAGER,
BRITISH COUNCIL IN HONG KONG

The British Council's engagement in international education has endured the changing global landscape and responded to the shifting priorities of institutions and governments in the UK and overseas. The first Prime Ministers Initiative for international education, PMI (1999 – 2005), focused on creating a national brand under which all UK institutions could market themselves internationally, and increase the number of international students studying in the UK. The successful development of the Education UK brand and more than 20 percent increase in the number of non-EU students studying in the UK led to part two of the initiative being introduced in 2006. The PMI2 reflected the global diversification by shifting focus from recruitment to the development of strategic alliances and partnerships and an emphasis on demonstrating the value of the UK as a partner in international education policy and delivery.

Through this emphasis on the development of partnerships, the British Council showed its recognition of, and reaction to, the shift in global higher education dynamics. The flight of human capital into one nation to the potential detriment of another, the so-called "brain drain," was recognized as unsustainable. The creation of mutually beneficial sustainable partnerships that linked institutions' students, faculty, and researchers and allowed the development of inter-institutional and international relationships showed immeasurable benefit to the global education community beyond traditional inward and outward mobility flows.

Among the stated aims and targets for the second Prime Ministers Initiative for international education (PMI2) was significant growth in the number of partnerships between the UK and other countries. It was anticipated that by 2011 the British Council would be working with governments, education providers, and industry in identified countries to build on the success of the BRIDGE (British Degrees in Russia), UKIERI (UK-India Education and Research Initiative), DelPHE (Development Partnerships in Higher Education), and INSPIRE (International Strategic Partnerships in Research and Education) projects that the British Council had already established outside the auspices of the PMI.

By providing seed-corn funding, all of these programs aim to ensure the long-term sustainability of the partnerships. To be successful, applications need to demonstrate how they will ensure longer term financial investment. Having reached the end of the PMI2, we can now reflect on these original aims, their continuing relevance, and the ingredients that constitute a successful higher education partnership post-seed-corn funding.

During the five-year initiative, the British Council facilitated 370 new partnerships. The focus of the first year involved research cooperation, the development of joint/dual award programs and collaborative delivery at undergraduate and graduate levels, and programs that facilitated the outward mobility of UK students and partnership development grants.[1] Year two funding focused on UK-Gulf research cooperation, facilitating UK outward mobility, and UK–China collaborative partnerships in entrepreneurship and employability.[2] Year three funding continued the focus on UK–China entrepreneurship and employability with further emphasis on UK students' outward mobility to China, India, Malaysia, and Thailand.

The fourth and final year of funding saw the U.S. prioritized alongside China and Nigeria in developing further collaborative programs. A report commissioned by the British Council, "UK–US Higher Education Partnership – Realising the Potential,"[3] ascertained the value and importance of the relationship between the two largest global knowledge economies and informed the strategy behind the launch of the UK–U.S. New Partnership Fund. The need to stimulate new networks of UK and U.S. institutions to facilitate growth in higher education partnerships was among the report's recommendations. A wider variety and geographic spread of institutions should be involved alongside enhancing the levels of engagement of existing partnerships. The report recommended that seed-corn funding be offered to institutions as initial investment to stimulate new partnerships.

The UK–U.S. New Partnership Fund

The UK–U.S. New Partnership Fund was launched in May 2010 at a one-day conference at the Royal Society of the Arts, London. Its aims were clearly stated: to grow mutually beneficial relationships between UK–U.S. higher education institutions; to deepen existing cooperation; to introduce new higher education institutions from a greater diversity of locations in both countries; to pilot new partnerships in third countries; to build the basis for future sustainable partnerships; and to strengthen the skills of higher education staff in developing and delivering partnerships. Prior to the May launch, 18 U.S. travel grants had been awarded to UK institutions to aid their planning process before application for the full grant funds. Although obtaining a travel grant was not a prerequisite for application to the New Partnership Fund, issuing travel grants clearly illustrated our understanding of the need for well-established communication and planning from early on in a new partnership.

Essential criteria for application to the fund were that projects should:

- be self-sustaining after initial funding has ended;
- evidence mutuality and complementarity;
- share lessons learned from the activities with the wider higher education community;
- grow mutually beneficial partnerships between UK and U.S. higher education institutions;
- provide opportunities to deepen and broaden existing cooperation between UK and U.S. higher education institutions;
- introduce new higher education institutions to UK-U.S. partnerships from a greater diversity of locations in both countries;
- pilot new UK and U.S. partnerships in third countries;
- build the basis for future sustainable partnerships between the collaborating institutions; and
- strengthen the skills of higher education staff in both countries in developing and delivering partnerships.

The clear communication of grant guidelines was therefore crucial for all partnership members. We held 12 web-seminars for over 120 participants, scheduled and structured so that both UK and U.S. participants could attend. The online delivery method was advantageous for many reasons, not only the financial and environmental cost savings but also the time saved by participants who attended.

We received a high number of inquiries from both UK and U.S. institutions. From these inquiries we were able to identify a trend from both U.S. and UK institutions interested in establishing a partnership, but who were unable to identify a partner institution. The British Council team created the UK–U.S. register of interest, allowing these institutions to submit a profile detailing their aims and objectives, favored activity area, and priority disciplines. These submissions were exchanged with interested parties from the UK or U.S.

By the October 2010 deadline, we had received 230 applications for the grant-funding awards. A thorough three-stage evaluation involving an extensive internal and external peer and panel review process was carried out. This included involvement from: 10 UK universities, 10 U.S. universities, the Institute of International Education, the American Council of Education, and the FCO Science and Innovation Network. The grant funds were awarded to support 31 new partnerships with the scope of involvement from: 31 UK and 35 U.S. institutions, and 16 trilateral partnerships including Australia, Brazil, Canada, China, Colombia, Cyprus, India, Italy, Kenya, Palestine, Rwanda, Saudi Arabia, South Africa, and Sweden. Twenty of the projects' priorities were in the STEM subject areas; 10 partnerships were research-based collaborations.

The high caliber of proposed partnerships was unprecedented, and the number of applications surpassed previous expectations of demand. The 31 partnerships granted seed-corn funding all showed innovation and excellence in their proposals. To illustrate the high standard, innovation, and originality of the new partnerships funded in March 2010, I'd like to focus on two particular applications involving the University of Wolverhampton, Stanford University, and Birzeit University, Palestine; and the University of Warwick, Boston University, and Monash University, Australia. Both these proposals give weight to mutuality and sustainability, but their strategic objectives and the practical components that comprise the core of their endeavors are unique.

The University of Wolverhampton and Stanford University hoped to develop a joint master's program in education development that would involve Birzeit University in Palestine and would use digital technology for mobile learning. All three institutions aimed for mutual benefit and sustainability to maintain course content on continuing syllabuses and embed further development elements for staff in the corresponding schools of education involved in this process, faculty-to-faculty.

The University of Warwick and Boston University endeavored to develop an institutional partnership, or core partnership, in order to make a step change in their relationship with a focus on research cooperation. This institutional-level partnership aims to build on complementary advantages of academic and administrative know-how, sharing resources and equipment to harness the combined research power of both partners and open up global opportunities. Mutual benefit and sustainability are aimed for through an exploration of institutional level funding, university donor funds, and the potential of developing a new paradigm for international collaboration that will be applied to future partnerships.

Much discussion and debate exists about what constitutes a successful international strategic partnership; in essence, what is the most successful combination of component parts that leads to a successful and sustainable partnership that can in theory be replicated across the sector. Continuing and easily accessible funding is a key component that in the most prosperous operating environment would be plentiful. However, it is obvious when studying examples like the British Council's New Partnership Fund, which saw an unprecedented number of applications, that funds are highly sought after and the high standard of innovative ideas grows over time.

There is huge potential benefit from programs like the New Partnership Fund. By taking advantage of the wealth of information available on strategic partnership, the innovative concepts grown from individual relationships, and the fresh definitions of sustainability and mutual benefit that they contain, we are one step closer toward a model of strategic international partnerships that can be replicated across the sector. Although PMI2 is now in its final phase, this process continues through monitoring and evaluation and subsequent reporting back to international audiences, cascading this learning to the sector. One particular area the New Partnership Fund can contribute to is a greater understanding of the operating environment in third countries, which proves to be especially challenging and sees much reinvention. Whether it is the faculty-to-faculty development of a highly innovative joint master's program with cost effective use of technology at its center, or an institution-to-institution core partnership focusing on widespread paradigm shifts and global positioning, all new initiatives that follow these principles will help the sector to move closer to a greater understanding of international strategic partnerships.

NOTES

[1] Countries involved: Thailand, Japan, Singapore, Malaysia, South Korea, Bangladesh, Vietnam, Pakistan, India, China, Sri Lanka, Hong Kong, Nigeria, Ghana.

[2] Not previously involved: Qatar, Oman, Saudi Arabia, United Arab Emirates, Kuwait.

[3] PMI2 Partnerships Connect, authors Neil Kemp and Christine Humphrey, 2010.

Chapter Twenty-five

ADVANCING FRENCH-AMERICAN PARTNERSHIPS: THE PARTNER UNIVERSITY FUND

PASCAL DELISLE, CULTURAL ATTACHÉ FOR HIGHER EDUCATION, FRENCH EMBASSY IN WASHINGTON, DC

Introduction

Research and higher education systems worldwide have entered a time of transition. National borders are not as relevant as they once were now that professors, students, and intellectual property have become increasingly mobile, following the trends set by international trade and direct investment. While the porosity of borders generates challenges for many, it also creates opportunities for intercultural innovation and understanding, all key ingredients for the 21st century knowledge economy.

For countries like France and the United States, both advanced industrialized nations with high levels of human capital, fostering these collaborative relationships should not be feared. Partnerships bring clear benefits both in the short and in the long term, adding to the knowledge bases that fuel our economies. In such a win-win game, it seems natural to invest heavily in funding and facilitating transatlantic partnerships.

In spite of the economic crisis that affected most of the industrialized world, France has increased its investment in higher education and research in recent years, strengthening the international dimension of its research and education through the *Plan Campus* and *Investissement d'avenir* in particular.[1]

At the initiative of Allan E. Goodman, President and CEO of the Institute of International Education, and of the French government, a high level meeting of governments and higher education agencies within the framework of the G8/G20 was held in Paris on May 5, 2011. It was entitled, "Raising the Profile of International Higher Education at the G8/G20." In her opening discourse, the French Minister for Higher Education and Research, Valérie Pécresse, emphasized the considerable influence of higher education and research on the competitiveness of the nation. The French government gave the biggest part of its "*Investissement d'avenir*" to higher education and research (25 billion Euros), making it a top priority. She also highlighted the key role universities play on the international scene, as they are at the crossroads of fundamental research, education, applied research, and technological innovation.

The French Minister of Foreign and European Affairs, Alain Juppé, echoed these priorities and emphasized that a priority for France was to foster partnerships between foreign and French universities, including joint and dual degrees. In particular, France hoped to increase the share of incoming international students coming through university partnerships from 20 percent to 50 percent by 2020.

In spite of these important transformations and the priorities set by the French government, France and the United States still largely rely on funding and regulatory mechanisms inherited from the postwar period, modeled after domestic, inward-looking principles. This is generally true for students and faculty, as numerous administrative and legal considerations, from visa regulations to credit transfer mechanisms, hamper the fluidity of their movement. It is also the case for funding, where each country tends to fund its own infrastructures and people in a "silo" mode while largely failing to fund the mutually beneficial "international bridges" through collaborative relationships. In other words, the economic obstacles to international partnerships stem from poor allocations of scarce resources, which in turn hamper the prosperity of the global economy, not to mention the benefits drawn from increased mutual understanding at the level of civil societies.

A Bold Experiment

Four years ago, then French Ambassador to the United States, Jean-David Levitte, and two American donors with deep attachments to France and faith in the productive power of the bilateral relationships were able to look beyond immediate circumstances and create a new tool to foster and fund transatlantic academic partnerships. They conceived the Partner University Fund (PUF) as a bold experiment to complement the existing domestic funding mechanisms and support beneficial research and education partnerships between France and the U.S.

When framing the contours of the Fund, the founders of PUF sought to alter the landscape of graduate training through an emphasis on the creation of new cross-disciplinary and multinational networks of research and academic inquiry. They also sought to provide sufficient funding flexibility and support over time to ensure sustainability for even the most complex partnerships; and to encourage a deep personal immersion in the academic, professional, and cultural experiences afforded by meaningful exposure to life in the U.S. and France.

Operating under the auspices of FACE, the French American Cultural Exchange in New York City, PUF has awarded 55 three-year grants over four funding cycles (2007-11) for a total commitment of over $10 million to date in the broadly defined categories of Business and Law (7 percent), Culture and the Humanities (23 percent), Earth Sciences (12 percent), Energy and Materials Science (38 percent), and the Life Sciences (20 percent). PUF provides up to $80,000 annually in co-financing to a maximum of $240,000 (or up to 30 percent of program costs) over three years. PUF programs are currently at work in 36 U.S. institutions in 18 states and 39 French institutions in 12 regions. PUF is proud of its record of identifying early-stage innovative projects and working with all types of institutions, from historic land-grant colleges, public universities, and Ivy League schools in the U.S. to *grandes écoles* and dedicated research centers such as the Commissariat à l'Énergie Atomique and Institut de Biologie Structurale Jean Pierre Ebel in France.

In 2010-2011, French and American participants included 1,837 master's and Ph.D. level candidates and 1,367 postdoctoral fellows and faculty. Approximately 40 percent, or 1,300 of these individuals, travel extensively between France and the U.S. for studies, teaching, administrative endeavors, research, and participation in conferences. In addition to France and the U.S., a number of these scholars are at work in Austria, Egypt, French Polynesia, and Japan. For instance, 2009 PUF laureates University of Maine School of Law and the Université de Nantes are currently working on extending their partnership in marine law to include participants in China. In 2010, the Andrew W. Mellon Foundation supported PUF by giving additional support to projects in the humanities, increasing the share of PUF funding to 60 percent of the cost of the collaboration, or up to $160,000 per year per project.

Measuring the Fund's Impact

How does one measure impact in an initiative that is still so young? The capacity of PUF-funded projects to expand geographically and obtain additional funds from the National Science Foundation, the European Union, and the French National Agency for Research, among others, is a good indicator; many such cases could be highlighted in different fields of research. Also, in March 2010, the PUF partnership between the California Institute of Technology and École Polytechnique in Aerospace Engineering was awarded the Institute of International Education's Andrew Heiskell Award for Innovation in International Education, while the partnership between North Carolina State University (Raleigh, NC) and Université Paul Cézanne-IAE Aix-en-Provence (France) received an honorable mention.

As the first cohort of PUF projects was about to graduate, (2008-11), PUF convened an international summit in Montpellier, France, in April 2011. It offered a candid appraisal of the strengths, consequences, and challenges of the PUF funding approach, and included reports from PUF principal investigators. Representatives from the French Ministry of Education, the French Embassy in the U.S., PUF jury members, Dr. Allan E. Goodman, President of IIE, and Mr. Phillip Lewis, Vice President of the Andrew W. Mellon Foundation, were among the participants of this evaluation seminar. Panels focused on higher education and scientific collaboration between France and the U.S.: Ecole Polytechnique and Caltech, Montpellier and Salk Institute.

The primary outcomes of PUF come from its ability to initiate and sustain transatlantic cooperation. PUF has had excellent results in structuring exchange programs and improving the quality and numbers of faculty mobility. The number of publications is impressive, and our partners wish to continue working closely together.

The most significant impact comes from providing life-changing experiences for PUF's scholars and students. PUF seeks to do this by making possible integrated courses of instruction and experimentation across national, institutional, and disciplinary boundaries, thus elevating the academic conversation for all involved. The freedom and security to pursue advanced studies in professionally rich environments and in challenging new settings is priceless. Living and working in foreign locations is profound and enriching on many levels. It demands both patience and a consideration of the larger context of the work.

Conclusion

Having laid the groundwork and built awareness and supportive networks across both countries, PUF is considered by many in the international education community as a success. PUF has provided a major tool for multilayered transatlantic collaborations. Ensuring the long-term sustainability of PUF will require greater fundraising efforts and increased visibility. In addition, PUF is currently exploring new partnerships within France and in the U.S. with individual philanthropists, research organizations and networks, and governmental organizations. Working toward sustainable funding streams, PUF will be able to develop its core program and address pressing challenges, such as capacity building in research and higher education in developing and emerging countries.

The lessons from these first years go well beyond PUF and even beyond France and the United States. PUF offers an example not only of the mutual benefits from international partnerships, but, more importantly, of the high returns that investments in such relationships produce. Postwar, nationally-centered funding mechanisms and regulatory systems are proving increasingly inadequate in the 21st century global knowledge economy. Higher education and research funding and regulatory regimes urgently need an *aggiornamento* inspired by the mutually supportive nature of international collaborations. PUF embodies this paradigm shift and offers an example of public-private partnerships to this effect. Together, with initiatives such as the recent UK-U.S. strategic partnership fund, our hope is for PUF to increase decision-makers' awareness and foster more globally-oriented higher education and research governance mechanisms to emerge for the benefit of students, professors, science, innovation, and mutual understanding.

NOTES

[1] For more details on those initiatives, please visit http://www.enseignementsup-recherche.gouv.fr/pid24591/operation-campus.html, and http://www.enseignementsup-recherche.gouv.fr/cid51892/investissements-d-avenir-mode-d--.html

Appendix A

International Academic Partnerships: Twenty-Five Sample Activities

By Susan Buck Sutton, Bryn Mawr College

1. One- or two-way movement of students who take courses or work in laboratories at either institution for short term, one semester, or full year.

2. One- or two-way movement of students who pursue internships or engage in service learning projects at either institution for short term, one semester, or full year.

3. 2+2, 1+2+1, and similar programs in which students at the partner institution take one to three years at their institution and then one to two years at yours, earning degrees at both.

4. Joint or coordinated degrees, enrolling students from both institutions as a unified cohort and requiring coursework at both institutions.

5. Tailored full-semester study abroad programs developed for your students at the partner institution, involving courses and in-country orientation aimed specifically at the visiting students.

6. Tailored short-term study abroad programs developed for your students at the partner institution, which can be stand-alone courses or complements to courses you teach (e.g., alternate spring break experiences).

7. Tailored full-semester or short-term study abroad programs developed at your institution for students from the partner institution.

8. Collaborative teaching in which students and faculty at both institutions are joined in a single virtual classroom through videoconferences, email exchanges, and web-based platforms, for either whole courses or components of whole courses.

9. Exchange of faculty for purposes of guest teaching, either whole courses or components of whole courses.

10. Provision of online, CD-Rom, or DVD courses and/or teaching modules from either institution to the other.

11. One-to-one faculty collaboration (through visits or electronic communication) for purposes of research or applied projects.

12. Collaborative research or applied projects that are pursued on a long-term, institutional level by both institutions working in partnership with each other.

13. Faculty development activities (e.g., workshops, videoconferences, short courses) in which faculty or staff at one institution provide sessions for personnel at the other.

14. Institution-building activities (e.g., workshops, site visits, videoconferences) in which personnel at one institution assist the other in terms of institutional assessment, faculty development, service learning, pedagogy, research development, accreditation, enrollment management, fund-raising, and similar activities.

15. Videoconferences involving faculty and other personnel at both institutions, for the purposes of getting to know one another, developing new projects, and exchanging ideas and information.

16. Videoconferences and other electronic communication involving students at both institutions for the purposes of getting to know one another, developing joint student activities, and understanding one another's countries.

17. Collaborating on lectures, film series, and performances that spread knowledge of the partner country at your institution, and/or knowledge of the U.S. at the partner institution.

18. Jointly sponsored conferences on topics of mutual interest, to be held at either institution.

19. Jointly sponsored publications or publication series on topics of mutual interest.

20. Sharing of library resources, especially those that are digital in nature.

21. Granting faculty or affiliate status to faculty from the partner institution, or vice versa; conferring honorary degrees.

22. Developing educational tours for your alumni or residents from your community to the country of the partner institution.

23. Using the partnership to collaborate with organizations such as Sister Cities, development agencies, travel companies, and/or multinational businesses that also operate both in your community and the country of the partner institution.

24. Collaborating with a third institutional partner to develop multinational projects in any of the above areas.

25. Jointly applying for funding to support any of the above activities.

Criteria for Selecting International Partner Institutions

By Susan Buck Sutton, Bryn Mawr College

General institutional compatibility with your institution
- Similar missions
- Similar areas of excellence (building synergy)
- Complementary areas of excellence (filling gaps)

Compatibility with the international goals of your institution
- Will support achievement of your goals in international teaching, research, engagement
- Fits with the role you have assigned partnerships in your internationalization

Fit with the range of your existing partnerships
- Building on areas of focused strength
- Filling in identified gaps
- Not stretching your resources too thinly

Quality and integrity of potential partner
- In terms of accreditation
- In terms of ranking
- In terms of academic programs
- In terms of business and partnership practices

Partner is in a part of the world of interest to your institution
- Building on your strengths or filling in gaps in targeted areas
- Mirroring the international connections of your surrounding community

Partner is in a nation that is a source of international students for your institution

Faculty and programs from your institution already have connections with the potential partner

Partnership will be of mutual benefit to all participating institutions
• Something to be gained on all sides

Partnership fits a range of constituencies at your institution

Productive discussions with the potential partner have taken place
• Trust and rapport have been built
• Mutual understandings (including what partnership means) have been reached
• Common projects and interests have been identified
• All relevant decision-makers have been engaged
• Level of commitment has been determined
• Possible roadblocks and negative impacts have been identified and addressed
• Resources and financial arrangements have been negotiated
• Regulatory issues have been addressed
• Language issues have been addressed

Resources and structures exist to support the partnership over time
• Faculty and departmental buy-in exists
• Funding for travel is available
• Revenue-neutral exchange structures are in place
• Course articulations are possible
• System of regular communication can be established
• Each side has a team or office to manage its part of the partnership
• Capacity to provide language instruction, cultural and national framing for work with partner exists (or can be developed)

Proposed partnership has undergone appropriate reviews at your institution
• Following agreed-on procedures
• Obtaining all necessary approvals
• Discussed by all relevant constituencies
• Reviewed by legal counsel
• System of ongoing review and re-evaluation is in place
• Exit strategy is in place

See also:
• Van De Water, J., Green, M. F., & Koch, K. (2008). *International partnerships: guidelines for colleges and universities.* Washington DC: American Council on Education.

Beyond Handshakes and Signing Ceremonies: Leveraging Institutional Agreements to Foster Broad and Deep International Partnerships

Tim Barnes, Director, Illinois Strategic International Partnerships Initiative, University of Illinois at Urbana-Champaign

A world-renowned professor from the Department of Atmospheric Sciences at a prominent U.S. research university is invited to give a short seminar on computational modeling of regional climate change at a leading research university in China. While there, he meets and exchanges pleasantries with the president of the hosting university. Hands are shaken, broad and somewhat vague ideas for collaboration are exchanged, and an invitation for a reciprocal visit to the U.S. campus is extended. Six months later, the president contacts the esteemed professor and proposes to visit the campus with a small delegation of senior academic and administrative personnel. During the visit, the president meets with the chancellor of the American school, and a general Memorandum of Understanding is signed with some fanfare. The MOU is a rather noncommittal document—essentially a formal way of saying, "Let's be friends." More hands are shaken, photographs taken.

Now what?

The scenario above is a common one. Most major U.S. research universities maintain hundreds of linkages with institutional partners around the world. These partnerships are memorialized in formal Memoranda of Understanding or Memoranda of Agreement, dutifully signed—with varying degrees of pomp and circumstance—by the senior leadership of the university and/or their governing boards. Often, as described above, these generic MOUs are just that: general expressions of the intent to collaborate, with the details to be worked out at some point in the future, in the form of more specific implementation agreements or legally binding contracts. Just as often, these good intentions result in little real collaborative activities. The challenge lies in translating these formal expressions of collegiality into vibrant, meaningful, and lasting partnerships that contribute to the core missions of both institutions.

Prominent U.S. research universities will typically receive scores of overtures each year from institutions of higher education around the world seeking partnerships of some sort. The overtures will sometimes come in the form of official delegations visiting the campus, often led by the president of the visiting university, accompanied by their senior international officer, or administrators of similar rank. Other times, the overtures will come in the form of email messages sent directly to the president, chancellor, provost, or senior international officer of the U.S. institution—the equivalent of a "cold call" by a salesman fishing for new clients. These overtures, directed at the highest ranks of the central administration, may occasionally result in signed MOUs, but rarely seem to foster any real collaboration. This is not to imply that the proposed partnerships themselves are ill-conceived; to the contrary, there are plenty of compelling reasons for U.S. universities to build partnerships with a wide variety of institutions abroad. Rather, the relative ineffectiveness of this basic approach to developing new partnerships often reflects differences in governance and management structures between the institutions (i.e, top-down versus faculty-driven, shared governance models), as well as a general lack of focus, coherence, and planning in the proposed collaborative activities. The latter highlights the increasing need for well-defined and articulated strategies to manage our international partnerships.

At the University of Illinois at Urbana-Champaign, we have recently undertaken an inventory of our various modes and models of international engagement, taking into consideration the costs and benefits, sustainability, funding sources, breadth and depth of impact, contributions to our core missions, and other considerations. This was the first attempt to catalogue and evaluate the different ways in which we engage with our institutional partners abroad; it is the result of the increasing importance and influence of our central, campus-level international offices, and in particular of the increased centralized oversight of the formal institutional agreements that support our international engagements. The goal of the exercise was not simply to compile a laundry list of international collaborations, but also to get some sense of the varied approaches taken to internationalization across a highly decentralized campus, and to learn which of these have been successful and sustained. One result is a set of general principles and guidelines that have proven useful in advising our faculty and administrators—and, perhaps more significantly, foreign institutions seeking to engage with us—when considering how best to foster meaningful international partnerships at the institutional level.

Principles and Guidelines

Think big, start small. In developing a new institutional partnership from the ground up, there should be a healthy balance between ambitious, long-term plans and more modest, short-term goals. We've been approached many times by potential partner institutions with proposals for joint degree programs, often in the initial communication or visit to our campus. This is somewhat like going out on a first date with a pre-nuptial agreement in your pocket—an optimistic approach that rarely results in marital bliss. For public institutions of higher education, answerable to their own faculty senates, their governing boards of trustees, their state higher education boards or commissions, and their regional accrediting agencies, the process of instituting a new joint degree program is daunting. Keep this in mind as a five- or ten-year goal, but also bring to the table proposals for more focused, easily-attainable outcomes. Some examples might include: four- or six-week summer research experiences for undergraduate students at either institution; a special topic graduate seminar co-taught via distance learning technologies; a shared design project or experiment involving cohorts of students for both institutions working together over a semester via the Internet and then coming together for a five-day workshop to present their results; co-sponsored invited lecture series on a topic of common interest to foster faculty exchange and interaction; shared service or outreach projects.

Define and articulate mutual benefit. It should go without saying that a vibrant, sustained partnership must benefit both institutions in somewhat equal measure. Yet, one of the most common questions raised in evaluating newly proposed partnerships is some variant of: "What's in it for us?" In these days of tightening budgets and frequent calls for our faculty to be "more entrepreneurial," the specific benefits to both partnering institutions must be articulated explicitly, and should be at least somewhat quantifiable. How will the proposed collaboration enhance the research and teaching activities on both campuses? Will joint or dual degrees really add value for the students who earn them? Is the flow of students and faculty between the two institutions likely to be balanced? Will the partnership open new opportunities for external funding? Will it provide access to research facilities, equipment, or sites previously unavailable? Will it aid in student recruitment? Alumni and/or corporate relations? Brand recognition? There many specific, demonstrable benefits to be realized from institutional partnerships, but too often we fall back on laudable, but vague clichés about broadening horizons, bridging cultures, and fostering good global citizens.

Engage the faculty. We've found that proposed partnerships originating with the highest reaches of the central university administration are rarely successful. Faculty typically take the initiative to form their own research collaborations, and it is generally more effective to identify and leverage these individual faculty connections into broader partnerships. When approaching a potential new institutional partner, go in knowing about the existing individual faculty connections. Are there alumni of doctoral programs from the proposed partner institution on your faculty, or vice versa? If so, there may be continuing ties between advisor and advisee that could be useful. Are their joint publications, successful co-written grant proposals, shared panels or presentations at scholarly meetings? One or two "faculty champions" at both institutions will go a long way toward ensuring that real collaborative activities take place, once the agreements are signed.

Ensure administrative infrastructure and support. Having key faculty supporters is crucial for developing institutional partnerships, but it is equally important to have established administrative support structures in place at both partner institutions. Faculty excel at identifying valuable research and educational opportunities for themselves and their students, but are typically less aware of—and less inclined to be interested in—the logistics of managing the emerging partnerships. Nor should they be, in fact. It is the job of the central international offices, under the leadership of the campus senior international officer, to facilitate new faculty-led initiatives by ensuring adequate and effective administrative support that attends to these details. Likewise, the international offices at the proposed partner institution must also be evaluated. Are they responsive, well staffed, and able to provide the support that your faculty and students need and expect?

Develop a funding model. An enthusiastic faculty member recently visited with her dean to "sell" the idea of a research and teaching collaboration that involved various departments in the college with a new international partner. In a sign of the changing culture in academia, the dean responded with interest, but then immediately asked, "What's your business plan?" This is not to say that the dean wanted to know how the college was to make a profit from the proposed project. Rather, he was looking for some clear sense that they had thought about the necessary human and financial resources, and come up with some plan for meeting those expenses beyond the initial "ask" for college-level support. Are educational activities to be funded primarily through student fees? If so, can the fees be kept in line with those charged for similar study abroad experiences, or with the cost of on-campus study? How will joint research be funded over the short, medium, and long term? Are there government agencies or foundations with opportunities that will be available to sustain the efforts? How will the exchange of personnel affect the departments' ability to meet their instructional demands?

The benefits of active, sustained institutional partnerships are many and manifest, and in an increasing global higher education "market," institutions of all sorts, from large public research universities to community colleges, are presented with new opportunities, and new mandates, to expand their international engagements. But along with this newly fertile soil for campus internationalization comes a heightened awareness of costs—in terms of both human and financial resources—and outcomes. Balancing and navigating the tension between these trends may be the key to moving beyond agreements and handshakes, and on to truly meaningful, transformative international partnerships.

What follows are several MOU and exchange templates from the University of Illinois at Urbana-Champaign, Kalamazoo College, and Purdue University. Most are specific rather than general, and define the mutual roles and responsibilities, funding models, and exchange purposes for each institution.

Templates for Establishing International Partnerships

A. Example of a General, Non-binding Memorandum of Understanding

MEMORANDUM OF UNDERSTANDING

BETWEEN

THE BOARD OF TRUSTEES OF THE UNIVERSITY OF ILLINOIS, USA

AND

[NAME OF PARTNER INSTITUTION]

IN

[CITY AND COUNTRY OF PARTNER INSTITUTION]

THE BOARD OF TRUSTEES OF THE UNIVERSITY OF ILLINOIS, acting on behalf of its [name of requesting/sponsoring academic or administrative unit], on its Urbana-Champaign campus, in Urbana, Illinois, U.S.A. ("ILLINOIS") and [name of partner institution], in [city and country of partner institution] ("[ABBR. NAME]"), each a "party" or "institution," wishing to establish a cooperative relationship through mutual assistance in the areas of education and research, agree as follows:

ARTICLE 1: SCOPE OF COLLABORATION

1.1 *General Scope.* Each institution may offer to the other opportunities for activities and programs, such as teaching, research, exchange of faculty and students, and staff development that will foster a collaborative relationship.

1.2 *Specific Activities.* Specific activities and programs implemented under authority of this MOU shall be subject to availability of funds and the approval of each institution's authorized representatives. The institutions contemplate implementation of programs or activities such as: (a) joint educational, cultural, and research activities; (b) exchange of faculty members and advanced graduate students for research, lectures, and discussions; (c) participation in seminars and academic meetings; (d) exchange of academic materials, publications, and other information; and (e) special, short-term academic programs.

1.3 *Separate Agreements.* Prior to initiating any specific activity or program, the parties will negotiate and enter into a separate agreement, signed by each party's authorized signatory, describing the terms of the arrangement, including the budgets. Each party will designate a Liaison Officer to develop and coordinate specific activities or programs.

1.4 *Student Exchange Limitations.* While advanced graduate and professional students may participate in cooperative activities as proposed in Article 1.2 above to conduct collaborative or independent research, this MOU does not provide for the exchange of undergraduate or graduate students who propose to enroll in classes and earn academic credit at the host institution. To implement student exchanges, the parties must enter into a separate agreement stipulating details of credit transfer, fees and participant qualifications prior to initiating the exchange of students or the acceptance of applicants as international non-degree students at either institution.

ARTICLE 2: RENEWAL, TERMINATION AND AMENDMENT

2.1 *Duration.* This MOU shall remain in force for five years from the date of the last signature. Either party may terminate this MOU by providing 60 days' advance written notice to the other party.

2.2 *Extension and Renewal.* The parties may extend or renew this MOU by agreement, confirmed in a written amendment signed by each party's authorized signatory.

2.3   *Amendment.* No amendment of the terms of this MOU will be effective unless made in writing and signed by each party's authorized signatory.

ARTICLE 3:   GENERAL MATTERS

3.1   *Use of Names.* Except in promoting the activities proposed in Article 1.2 above among its faculty and students, neither party may use the name of the other party in any form of advertising or publicity without express written permission. The parties must seek permission from one another by submitting the proposed use, well in advance of any deadline, to the liaison officers designated in Article 3.2 below.

3.2   *Notices.* The parties must give all notices under this MOU in writing via one of the following methods: (a) confirmed facsimile transmission; (b) postage prepaid registered or certified mail, return receipt requested; or (c) commercial overnight carrier. All communications must be sent to the addresses set forth below or to such other address designated by the parties by written notice. Notices are effective upon receipt.

ILLINOIS: [liaison officer/sponsoring unit name]
[campus address]
University of Illinois at Urbana-Champaign
[street address]
[city, state, zip]
USA
Tel: [217-###-####]
Fax: [217-###-####]
email: [liaison officer email address]

[ABBR. NAME]:   [liaison officer/sponsoring unit name]
[address line 1]
[address line 2]
[address line 3]
[city, state/province, postal code as appropriate]
[country]
Tel: [###-####]
Fax: [###-####]
email: [liaison officer email address]

3.3   *Binding Obligations.* With the exception of Articles 2 and 3, this MOU is not intended to create any legally binding obligations on either institution but, rather, is intended to facilitate discussions regarding general areas of cooperation.

3.4   *Authorized Signatories.* Each party represents that the individuals signing this MOU have the authority to sign on its behalf in the capacity indicated.

**FOR THE UNIVERSITY OF ILLINOIS
AT URBANA-CHAMPAIGN**

FOR [NAME OF PARTNER INSTITUTION]

_____
Chancellor

_____
[name of partner signatory], [title]

Date: _____

_____
Associate Provost
for International Affairs

**FOR THE BOARD OF TRUSTEES
OF THE UNIVERSITY OF ILLINOIS**

_____
Comptroller

Date: _____

Approved for legal form: LMP/20100127
Changes to form require legal review.

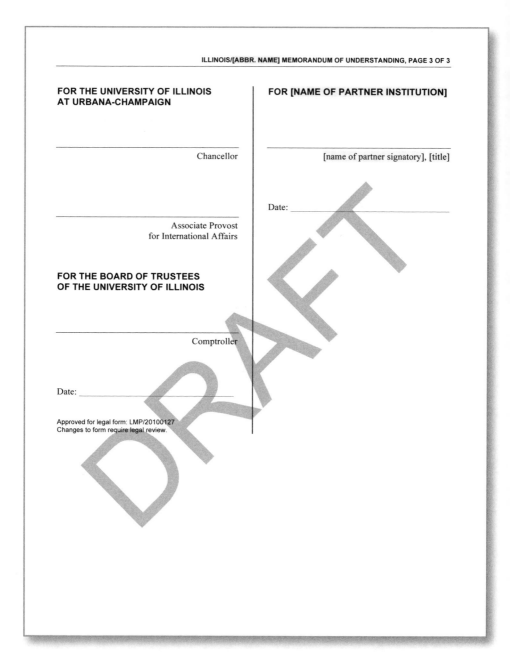

B. Example of a General MOU with a Focus on Exchange of Research Personnel

MEMORANDUM OF UNDERSTANDING

BETWEEN

THE BOARD OF TRUSTEES OF THE UNIVERSITY OF ILLINOIS, USA

AND

[NAME OF PARTNER INSTITUTION]

IN

[CITY AND COUNTRY OF PARTNER INSTITUTION]

THE BOARD OF TRUSTEES OF THE UNIVERSITY OF ILLINOIS, acting on behalf of its [name of requesting/sponsoring academic or administrative unit], on its Urbana-Champaign campus, in Urbana, Illinois, U.S.A. ("ILLINOIS") and [name of partner institution], in [city and country of partner institution] ("[ABBR. NAME]"), each a "party" or "institution," wishing to establish a cooperative relationship through mutual assistance in the areas of education and research, agree as follows:

ARTICLE 1: SCOPE OF THE COLLABORATION

1.1   The areas of collaboration include activities or programs offered at either institution that will contribute to the fostering and development of the cooperative relationships between them.

1.2   Each institution may offer to the other institution opportunities for activities and programs, such as teaching, research, exchange of faculty and students, and staff development that will foster and develop the collaborative relationship.

ARTICLE 2: GENERAL AREAS OF COOPERATION

2.1   Except for Articles 4 and 5, this MOU is not binding on either institution but is intended to facilitate discussions relative, but not limited, to the following general areas of cooperation. Specific activities and programs implemented under authority of this MOU shall be subject to availability of funds and the approval of each institution's authorized representatives, and may include:

    2.1.1   joint educational, cultural, and research activities;

    2.1.2   exchange of faculty members for research, lectures, and discussions;

    2.1.3   exchange of advanced graduate and professional students for collaborative or independent research;

NOTE: This MOU does not provide for the exchange of undergraduate or graduate students who propose to enroll in classes and earn academic credit at the host institution. The institutions will enter into a separate agreement that stipulates details of credit transfer, fees and participant qualifications prior to initiating the exchange of students or accepting applicants as international non-degree students.

    2.1.4   participation in seminars and academic meetings;

    2.1.5   exchange of academic materials, publications, and other information; and

    2.1.6   special short-term academic programs.

2.2   Prior to initiating any specific activity or program contemplated by this MOU, the institutions will enter into a separate agreement signed by each of their authorized signatories that describes the terms of the arrangement, including the budgets. Each institution will designate a Liaison Officer to develop and coordinate specific activities or programs.

ARTICLE 3:   EXCHANGE OF RESEARCH PERSONNEL

3.1   This MOU is intended, among other objectives, to foster increased interaction among faculty and advanced graduate students engaged in scientific and scholarly research in areas of mutual interest. In support of this effort, each institution will promote the exchange of research personnel, especially young faculty and advanced graduate students, for short periods of time so that they may become familiar with the facilities, methodologies, research culture and particular areas of focus of the other institution.

3.2   As a general principle, funding for the exchange of such personnel ("Participating Researchers") shall be based on a reciprocal sharing of costs:

3.2.1   Each institution will provide funding for roundtrip transportation to and from the host institution for its own Participating Researchers.

3.2.2   Each host institution will provide housing accommodations free of charge, as well as a modest living allowance in accordance with the standard per diem rates established by their governing bodies at the time of the exchange, to the Participating Researchers.

3.2.3   Each institution will provide assistances and/or the necessary letters of invitation or affiliation to facilitate the visa applications of Participating Researchers.

3.2.4   Individual Participating Researchers shall be responsible for ensuring adequate medical insurance coverage, applicable in the country of the host institution, for the duration of their visits.

3.2.5   Specific funding allocations for this exchange of Participating Researchers shall be subject to the approval of the institutions.

3.3   Each institution acknowledges that the Participating Researchers may engage only in general, collaborative activities involving basic, non-proprietary research during exchange visits under this MOU. The institutions do not intend for the Participating Researchers to create or develop new intellectual property as a result of such visits. If intellectual property is created or developed by Participating Researchers under this MOU, the institutions will negotiate in good faith to resolve issues including but not limited to ownership, responsibility for patent or other statutory protection, and licensing.

3.4   If, during the visits, the Participating Researchers identify specific collaborative research projects that they wish to pursue, the institutions will enter into a separate written agreement ("Specific Collaborative Research Project MOU") before commencing any research activity. Specific Collaborative Research Project MOUs will delineate the institutions' rights and obligations and will address, among other things, sources of funding and intellectual property rights. Each institution shall inform its Participating Researchers that they are responsible for reporting to their respective Liaison Officer regarding any proposed specific collaborative research projects that may arise from their initial visits and their interactions with one another under this MOU, prior to initiating projects or applying jointly for external funding for such projects. Each institution also shall inform its Participating Researchers of their obligations to abide by all regulations, policies and procedures of their employing institutions regarding the disclosing and handling of intellectual property and developed technologies that may arise under this MOU or under any Specific Collaborative Research Project MOU.

ARTICLE 4: DURATION

This MOU shall remain in force for a period of five (5) years from the date of the last signature, with the understanding that it may be terminated by either institution by providing sixty (60) days' advance written notice to the other.

ARTICLE 5: GENERAL MATTERS

5.1 USE OF NAMES. Except in promoting the activities proposed in Article 1.2 above among its faculty and students, neither institution may use the name of the other in any form of advertising or publicity without express written permission. Each institution must seek permission from the other by submitting the proposed use, well in advance of any deadline, to the liaison officers designed in Article 5.4 below.

5.2 AMENDMENTS. The institutions may amend this MOU only in a writing signed by each of their authorized signatories.

5.3 COUNTERPARTS. The institutions may sign this MOU in counterparts, all of which together constitute the complete MOU. Duplicated or facsimile signatures shall be originals for all purposes.

5.4 NOTICES. Any notice to given under this MOU must be in writing and will be effective upon receipt evidenced by: (a) confirmed facsimile transmission; (b) return receipt of postage prepaid registered or certified mail; or (c) delivery confirmation by commercial overnight carrier. All communications will be sent to the addresses set forth below or to such other address designated by each institution by written notice to the other:

ILLINOIS: [liaison officer/sponsoring unit name]
[campus address]
University of Illinois at Urbana-Champaign
[street address]
[city, state, zip]
USA
Tel: [217-###-####]
Fax: [217-###-####]
email: [liaison officer email address]

[ABBR. NAME]:   [liaison officer/sponsoring unit name]
[address line 1]
[address line 2]
[address line 3]
[city, state/province, postal code as appropriate]
[country]
Tel: [###-####]
Fax: [###-####]
email: [liaison officer email address]

5.5 AUTHORIZED SIGNATORIES. Each institution represents that the individuals signing this MOU have the authority to sign in the capacity indicated.

FOR THE UNIVERSITY OF ILLINOIS AT URBANA-CHAMPAIGN

_____

Chancellor

_____

Associate Provost
for International Affairs

FOR THE BOARD OF TRUSTEES OF THE UNIVERSITY OF ILLINOIS

_____

Comptroller

Date: _____

Approved for legal form: LMP/20100127
Changes to form require legal review.

FOR [NAME OF PARTNER INSTITUTION]

_____

[name of partner signatory], [title]

Date: _____

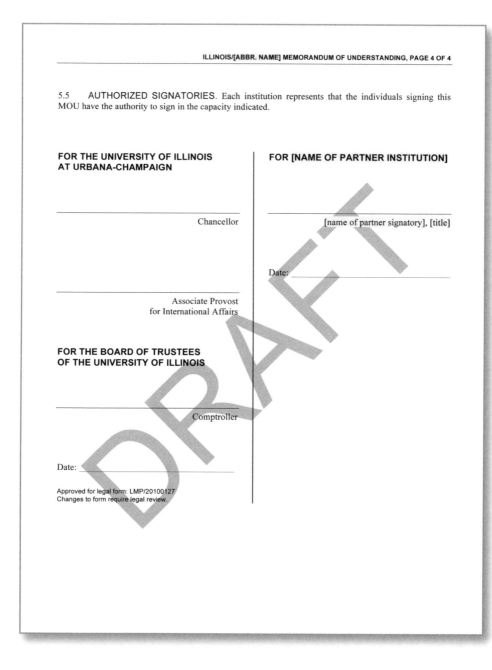

C. Example of a Student Exchange Program Agreement

A STUDENT EXCHANGE PROGRAM AGREEMENT

BETWEEN

THE UNIVERSITY OF ILLINOIS AT URBANA-CHAMPAIGN, USA

AND

[NAME OF PARTNER INSTITUTION]

IN

[CITY AND COUNTRY OF PARTNER INSTITUTION]

This Student Exchange Program Agreement ("Agreement") is between The Board of Trustees of the University of Illinois, acting through its Urbana-Champaign campus in Urbana, Illinois, U.S.A., on behalf of its [name of requesting/sponsoring academic or administrative unit] ("ILLINOIS"), and [name of partner institution], in [city and country of partner institution] ("[ABBR. NAME]"). The purpose of this Agreement is to promote and guide the ongoing exchange of students between the institutions.

ARTICLE 1:   DEFINITIONS

1.1   Unless otherwise specified in article 2 (Numbers) below, "Exchange" means a one-for-one exchange of students between the institutions.

1.2   "Home Institution" means the institution from which the student intends to graduate.

1.3   "Host Institution" means the institution that has agreed to receive the students from the Home Institution.

ARTICLE 2:   NUMBERS

2.1   Beginning with the 2011–2012 academic year, and in each subsequent academic year, ILLINOIS may send up to [number] Exchange Students to [ABBR. NAME], and [ABBR. NAME] may send up to [number] Exchange Students to ILLINOIS.

2.2   ILLINOIS and [ABBR. NAME] will review the program annually for any imbalances in the number of students exchanged and will adjust the numbers the following year to maintain a balance. By December 15 of each year, the administrators of this exchange for each institution will agree upon the number of allotted exchange spaces on each side for the upcoming academic year.

2.3   To determine balance, the institutions will use a person-per-semester formula so that two students attending the Host Institution for one semester equals one student attending the Host Institution for one academic year.

ARTICLE 3:   NOMINATION OF PARTICIPANTS AND ENROLLMENT

3.1   Each institution, as Home Institution, will accept applications from its students to participate in the Exchange, will screen the applications as it deems appropriate and will nominate the appropriate number of students for Exchange.

3.2   Each Home Institution will send to the Host Institution the applications for the nominated students by a date to be determined by the Host Institution. At ILLINOIS, unless otherwise agreed upon by both parties, applications for incoming students proposing to attend ILLINOIS during the fall semester (roughly mid-August through mid-December of each year) must be received no later than April 1; applications for students proposing to attend ILLINOIS during the spring semester (roughly mid-January through mid-May of each year) must be received no later than September 1. The Host Institution shall have the right to make final judgments on the admissibility of each student nominated.

3.3   The Home Institution will make sure that its nominees for students: (a) satisfy the language proficiency requirement for admission or take appropriate language instruction prior to the beginning of their academic program, as determined by the Host Institution; and (b) have completed at least one year of continuous study at the Home Institution before the exchange year.

3.4   The Host Institution will permit the students to apply to any academic program offered at the Host Institution as full-time, non-degree students, at a level determined by the Host Institution. The Host Institution may exclude students from restricted enrollment programs. Incoming students may not have access to courses in high demand at the Host Institution because enrollment priority is given to degree-seeking students. The study abroad administrators at each institution shall endeavor to inform their counterparts as to which specific academic programs or particular courses are likely to be unavailable to incoming students in any given semester.

3.5   The Home Institution will evaluate coursework completed by each student at the Host Institution and determine the type and amount of academic credit earned by the student, in accordance with the policies, procedures and regulations of the Home Institution.

3.6   Each Home Institution shall advise its students that they must return to the Home Institution upon completion of the Exchange period and in accordance with their visa status and expiration date. Any extension of stay beyond the initial program period must be approved by both institutions and supported by the necessary extension of the student visa status.

3.7   Students wishing to pursue undergraduate or graduate degrees at the Host Institution must first return to their Home Institution and apply for admission as degree-seeking students under the standard international admissions application process.

3.8   The institutions will cooperate to inform the students that they must abide by all policies, rules and regulations of the Host Institution and all relevant laws.

ARTICLE 4:   RESPONSIBILITIES OF ILLINOIS

4.1   ILLINOIS will accept the prescribed number of [ABBR. NAME] students and will enroll them as full-time non-degree students for one or two regular semesters of the academic year (roughly late August to mid-December and/or mid-January to mid-May).

4.2   ILLINOIS will provide [ABBR. NAME] students with tuition and partial fee waivers.

4.3   ILLINOIS will provide the appropriate counseling and other assistance to [ABBR. NAME] students and will assist in finding housing in ILLINOIS-approved residence halls.

4.4   ILLINOIS will send the student's official transcript of credits to [ABBR. NAME] at the end of the student's academic program at ILLINOIS, after receiving the student's written consent and payment in full of any outstanding charges on the student's account. .

ARTICLE 5: RESPONSIBILITIES OF [ABBR. NAME]

5.1   [ABBR. NAME] will accept the prescribed number of ILLINOIS students and will enroll them as full-time, non-degree students for the regular semesters of the academic year (roughly September 1 to July 1).

5.2   [ABBR. NAME] will provide the ILLINOIS students with tuition and partial fee waivers.

5.3   [ABBR. NAME] will provide the appropriate counseling and other assistance to the ILLINOIS students and will assist them in finding appropriate housing in residence halls, apartments, or private homes.

5.4   [ABBR. NAME] will send the student's official transcript of credits to ILLINOIS at the end of the student's academic program at [ABBR. NAME], after receiving payment in full of any outstanding charges on the student's account.

ARTICLE 6: FINANCE AND SERVICES

6.1   The Home Institution will require exchange students to register and to pay tuition and other required fees at their Home Institutions.

6.2   Each Host Institution will provide tuition and service fee waivers for the visiting students. The Host Institution also will provide to the Home Institution the necessary documents for obtaining visas.

6.3   [ABBR. NAME] will not disburse U.S. Federal Student Aid ("financial aid") to ILLINOIS students participating in the Program. ILLINOIS will process and disburse all financial aid for ILLINOIS students. ILLINOIS will maintain all records necessary to document student eligibility and receipt of financial aid.

6.4   The Host Institutions will not be responsible for the following costs incurred by Exchange students:

  6.4.1   transportation to and from the Host Institution

  6.4.2   room and board expenses

  6.4.3   textbooks, clothing, and personal expenses

  6.4.4   student fees at the Host Institution, including adequate health insurance coverage, which are not included in the standard tuition and fee waiver. Each institution will disclose to the other all non-waived fees for the subsequent academic year as soon as these fees are set by the Host Institution and made public

  6.4.5   passport and visa costs

  6.4.6   all other debts incurred during the course of the year

ARTICLE 7: DURATION

This Agreement shall remain in force for five years from the date of the last signature, with the understanding that it may be terminated by either institution providing 60 days' advance written notice to the other. Students participating in this exchange at the time of the intended termination will be permitted to complete the agreed upon exchange period at the Host Institution.

ARTICLE 8: GENERAL MATTERS

8.1 USE OF NAMES. Except in promoting the Exchange, neither institution may use the name of the other in any form of advertising or publicity without express written permission. Each institution must seek permission from the other by submitting the proposed use, well in advance of any deadline, to the liaison officers designated in Article 8.4 below.

8.2 AMENDMENTS. The institutions may amend this Agreement only in a writing signed by each institution's authorized signatory.

8.3 COUNTERPARTS. The institutions may sign this Agreement in counterparts, all of which together constitute the complete Agreement. A facsimile or PDF copy of a signature of a party hereto shall have the same effect and validity as an original signature.

8.4 NOTICES. Any notice given under this Agreement must be in writing and will be effective upon receipt evidenced by: (a) confirmed facsimile transmission; (b) return receipt of postage prepaid registered or certified mail; or (c) delivery confirmation by commercial overnight carrier. All communications will be sent to the addresses set forth below or to such other address designated by the parties by written notice to the other:

ILLINOIS:
[liaison officer/sponsoring unit name]
[campus address]
University of Illinois at Urbana-Champaign
[street address]
[city, state, zip]
USA
Tel: [217-###-####]
Fax: [217-###-####]
email: [liaison officer email address]

[ABBR. NAME]:
[liaison officer/sponsoring unit name]
[address line 1]
[address line 2]
[address line 3]
[city, state/province, postal code as appropriate]
[country]
Tel: [###-####]
Fax: [###-####]
email: [liaison officer email address]

8.5 AUTHORIZED SIGNATORIES. Each institution represents that the individuals signing this Agreement have the authority to sign in the capacity indicated.

**FOR THE UNIVERSITY OF ILLINOIS
AT URBANA-CHAMPAIGN**

FOR [NAME OF PARTNER INSTITUTION]

_____

Robert A. Easter, Interim Chancellor

_____

[name of partner signatory], [title]

Date: _____

_____

Wolfgang Schlör, Interim Associate Provost
for International Affairs

**FOR THE BOARD OF TRUSTEES
OF THE UNIVERSITY OF ILLINOIS**

_____

Walter K. Knorr, Comptroller

Date: _____

D. Example of an MOU for the Development of Academic Cooperation

MEMORANDUM OF UNDERSTANDING

*** U,

AND

KALAMAZOO COLLEGE,
MICHIGAN, USA

FOR THE DEVELOPMENT OF ACADEMIC COOPERATION
IN INTERNATIONAL EDUCATION

The general objective of this Memorandum of Understanding (MOU) is to stimulate and facilitate the development of collaborative and mutually beneficial programs which serve to enhance the intellectual life and cultural development on both campuses, and to contribution to increased international cooperation. Thus, *** U (*** U) and KALAMAZOO COLLEGE (KC) have agreed that in support of their mutual interests in the field of education and research:

1. The two Educational Institutions will:

    a) cooperate in the exchange of information relating to their activities in teaching and research in fields of mutual interests;

    b) promote appropriate joint research projects and joint courses of study, with particular emphasis on internationally funded projects;

    c) endeavor to encourage students and staff to spend periods of time in the host University. The exchange of students will be dependent on the execution of a formal Student Exchange Agreement prior to commencement of this activity;

    d) conduct short courses, as mutually agreed in writing between the parties prior to commencement of this activity;

    e) conduct cultural projects, as mutually agreed in writing between the parties prior to commencement of this activity;

    f) conduct study tours, as mutually agreed in writing between the parties prior to commencement of this activity.

2. Facilitate the exchange of undergraduate students. Such exchanges may take place for a period normally of one academic year (or at least one term or semester). The academic standing of such students shall be determined by the host University. Exchange students will be accorded the rights and privileges of students in the host country in accordance with the regulations of the host University relating to students and will be admitted under the terms and conditions relevant to the host University.

    Accreditation for the academic work carried out by an undergraduate student during the period of study at the host University will be at the discretion of the student's home University.

3. Work to develop an articulation agreement that provides a means for Kalamazoo College graduates to apply for admission to selected graduate degree programs at *** U.

4. Admission to a specific department or course is subject only to a student being satisfactorily qualified for the chosen area of study and to the availability of resources in the period for which admission is sought.

5. The aim of the Memorandum of Understanding shall be to achieve a broad balance in the respective contributions and benefits of the collaboration, and this shall be subject to periodic review by both Universities.

6. Academic members of staff and other personnel of one partner institution may spend periods not normally exceeding one academic year in the other partner institution. In supporting such an arrangement, the home institution undertakes to continue the salary of the participant. All other financial matters, including travel costs, are subject to individual negotiation, and will normally be the responsibility of the persons involved and their home institution.

7. The host institution agrees to assist in the seeking of appropriate housing, and to supply work space, library and technical facilities as appropriate.

8. In the implementation of specific cooperative programs, a written agreement covering all relevant aspects including funding and the obligations to be undertaken by each party will be negotiated, mutually agreed and formalized in writing, prior to the commencement of the program.

9. KC shall not hold *** liable for any damage that is caused, whether directly or indirectly, by KC. *** shall not hold KC liable for any damage that is caused, whether directly or indirectly, by ***.

10. KC will indemnify any loss suffered by *** that is caused, whether directly or indirectly, by the KC. *** will indemnify any loss suffered by the KC that is caused, whether directly or indirectly, by USL.

This agreement will take effect from the date of its signing and shall be valid for an unlimited period from that date unless sooner terminated, revoked or modified by mutual written agreement between the parties, and may be extended by mutual written agreement.

Either party may terminate the Agreement at any time during the term by the provision of three months written notice to the other party.

SIGNATURES

Signed for and on behalf of   Signed for and on behalf of
*** U   Kalamazoo College

_____   _____
                                            Prof. Eileen Wilson-Oylaren, President

_____   _____
        Date   Date

E. Example of a Memorandum of Understanding

MEMORANDUM OF UNDERSTANDING

THIS AGREEMENT, entered into this _____ day of _____, 20___, by and between Purdue University, West Lafayette, Indiana, U.S.A. and _____ .

WITNESSETH THAT:

WHEREAS, Purdue University and _____ desire to promote the enrichment of their teaching and learning, research and discovery, and engagement missions; and

WHEREAS, Purdue University and _____ desire to strengthen and expand the mutual contacts between the two universities; and

WHEREAS, Purdue University and _____ desire to provide for an exchange of faculty and students and other collaboration between the two universities on the terms and conditions hereinafter set forth;

NOW THEREFORE, it is mutually agreed as follows:

I. **Scope of Agreement** - The Agreement, together with Faculty and Student Exchange Agreements, shall include, but not be limited to, the following types of collaboration:

    A.   Short and Long-term Faculty Exchange

    B.   Undergraduate and Graduate Student Exchange

    C.   Collaborative Research and Discovery, Learning and Teaching, and Engagement

    D.   Other mutually agreed educational programs

II. **Definitions** - As used herein the terms "host university" and "home university" shall have the following meanings:

    A.   Host University - the university accepting the exchanged faculty member or student.

    B.   Home University - the university providing the exchanged faculty member or student.

III. **Period of Agreement** - This Agreement shall be effective _____ and will remain in force for a period of five years. Prior to the expiration date, this agreement may be reviewed for possible renewal for a further five-year period. In addition, either university may terminate the agreement in advance of it's normal expiration date by providing the other university with one year prior notice. In this case, personnel already participating in the exchange shall serve out their terms under the conditions specified at the time of their appointment.

IV. **Activities Under This Agreement** - It is expected that activities taking place under this Agreement will be initiated primarily by academic units within each university, and in coordination with their respective administrative units concerned with international activities. All activities undertaken must conform to the policies and procedures in place at each institution. For Purdue University, faculty and student exchanges will follow university guidelines for faculty and student exchange.

V. **Planning and Management of Activities** – Each distinct collaboration program or activity will be described in a separate Activity Agreement drawn up jointly by the collaborating units, and signed by the heads of these units. Such agreements will specify the names of those individuals on each campus responsible for the implementation of the program. Activity Agreements will also be approved by the Dean of International Programs at Purdue University and the _____ of _____.

VI. **Funding of Activities** – Activity Agreements should make financial costs and obligations explicit. Collaborating units are encouraged to work together to identify and secure any outside funding which may be needed. Projects requiring funding must be approved by both institutions.

VII. **Nondiscrimination** - Purdue University and _____ agree that no person shall on the grounds of race, color, national origin, gender, sexual orientation, or creed be excluded from participation under the terms of this Agreement.

VIII. **Modification** - The terms of this Agreement may be changed or modified only by written amendment signed by authorized agents of the parties hereto.

IN WITNESS WHEREOF, Purdue University and _____ have executed this Agreement as of the date first above written.

Signing for Purdue University   **Signing for (*international institution*)**

_____   _____

(name and title of department chair or dean   (name and title of counterpart at

of sponsoring unit)   international institution)

_____   _____

Date   Date

Sponsored Programs Services

_____

Date

F. Example of a Letter of Intent

LETTER OF INTENT ("LOI")

between

PURDUE UNIVERSITY
West Lafayette, Indiana, USA

and

Name of International Institution)
Name of unit (College/School, Department)
(City and Country)

Purdue University on behalf of its (unit name) and (International Institution) on behalf of its (unit name) establish this Letter of Intent to foster international cooperation in education and research.

1. Both parties will encourage the following activities to promote international academic cooperation:

    a) Exchange of materials in education and research, publications, and academic information;

    b) Exchange of faculty and research scholars;

    c) Exchange of students;

    d) Joint research and meetings for education and research;

    e) Technical assistance.

    Before implementing these activities, the parties will discuss the opportunities and challenges presented and may thereafter enter into specific agreements based on the mutually agreed objectives and outcomes.

2. This Letter of Intent forms the framework for cooperation between the parties to identify and achieve shared goals and objectives, and to facilitate and develop a genuine and mutually beneficial exchange process and research relationship. This Letter of Intent is non-binding and does not impose any legal or financial obligations or liabilities on either party.

3. This Letter of Intent shall remain in effect for five years, unless (i) either party terminates sooner by notifying the other party in writing, or (ii) the joint activites contemplated by this Letter of Intent are completed before the end of the five-year period. The parties may extend this Letter of Intent beyond five years by mutual agreement.

4. Each party shall designate a person or office to serve as liaison for implementing this Letter of Intent. For Purdue University, the contact person will be (name, address, phone, fax, email). For (international institution), the contact person will be (name, address, phone, fax, email).

Purdue University   (International Institution)

By: _____   By: _____

(Name and title of department chair or dean of   (Name and title of counterpart at international
sponsoring unit)   institution)

Date: _____   Date: _____

This document is approved in form by Purdue University Sponsored Program Services ("SPS"). Any changes to language effecting terms and conditions not approved by SPS renders this document invalid and unenforceable.

G. Example of a Letter of Agreement

LETTER OF AGREEMENT

BETWEEN
PURDUE UNIVERSITY
AND

This Agreement is made between the   (hereafter referred to as "Organization"), and Purdue University (hereafter referred to as "University"), West Lafayette, Indiana.

PROGRAM PURPOSE

Purdue University and the   wish to create a mutually beneficial partnership that will strengthen mission of the University, the business plans of the Organization and the economy of the State of Indiana.

PROGRAM PERIOD

This program period extends from   to   .

RESPONSIBILITIES

Purdue University

1.

1.

USE OF UNIVERSITY NAME

The Organization will not use the name of the University, nor of any member of University's Program staff, in any publicity, advertising, or news release without the prior written approval of an authorized representative of the University. The University will not use the name of Organization, or any employee of the Organization, in any publicity, advertising, or news release without the prior written approval of the Organization.

INSURANCE

Each party hereby assumes any and all risks of personal injury to its personnel and of property damage that occurs on its premises. As evidence of insurance coverage, Organization will provide a certificate of insurance to the University at the start of the program.

TERMINATION

The University or Organization may terminate this Agreement with or without cause at any time by giving thirty (30) days written notice when it is determined that termination is in either party's best interest.

RENEWAL

It is understood that the University and Organization may renew this Agreement at the termination date, subject to approval and written agreement of the parties.

ASSIGNMENTS

Either party without the prior written consent of the other party hereto shall not assign this Agreement.

EQUIPMENT/INSTRUCTIONAL MATERIALS

Equipment provided by the University remains the property of the University. All instructional materials developed by or provided by the University remains the sole and exclusive property of the University.

GOVERNING LAW

This Agreement shall be governed and construed in accordance with the laws of the State of Indiana.

RELATIONSHIP OF THE PARTIES

The parties agree that in the performance of this contract, the parties are acting as independent contractors and not as agents, an employee, partners, joint ventures or associates of one another. Neither party is authorized to act on behalf of the other for any purpose.

NON-DISCLOSURE OF CONFIDENTIAL INFORMATION:

The parties hereto agree that in their performance under this memorandum all information or intellectual property marked or characterized as confidential or proprietary to the University or the Organization or their client companies will be managed pursuant to a standard of care normally given to sensitive or confidential information. When further warranted or requested by either of the parties hereto, acceptable forms of Non-Disclosure Agreement will be executed as further evidence of the mutual commitment.

NOTICES

A. **Purdue University**

Purdue University

Phone: (   )
Fax: (   )
E-mail: @

B.

Phone:
Fax:
E-mail:

GENERAL

This instrument contains the entire agreement between the parties with respect to the subject matter hereof, and any representation, promise or condition in connection therewith not incorporated herein shall not be binding on either party. If any term of this Agreement is held invalid or unenforceable, such term shall be considered omitted from this Agreement and shall not affect the validity or enforceability of the rest of this Agreement. No modification of the terms of this Agreement shall be valid unless made in writing and signed by authorized representatives of the parties.

IN WITNESS THEREOF, the parties have executed this agreement as of the day and year last written below.

PURDUE UNIVERSITY

By: _____   By:_____

Date:_____   Date:_____

                                        By: _____

                                        Sponsored Program Services

                                        Date:_____

H. Example of an Information Collection for the Development of Exchange Agreement

Information Collection
For the development of an Exchange Agreement at Purdue

Sponsored Programs Services (SPS) with the International Programs (IP) is charged by the University Board to review contracts and linkages with overseas programs to ensure that proposed agreements meet Purdue University standards. In order to assist interested parties with the review process, this form is designed to assist you when collecting information about the proposed exchange partner.

About the international partner: (_____)
Name

1. Describe the type of schools/colleges that make up the institution, including the accreditation body and ranking:

2. How many faculty members are associated with this institution?

3. How many undergraduate and graduate students are enrolled in this institution?

4. What are the demographics of the student body (e.g., who has access to matriculation)?

5. How is the institution funded (publicly or privately)?

6. Describe any previous and/or current agreements or relationships with Purdue.

2011

About the Agreement

7. Describe the purpose of the agreement

   7a In view of the purpose of this agreement, describe the expected outcomes of the proposal to both institutions and the public they serve.

   7b If this is a renewal agreement, discuss the outcomes achieved over the years the linkage was in effect and evaluate the extent to which the purpose of the agreement was met.

8. Describe any agreement about financial arrangements (e.g., tuition, health insurance, travel, student exchange, etc.). Does Purdue University have the resources to carry out the proposal? (If financial commitments are made, Sponsored Programs Services (SPS) will not approve or sign the document until the appropriate fiscal officer has approved the commitments. (Department requesting – Business Manager must approve, College requesting – Director of Financial Affairs must approve. For Discovery Park, Director of Financial Affairs for Discovery Park must approve).

9. Who are the principal contacts at both institutions?

	Partner Institution	Purdue University
Contact Name:	_____	_____
Title:	_____	_____
Department:	_____	_____
Campus Address:	_____	_____
	_____	_____
Phone:	_____	_____
Fax:	_____	_____
E-Mail:	_____	_____

Appendix C

IIE Center for International Partnerships in Higher Education

The IIE Center for International Partnerships in Higher Education (CIP) assists higher education institutions in developing and sustaining partnerships around the world. CIP provides strategic planning, advisory services, and program development and management to support international higher education initiatives. The Center's consultative services, trainings, and resources allow institutions, organizations, and government ministries to develop internationalized or "global" campuses and programs that encourage the exchange of students and scholars across borders.

The Center engages in the following activities:

- Organizing U.S. study tours for higher education administrators and experts from around the world to enrich their understanding of U.S. higher education's diversity and bring them together with potential partners.

- Delivering the IIE Global Partnership Service (GPS), which assists international institutions in identifying potential U.S. partners.

- Providing advice and liaison services through IIE's network of international offices and partners.

- Collecting and disseminating best practices in developing institutional linkages and programs.

- Convening conferences and symposia of international educators and other leaders in the field.

- Producing timely policy research papers on critical issues.

WEBSITE: www.iie.org/cip

The International Academic Partnership Program

The International Academic Partnership Program (IAPP), originally funded by the U.S. Department of Education's Fund for the Improvement of Postsecondary Education (FIPSE), is a major initiative of IIE's Center for International Partnerships in Higher Education that seeks to increase the number of international partnerships between higher education institutions in the U.S. and their counterparts abroad.

To meet the demand for creating international partnerships in these countries, this program aims to:

- Identify best practices in building academic linkages.

- Provide customized training in the form of webinars, study tours, and mentorship programs to ten institutions selected to participate in a year-long International Academic Partnership Program.

- Share training materials and resources on establishing institutional partnerships with the U.S. higher education community at large.

- Provide guidance to institutions on how to develop and implement sustainable partnerships with a focus country. This is achieved by forming a campus task force, conducting an institution-wide inventory of activities pertaining to the focus country, and developing a strategic partnership plan.

U.S.-accredited institutions may apply to participate. Previous focus countries include India, China, and Brazil.

WEBSITE: www.iie.org/iapp

The U.S.-Indonesia Partnership Program

The U.S.-Indonesia Partnership Program (USIPP) is a two-year initiative sponsored by the U.S. Department of State, Bureau of Educational and Cultural Affairs (ECA). USIPP brings together six U.S. institutions with six Indonesian institutions to develop new, innovative study abroad strategies with the aim of increasing the number of U.S. undergraduate students studying abroad for credit in Indonesia.

Over the two-year period, USIPP will work to develop and pilot new study abroad programs for students from the United States. The initiative includes interviews with the participating students and university administrators to identify lessons learned and next steps, so that institutions can provide high quality study abroad programs and prepare to host more international students in Indonesia. A final written report will serve as a hands-on tool for international education practitioners.

The program aims to expand academic partnerships between other U.S. and Indonesian institutions, enabling faculty and students at home and host campuses to deepen mutual understanding and broaden the ongoing exchange of individuals and ideas between the U.S. and Indonesia. These aims will be met by identifying both general and country-specific best practices in preparing for and building study abroad capacity; disseminating these resources to the wider higher education community; and deepening the academic engagement of faculty and institutions in the U.S. and Indonesia.

WEBSITE: www.iie.org/usipp

IIE Global Partnership Service (GPS)

The Institute of International Education's Global Partnership Service (GPS) offers expertise to higher education institutions around the world seeking academic partnerships in the United States. GPS utilizes the IIE membership network of over 1,000 institutions to assist higher education institutions in identifying potential partners.

The Standard Global Partnership Service Package includes the following five services:

1) **IIE Global Partnership Toolkit:** A comprehensive set of materials compiled by IIE outlining strategies for partnership building. It includes case studies, articles, best practices for partnership building, and practical tools, such as MOU templates.

2) **IIE's Strategic Planning Worksheet:** A self-guided planning document to help determine institutional partnership priorities and strategies.

3) **Strategy Meeting:** A phone call with an IIE GPS staff member to discuss partnership strategies.

4) **Partner Search Announcement:** IIE will send a customized announcement via the IIE.Interactive, a weekly email newsletter reaching the IIENetwork of over 1,000 member institutions worldwide, to facilitate your partner search.

5) **Shortlist of Potential Partner Institutions:** IIE's GPS staff will develop a list of up to eight potential U.S. partner institutions, including contact information, based on stated criteria.

For information or to apply, please visit: www.iie.org/gps

About the Contributors

Nader Asgary is a professor of management and economics at Bentley University. He has taught courses in international business, international economics, international management behavior, economic development, econometrics, and finance at the undergraduate and graduate levels for more than 20 years, and he has been the recipient of many educator awards and grants. He was named Associate Provost for International Relations and Director of the Cronin International Centre at Bentley in 2006. As associate provost, he manages all things "international" at Bentley University and led many initiatives to enhance the globalization agenda of the University. He has received grants from the Fund for the Improvement of Postsecondary Education (FIPSE) to develop dual degree program with universities in Europe and to build comprehensive relationship with institutions in Brazil. Dr. Asgary has published in numerous national and international journals, such as *Economic Inquiry* and *Journal of Business Ethics*, has participated in many international and national conference presentations, has been a guest speaker, and professional journal reviewer. Dr. Asgary studied at Texas A&M University, where he received a B.S. in Civil Engineering, and then worked in the public and private sector in the Middle East for several years. He received his MA and Ph.D. in economics at the University of Houston.

Fanta Aw is the Assistant Vice President of Campus Life and Director of International Student and Scholar Services at American University in Washington D.C. Dr. Aw received her bachelor's degree in business administration, her master's in public administration with a concentration in organization development, and a Ph.D. in sociology from American University. Dr. Aw oversees all administrative, programmatic, and personnel operations related to international/intercultural programs and services in the Office of Campus Life. She advises the university leadership on matters related to campus internationalization as well as on issues of inclusion, diversity, and equity. Dr. Aw has close to 20 years of experience in higher education administration and international educational exchange.

Jessica Bailey received her undergraduate degree in mathematics and early childhood education and her first graduate degree in vocational rehabilitation counseling from Coppin State College in Baltimore. She received her MBA and Ph.D. in marketing from the University of Missouri-Columbia. She taught at Seattle University and American University, before moving into administration. She served as the Dean of the Sydney Lewis School of Business at Virginia Union University in Richmond before assuming the deanship of the School of Business and Economics at Winston-Salem State University. Recently, she served as Interim Provost of Winston-Salem State University. Much of her scholarly work has been in the area of international marketing. She is currently President-Elect of the HBCU Deans Roundtable, and active with the AASCUBS, North Carolina SBTDC, Leadership Winston-Salem, Senior Services, and Forsyth Futures.

Adria L. Baker, Associate Provost for International Education/Executive Director, Office of International Students & Scholars at Rice University, has held a variety of international education leadership positions. Her focus on public policy issues in international education allowed her to serve several years on NAFSA's State Whip Network as Texas's key congressional liaison, the Educational Subcommittee for the Mayor's Task Force for International Visitors, and the Governor's Council for the Department of Homeland Security. She led the Committee for an International Education Policy in Texas, which resulted in Texas H.R. 143 and Texas S.R. 532. Baker has written several articles and presented on subjects including advocacy in international education, international student and scholar advising, foreign credentials evaluation, and immigration topics. She is a past Chair of NAFSA Region III and is presently on the boards for the Fulbright Association-Houston Area Chapter and the Houston Greeters. She has received various recognitions for work in international education, including the inaugural award for excellence of KCISSS (Knowledge Community for International Students & Scholars Services) in NAFSA. She studied as a Rotary International Research Fellow and graduate international student at the University of Costa Rica, and worked in Mexico City teaching English. She received her doctorate from the University of Houston, and MA and BA from Texas Tech University.

Tim Barnes joined International Programs and Studies at the University of Illinois at Urbana-Champaign in 1998, and now serves as the Director of the newly inaugurated Illinois Strategic International Partnerships (ISIP) initiative, which focuses on identifying, cultivating, evaluating, and sustaining broadly and deeply impactful institutional relationships with a small, highly selective group of peer institutions around the world. In addition to launching ISIP, Barnes continues to manage more than 300 individual institutional partnerships, as well as drafting, negotiating, and tracking all written memoranda of understanding or contractual instruments that formalize institutional linkages for the campus. He also serves as the campus representative for the Fulbright Scholar, Specialist, and Distinguished Chair Programs, and was selected to participate in the 2011 Fulbright International Education Administrators (IEA) Program in Korea. His past contributions toward enhancing international engagement at one of the world's pre-eminent public research universities have included administering a multi-year, interdisciplinary grant from the Ford Foundation's "Crossing Borders" initiative, and administering a campus-wide cooperative research program with France's Centre National de la Rechercheé Scientifique (CNRS). Barnes first came to the University of Illinois at Urbana-Champaign in 1990 to pursue doctoral studies in musicology and ethnomusicology. He has presented papers for the Society of Ethnomusicology, the American Musicological Society, and the International Association for the Study of Popular Music on topics including sixteenth-century Spanish instrumental music, eighteenth-century Japanese koto music, and Christian heavy metal. His current research focuses on Hawaiian music on the U.S. mainland during the first half of the twentieth century.

Joseph L. Brockington is Associate Provost for International Programs and Professor of German language and literature at Kalamazoo College. He holds BA, MA, and Ph.D. degrees from Michigan State University. A former Chair of the Section on U.S. Students Abroad (SECUSSA) of NAFSA, Dr. Brockington has served as a member of the founding board of the Forum on Education Abroad, the Association of International Education Administrators (AIEA) executive committee, as well as the national team of the International Education Leadership Knowledge Committee of NAFSA. He currently serves as chair of the Ethics working group of the Forum on Education Abroad. He has published and presented numerous papers at international, national, regional, and consortial conferences on topics in study abroad, international programs administration, campus internationalization, legal and risk management issues in education abroad, and modern German literature. From 2005-2009, he organized and led the workshop on Best Practices in Legal and Risk Management Issues in Education Abroad at the NAFSA annual conference. He is one of the co-editors of the 3rd edition of *NAFSA's Guide to Education Abroad for Advisers and Administrators*.

William I. Brustein is Vice Provost for Global Strategies and International Affairs and Professor of Sociology, Political Science, and History at The Ohio State University. His work at Ohio State is dedicated to fully integrating international and multicultural experiences to the academic units within the university and expanding and enhancing its global reach. Before coming to Ohio, he was the Associate Provost for International Affairs and Director of International Programs and Studies at the University of Illinois at Urbana-Champaign. Dr. Brustein has published widely in the areas of political extremism and ethnic/religious/racial prejudice. His most recent books are *The Logic of Evil: The Social Origins of the Nazi Party, 1925 to 1933* (Yale University Press, 1996) and *Roots of Hate: Anti-Semitism in Europe before the Holocaust* (Cambridge University Press, 2003). He is past-president of the Association of International Education Administrators (AIEA) and past-Chair of NAFSA's International Education Leadership Knowledge Community. He has served on the Board of Directors of the Association for Studies in International Education, the editorial advisory boards of the *Journal of Studies in International Education* and the *International Education Report,* and on the executive committee of the Commission on International Programs of the Association of Public and Land-Grant Universities (APLU). In 2003, he was appointed to the NASULGC's Task Force on International Education and helped draft the published report entitled *A Call to Leadership: The Presidential Role in Internationalizing the University.*

Joan-Anton Carbonell was born in Barcelona in 1958. He has been involved in international education since 1990, when he was appointed as the Head of European Programmes at the Universitat Autònoma de Barcelona. In 1995, he became the head of the International Office, where he implemented a policy of developing partnership with institutions across the world. In December 2004, he moved to the United Kingdom and was appointed by Kingston University, London, as the Manager of the European Office. Since August 2010, Carbonell has been the Manager of the European and Study Abroad Office. He was the President of the EAIE (European Association for International Association) in 2000 and a member of its Executive Board from 1996 to 2001. Since 2006, he has been a member of the Executive Committee of HEURO, the Association of UK Higher Education European Officers. He has published several articles about international education and has made presentations in five continents. He has been writing an annual report on UK student mobility and its evolution since 2008. He started working in the creation of the Dorich House Group of European Universities in 2007.

Rosina C. Chia was born and raised in China, came to the U.S. and obtained her Ph.D. in social psychology from the University of Michigan. She is a professor in the Department of Psychology at East Carolina University. Her main research interest is in the areas of cross-cultural attitudinal comparison and locus of control. She serves as Assistant Vice Chancellor for Global Academic Initiatives and is responsible for the internationalization of curriculum on campus. Together with Dr. Elmer Poe, she co-developed the ECU Global Understanding Project that was piloted in 2003, and taught in fall 2004. In this course students are video linked in real-time with students from another country to learn about each other's culture and work on joint projects. In five years the project grew to 28 partners in 22 countries across five continents. Other programs have sprung from this project, including the ILEP (international lecture exchange program), the ICEP (international course exchange program), and the IREP (international research exchange program). Together, these programs have led to the effective internationalization of curriculum across the 10 colleges at ECU. This has been expanded outside the university to elementary and high schools. The institutions working in the program formed the Global Partners in Education to provide access to the global community. The program was awarded the Heiskell Award for

Innovation in International Education from the Institute of International Education and was highlighted in the *Chronicle of Higher Education* as a "best practice" of innovative approaches to internationalization.

Cathryn Clement has worked with international education and agriculture development programs for more than 25 years. She is the Coordinator for International Academic Programs for the College of Agriculture and Life Sciences as well as for the Borlaug Institute for International Agriculture at Texas A&M University. She also serves as a lecturer in the Department of Agricultural Leadership, Education and Development, where she teaches a course on cultural orientation and adaptation. Clement coordinates international academic programs—reciprocal exchanges, faculty-led study abroad, a graduate certificate program, workshops, seminars, sponsored students, internships, and the Peace Corps Master's International program at Texas A&M—and provides development leadership and logistical support for international academic programs for Texas A&M AgriLife faculty. She also manages and/or backstops international agriculture development and education projects in countries such as Brazil, Tunisia, South Africa, Namibia, and Indonesia. In 2010, she worked with graduate and undergraduate students to develop a new student group, Aggies in International Development. Clement has a B.A. in Spanish, and an MA in horticulture, both from Texas A&M.

Kiran Cunningham is Professor of Anthropology at Kalamazoo College and Faculty Fellow with Kalamazoo College's Arcus Center for Social Justice Leadership. She is an applied anthropologist whose areas of expertise include action research, community-based research, social change, deliberative democracy, community development, international and intercultural education, experiential learning, and transformative learning. At the core of her teaching, scholarship, and service is using action research to catalyze social change. As an action researcher, she uses participatory research methods to bring a broad range of community members into the change process. She has designed workshops and trainings for numerous groups and organizations in the areas of leadership development, transformative learning, and mindset change. This work has led to numerous publications, including *Tapping the Power of City Hall to Build Equitable Communities* (National League of Cities, 2007) and *Integrating Study Abroad into the Curriculum: Theory and Practice across the Disciplines* (Stylus Press, 2010).

Pascal Delisle was until recently the Cultural Attaché for Higher Education at the French Embassy in Washington DC, and the founding director of the Partner University Fund. Under the auspices of a private American foundation (FACE), this Fund promotes innovative partnerships in research and higher education between France and the United States. Previously, Delisle was the director of the Center of the Americas at Sciences Po in Paris, where he oversaw Sciences Po student exchanges, academic partnerships, and joint and dual degrees with the Americas. From 2002 to 2004, he was a visiting professor at Columbia University in New York, where he founded the Alliance Program, a strategic joint venture between Columbia University, Science Po, Ecole Polytechnique, and Université Paris I Panthéon-Sorbonne. Formerly, Delisle held several faculty positions in France, Colombia, and the United States, publishing articles and book chapters, and contributing to collective books on environmental economics and policy as well as European economics and policy. A native of France, Delisle holds a Ph.D. in environmental economics from Université Paris I Panthéon Sorbonne. He is a graduate of Sciences Po, where he obtained a master's degree in public policy, and a graduate of Ecole Normale Supérieure.

Kim E. Dooley is a professor in the Department of Agricultural Leadership, Education and Communications at Texas A&M University. She has conducted professional presentations and distance training programs around the globe. Her publications include 51 refereed journal articles and a book entitled *Advanced Methods in Distance Education: Applications and Practices for Educators, Administrators, and Learners.* She received the Distinguished Research Award (2008) from the Association of Agricultural Educators, Southern Region. She currently serves as executive editor of the *Journal of International Agricultural and Extension Education* and on the managing editorial board for the *Journal of Agricultural Education.* She also serves as an elected representative to the Council of Principal Investigators.

Leeanne Dunsmore is the Associate Dean for Program Development and Graduate Admissions at American University's School of International Service. Dean Dunsmore received her BA from the College of Wooster and her MA in international political economy from American University. She pioneered the first dual degree program between a Japanese and a U.S. university in the early 1990s, and has spent the last twenty years building global partnerships. As a result, international students currently comprise 20 percent of the entering class in the largest school of international affairs in the United States. Additionally she established Graduate Study Abroad, and graduate student participation is currently at forty percent.

Helen Foster is a University Manager and her current role is Head of Partnership Development in the International Office at The University of Nottingham. She manages, supports, and coordinates activities around teaching partnerships with overseas institutions. Since 2005, Helen has been closely involved in the development and set-up stage of the University of Nottingham Ningbo, China, giving support and advice to senior management. She regularly speaks about how universities set up campus activities abroad and leads major projects at the overseas campuses in China and Malaysia, including management of a range of summer schools. Helen has held a number of roles within higher education management, including Head of Postgraduate Admissions, Postgraduate Funding Manager in a Graduate School, and University Planning. She also co-founded the University of Nottingham Survey Unit.

Cheryl Francisconi, MSW/MPH, is based in Addis Ababa, Ethiopia, as the Director of the Institute of International Education's office in sub-Saharan Africa. She is also the director of two leadership development programs that IIE implements in Ethiopia and the region. Prior to joining IIE, Cheryl directed international program operations for the David and Lucile Packard Foundation's Population Program in eight countries in the developing world. She has also previously served as a consultant in the area of organizational development, leadership, and capacity building both in the U.S. and abroad. She holds master's degrees in social welfare and public health from the University of California, Berkeley, and is a certified trainer in a variety of leadership development and large scale meeting methodologies.

Eckhard A. Groll is a professor of Mechanical Engineering and the Director of the Office of Professional Practice at Purdue University. He joined Purdue University as an Assistant Professor in 1994 and was promoted to Associate Professor in 2000 and to Full Professor in 2005. He received his diploma in mechanical engineering from the University of the Ruhr in Bochum, Germany, in 1989 and a doctorate in mechanical engineering from the University of Hannover, Germany, in 1994. Since joining Purdue, he has been the principal investigator (PI) or Co-PI on 79 research grants and 40 educational grants with a total budget of $8.5 million. Dr. Groll has authored or co-authored 72 archival journal articles and 126 conference papers. He has been the co-author of two handbook chapters and the editor or co-editor of seven conference proceedings. He has given 45 invited lectures or seminars and four keynote lectures. He serves as the Regional Editor for the Americas for the *International Journal of Refrigeration* and is a Fellow of the American Society of Heating, Refrigerating, and Air Conditioning Engineers (ASHRAE). He is a 2010-2011 Fellow of the American Council on Education (ACE) and participated in the Academic Leadership Program of the Committee on Institutional Collaboration (CIC-ALP) during 2009-2010. He has received numerous awards for his research and teaching excellence, including the 2010 E. K. Campbell Award from ASHRAE, induction into the Book of Great Teachers at Purdue University in 2008, and the 2007 Purdue University Faculty Scholar Award.

Yating Haller is the Assistant Director of Global Professional Practice at Purdue University. She also served as a Program Director of International Research and Education in Engineering (IREE), a NSF funded program that sent 58 U.S. engineering researchers to conduct research in China. Born in Taiwan and raised in Singapore, Haller has traveled to over 30 different countries. She has an MS in cross-cultural psychology and an Ed.D. degree in higher education leadership and policy at the Peabody College at Vanderbilt University in 2007. Haller's research interests include global engineering competencies and the impact of internationalization on the engineering profession. At Purdue University, Haller's main responsibilities include engagement of both students and faculty members to embrace global engineering mindsets and practice. She builds and develops Co-op and internship programs by leveraging global engineering education. Her office manages the Co-Op and internship programs for over 600 Purdue University students per year.

Stevan Harrell is an anthropologist at the University of Washington, specializing in ecology, ethnicity, education, demography, and material culture in China and Taiwan. In the late 1990s, three formerly separate aspects of his professional life converged. His research interests in ethnic relations and in the society and culture of the Nuosu led to a collaboration with local scholar Ma Lunzy, which in turn led to working with a group of local and international friends to raise money to build a primary school in Ma's home village of Yangjuan. His institutional interests in collaboration with Chinese scholars led to his work with Gretchen Kalonji and Thomas Hinckley in establishing the multi-stranded relationship between the University of Washington and Sichuan University described in chapter 4 of this volume. And his pedagogical interests in interdisciplinary teaching led him to invite natural and social scientists from Sichuan University and their students to collaborate on a variety of research and teaching exchanges. Out of this mix he has published *Cultural Encounters on China's Ethnic Frontiers* (edited, 1995), *Mountain Patterns: The Survival of Nuosu Culture in China* (with Ma Lunzy and Bamo Qubumo, 2000), *Perspectives on the Yi of Southwest China* (edited, 2001), *Ways of Being Ethnic in Southwest China* (2001), and *Fieldwork Connections* (with Bamo Ayi and Ma Lunzy, 2007). He is also co-founder and president of the Cool Mountain Education Fund, a small public charity that provides scholarships and other help to graduates of the Yangjuan Primary School.

Thomas M. Hinckley is Interim Director and David R.M. Scott Professor of Forest Biology at the School of Forest Resources at the University of Washington. For most of his career, his research interest has been in the water and carbon physiology of trees and woody shrubs. For the last decade, he has become increasingly interested in educational pedagogy that supports group, place-based, hands-on learning and interdisciplinary research on the interaction between history, people, and current land-use practices that may or may not be sustainable. He graduated in 1966 with distinction in biology from Carleton College, Minnesota, and received a Ph.D. in 1971 from the University of Washington. He has taught at the University of Missouri–Columbia, the Agricultural University of Vienna, and the University of Washington.

Ian Jones has been The University of Nottingham's International Officer for Partnership Development since March 2009. He manages the University's Transnational Education (TNE) activities, working with existing partners and identifying and developing new partnerships. His responsibilities extend across The University of Nottingham's three campuses in the United Kingdom, Malaysia, and China. He is Secretary to the University's TNE Committee and provides advice and guidance on TNE policy and strategy to senior management in the institution. He also contributes to international student recruitment activity and other special projects relating to the

University's international strategy on an *ad hoc* basis. Jones was the co-founder of the United Kingdom's International Partnership Development Forum, which has membership from over 100 higher education institutions in the UK and meets biannually in Nottingham to discuss TNE practice and developments in the sector. In 2011 he led a team of nine UK higher education professionals on a ten-day study tour to Brazil, facilitated by the United Kingdom's Association of University Administrators (AUA), which considered various aspects of Brazilian higher education. He is also the AUA's Travel Award Coordinator, responsible for promoting travel awards and selecting recipients, which are often people who would otherwise be unable to gain international experience. His previous professional experience includes quality assurance of international and UK-based collaborative partnerships at Birmingham City University and the University of Wolverhampton. Jones holds a postgraduate diploma in management and a bachelor's degree in law.

Joseph V. Jones serves as Interim Assistant Vice President in the Office of International Education and Development at Florida A&M University (FAMU). Mr. Jones's international programs management includes implementation of the following grant projects: a training workshop for Tajikistan Solid Waste Managers in Budapest; Fulbright Groups Abroad Project Coordinator to three cities in Brazil; FAMU academic overseas course offerings in Nassau; and faculty/students short-term groups to the Dominican Republic and Brazil. Mr. Jones is the current principal investigator of two exchange projects in biofuels production and sustainable development with five universities in Brazil. Mr. Jones's professional work experiences include: coordinated study abroad program; oversees the Student and Visitors Exchange Program J-1 and F-1 visas; served as panelist for three consecutive years on the Boren/NSEP Undergraduate Scholarship for Study Abroad in Houston; coordinated the Statewide African-American Educational Conference in Orlando; and served as pastor of a Baptist church. Mr. Jones earned his master of science degree in counselor education from Florida A&M University and his bachelor of arts degree in religion from Florida State University.

Terry-Ann Jones is Associate Professor of Sociology and Anthropology at Fairfield University. Her main areas of research and teaching interest are in international migration, particularly movement between Latin America and the Caribbean and North America. Her research has compared Jamaican immigrants in the metropolitan areas of Miami and Toronto, examining the racial and ethnic setting and labor markets of the two areas, and the immigration policies of the two countries. Her book on this theme, *Jamaican Immigrants in the United States and Canada: Race, Transnationalism, and Social Capital*, was published in 2008. Her second book, *Mass Migration in the World-System: Past, Present, and Future*, was co-edited with Eric Mielants and published in 2010. Professor Jones is currently doing research on seasonal labor migration in Brazil. She studies the migration patterns of Brazilian sugar cane workers who travel from Brazil's northeast to the central and southeastern regions, with an emphasis of their living and working conditions. The role of migration as a livelihood strategy among both domestic and international migrants is central to this research. She received her Ph.D. in international studies from the University of Miami in 2005.

Sabine C. Klahr is the recently appointed Director of the International Center at the University of Utah in Salt Lake City. She previously served in positions in international education at Chatham University, Boise State University, Western Michigan University, and Colorado State University. During her tenure at Chatham and Boise State, Klahr developed over 50 international partnerships. Altogether, she has 15 years of experience in international education and earned a doctorate in higher education leadership from Montana State University-Bozeman in 1998 with an emphasis on international education leadership. Her dissertation research focused on internationalizing engineering education and addressing the barriers to study abroad for students in engineering. Prior to her doctorate, she earned a BS and MS in botany and served as a teacher in secondary science education, mathematics, and German language. Klahr has served on numerous committees and task forces for NAFSA: Association of International Educators, the Association for International Education Administrators (AIEA), and for the German Academic Exchange Service (DAAD). She currently serves as Chair of the AIEA Membership Committee and as a member of the AIEA Strategic Planning Task Force. Klahr has been involved in international education since arriving in the U.S. as a high school exchange student from Germany.

K. Peter Kuchinke, Ph.D., is Professor at the University of Illinois at Urbana-Champaign. A native German, he holds a doctoral degree from the University of Minnesota in human resource development and strategic management. His current research focuses on the development of capacity of workforce and human resource professionals to lead organizational and individual growth and development efforts. He further explores the changing meanings of work and career in this era of rapid technological, economic, political, and social rates of change. Professor Kuchinke is published widely and frequently lectures at conferences and universities around the world.

Nita Kumar is Brown Family Professor of South Asian History at Claremont McKenna College, Claremont, California. She has been studying Indian education for the last 25 years from numerous perspectives. Her work has included: the history of education, particularly in the modern period; the rise of a new intelligentsia, "new" in the sense of gender, class, community, profession, and subject-position; the ethnography of schools; the teaching in cities, peer groups, work sites and the media; curricula; teachers; children, families, and the intersections of home and school; modernity and democracy in schooling; and the methodologies of history, anthropology and postcolonialism. Her books and articles include *Artisans of Banaras* (Princeton, 1998); *Friends, Brothers and Informants* (Berkeley, 1992); *Women as Sub-*

jects (Virginia, 1994); *Mai: A translation* (Kali, 2001); *Lessons from Schools* (Sage, 2001), *The Politics of Gender, Community and Modernities* (Oxford, 2007); and she is working on two books called *Managing a School in India* and *Education and the Rise of a New Indian*. Since 1990, she has also been engaged in innovative education in Varanasi, India, through both service and advocacy, working with children, teachers, and families to develop curricula, fiction for children, arts materials, and teachers' training units (www.nirman.info).

William B. Lacy is Vice Provost–University Outreach and International Programs and Professor of Sociology in the Department of Human & Community Development at the University of California, Davis, since August 1999. Vice Provost Lacy is responsible for leadership of campus international initiatives, including Faculty New Initiatives Seed Grant Program, Services for International Students and Scholars, UC Education Abroad Program, UC Davis Quarter Abroad and Summer Abroad, International Agreements of Cooperation, International Alumni and Development, the Hubert H. Humphrey Fellowship Program, and the Fulbright Programs. Prior to arriving at Davis, Dr. Lacy was the Director of Cornell Cooperative Extension and Associate Dean of the Colleges of Agriculture and Life Sciences, and Human Ecology at Cornell University 1994-1998, and Assistant Dean for Research, College of Agricultural Sciences, Penn State University 1989-1994. Dr. Lacy received his BS in 1964 from Cornell University, MA in higher education administration in 1965 from Colgate University, and his MA and Ph.D. from the University of Michigan in sociology/social psychology. Dr. Lacy has authored/co-authored/co-edited over eighty journal articles and book chapters and six books on education, science policy, agricultural research and extension, biotechnology, and biodiversity. Dr. Lacy is a Fellow of the American Association for the Advancement of Science and a recipient of two Fulbright awards for international education administrators and the German Academic Exchange Services award. He founded the UC Senior International Leader's Council, and is the past President of three professional organizations: the Agriculture, Food, and Human Values Society (1993), the Rural Sociological Society (1999), and the Association of International Education Administrators.

P.J. Lavakare obtained his Ph.D. degree from the University of Rochester in 1963 during a Fulbright fellowship to the U.S. After two decades of research at the Tata Institute of Fundamental Research, Bombay, he secured a diploma in systems management from Bombay University and joined the Ministry of Science and Technology, as an Advisor to Government of India. From 1986-90, he served as the Secretary of the Science Advisory Council to the Prime Minister. He was also Adviser to the Planning Commission. On his retirement from government service, he served as the Executive Director of the U.S. Educational Foundation in India until 1999. He is presently the India Country Program Representative of the Institute of International Education for the GE Foundation Scholarship Program in India. He is a Member of the Board of Governors of the Mody Institute of Technology and Science University (Rajasthan, India) and also a Member of the Board of Management of the Symbiosis International University (Pune, India). He has published over 100 papers, edited four books, and authored two popular science books. He is a member of the Education Committee set up by the Federation of Indian Chambers of Commerce and Industry (FICCI). He presently specializes in international education.

Clifford Louime is an Assistant Professor in the College of Engineering Sciences, Technology and Agriculture at Florida A&M University (FAMU). His current academic work is centered on the question: "How can we secure the planet's future energy needs?" In 2009, he co-founded the FAMU BioEnergy Group, whose main goal is to address the issue of national energy security from a holistic perspective, namely by addressing the social, economic, and environmental challenges at hand. Louime published numerous manuscripts on the subject. Presently, he is serving as the Editor in Chief of a special biofuels issue that will be published by the *International Journal of Molecular Sciences* in Switzerland. Louime earned a BS degree in international agriculture from the University of Kassel, Germany, and a Ph.D. from FAMU in environmental sciences. Prior to returning to FAMU, Louime co-founded the Foundation for the Advancement of Higher Education (FAdHiEd), a nonprofit organization registered in Miami, Florida, whose vision is to provide educational missions in developing countries. In his capacity as Vice-President of FAdHiEd, Louime participated in educational exchanges in Haiti, the Dominican Republic, the Cayman Islands, Germany, Sweden, and Brazil.

Minnie Battle Mayes is the founding Director of the Office of International Programs (OIP) and its nationally recognized interdisciplinary Global Studies Certificate Program at North Carolina Agricultural and Technical State University (NC A&T). Mayes began her career in international affairs at the United Nations in New York in 1975. This was followed by positions in Cameroon with CARE, Inc. and the American Council for Nationalities Services/Joint Voluntary Agency, in the Vietnamese refugee camps of Singapore and Indonesia. Mayes came to NC A&T from the U.S. Department of State and the U.S. Information Agency, where she spent 20 years as an independent contractor for its educational and cultural exchange programs. Mayes received her Bachelor of Arts degree in political science from the State University of New York (now Binghamton University) in 1975 and earned a master's degree in international administration from the School for International Training in Brattleboro, Vermont, in 1981. Mayes currently serves as a member of the Gilman International Scholarship National Review Panel, the School for International Training (SIT) Partnership Council and Arcadia University College of Global Studies National Advisory Board. At NC A&T, she serves as the Chair of the SACS Subcommittee on Operations, and Chair of the University's Strategic Planning Committee on Global Readiness.

Maureen E. Miller is Director of Communications for the Office of International Affairs at The Ohio State University. She is responsible for the strategic communications and marketing of study abroad, international student and scholar services, and international initiatives through a variety of publications, special events, the Internet, and social media. Miller has more than 25 years of public relations, media relations, and news reporting experience, and has worked in the public, private, government, and nonprofit arenas. She earned a master's in business administration from Ohio Dominican University and a bachelor's in journalism from Ohio State. Miller has been actively involved in the Public Relations Society of America (PRSA), Central Ohio Chapter, and served as its president in 2003. She is the 2006 recipient of the PRSA Central Ohio Chapter's Tom Poling Practitioner of the Year award and has been recognized for successfully leading media relations and promotional campaigns. Miller has served as a member of the board of trustees for YWCA Columbus and has helped raise awareness for nonprofit organizations including Make Room Columbus, Mid-Ohio Food Bank, Special Olympics, and BalletMet Columbus.

Daniel Obst is Deputy Vice President of International Partnerships at the Institute of International Education (IIE) in New York. Obst provides strategic leadership in the creation and implementation of international academic partnerships, and oversees all the activities of IIE's network of 1,000 member institutions, IIE's publications and higher education services, and IIE's Center for International Partnerships in Higher Education. Obst has recently worked on a number of international partnership projects, including a British Council-funded project on academic linkages between the U.S. and the UK, the U.S. Department of Education-funded International Academic Partnership Program, and the U.S. Department of State-funded U.S.-Indonesia Partnership Program for Study Abroad Capacity. Obst recently co-edited several publications, including *Joint and Double Degree Programs: An Emerging Model for Transatlantic Exchange* and *Innovation through Education: Building the Knowledge Economy in the Middle East,* and co-authored two white papers in IIE's series on *Meeting America's Global Education Challenge*. Obst received his BA in international relations from The George Washington University and holds a master's degree in European studies from the London School of Economics.

Samuel Owusu-Ofori is the chair of the Mechanical Engineering Department, Boeing Professor of Manufacturing, and Professor of Mechanical Engineering at North Carolina A&T State University (NC A&T). He earned a Ph.D. from University of Wisconsin-Madison in 1981. His research is in the area of modeling, analysis, and control of mechanical systems, manufacturing processes, and tribology of manufactured surfaces. He joined the NC A&T faculty in the fall of 1983. As the Boeing Endowed Professor of Manufacturing, he coordinates all the manufacturing activities within the College of Engineering and serves as the Chair of the manufacturing committee. He has received the Outstanding Professor and the Mechanical Engineering Research Excellence Award both from NC A&T State University. He has also received awards for excellence in teaching at NC A&T State University. He is a member of the American Society of Mechanical Engineers and American Society for Engineering Educators. He has published over 50 articles in conference proceedings and journals. He initiated the Exchange Agreement between NC A&T and Kwame Nkrumah University of Science and Technology in 1995 and has been its coordinator since its inception.

Elmer C. Poe is currently the Assistant Vice Chancellor for Emerging Academic Initiatives at East Carolina University (ECU). He helped ECU become the UNC system leader in distance and online learning. Poe served as the interim dean in the School of Industry and Technology and as the director of graduate studies. Current projects include creating the East Carolina campus in Second Life, and social networking/presence tools in a variety of learning settings. Poe was a member of the consortium team that created the Internet-based Ph.D. in technology management hosted at Indiana State University. In 2003 Poe worked with Dr. Rosina C. Chia to develop a world cultures course that uses real-time video, chat, and W2 tools, bringing students from around the world together in a common classroom. The structured experiences in this course provide a venue for the development of global perspectives and an appreciation for diverse cultures. There are more than 30 university partners in Europe, Asia, Africa, and South America. The universities participating in the program formed the Global Partners in Education to provide access to the global community. The program was awarded the Andrew Heiskell Award for Innovation in International Education from the Institute of International Education and was highlighted in the *Chronicle of Higher Education* as a "best practice" of innovative approaches to internationalization.

Ann B. Radwan received her BA degree in international labor relations from the School of International Service of the American University in Washington, DC. Her first Fulbright grant was to India and after returning to the U.S., she entered the University of Pennsylvania, receiving her Ph.D. in South Asia regional studies and economic history. She has received both pre- and post-doctoral Fulbright-Hays grants to complete her dissertation research and to engage in comparative research in Egypt and India. At the University of North Florida, she was an Associate Professor and Director of International Programs, where she initiated internationalization with funding from the U.S. Department of Education. Before moving to Egypt to be the Executive Director of the Bi-national Fulbright Commission, she served as Branch Chief in the Office of Academic Programs at the United States Information Agency for the Near East and South Asia region. During her tenure at USIA, she expanded and administered the worldwide University Affiliation Program. Her international experience includes being chosen as a consultant to assist in the establishment of an American-style university in Saudi Arabia. Currently, she is responsible for the Center for International Studies at St. Cloud State University, which includes recruitment and admissions, international student and scholar services, and education abroad. She also chairs the University's International Vision Task Force, which has developed the strategic plan for internationalizing St. Cloud State University.

Jonas Redwood-Sawyerr is acting Vice Chancellor and Principal of the University of Sierra Leone (Sierra Leone). He received his Ph.D. in electrical systems engineering from the University of Essex (UK). Dr. Redwood-Sawyerr has previously served as Head of the Department of Electrical & Electronic Engineering, Dean of the Faculty of Engineering, Acting Principal and also Dean of the Board of Postgraduate Studies at Fourah Bay College, University of Sierra Leone. Dr. Redwood-Sawyerr serves as the managing editor of the *Journal of Pure and Applied Science*. He is one of three Vice Presidents of the Sierra Leone Institution of Engineers and a member of the Professional Engineers Registration Council of Sierra Leone. Dr. Redwood-Sawyerr has presented papers in many conferences, workshops, and seminars and has research publications in many international journals. He co-authored a book in telecommunications that was published in Germany in 2000. He has published papers in telecommunications, information technology, energy, power sector reforms, technology management, and renewable energy with special interest in solar energy and biogas for rural electrification. Dr. Redwood-Sawyerr is the current Chairman of the West African Examinations Council (WAEC).

Joti Sekhon is the Director of International Programs at Winston-Salem State University, where he provides leadership and coordination for programs and initiatives designed to promote internationalization. These include: international exchange partnerships; promoting faculty scholarship and research to internationalize the curriculum; oversight of study abroad programs and international student services; seeking resources to support program activities; coordinating internationalization extracurricular activities. Dr. Sekhon received her BA degree at the University of Delhi; her MA and M.Phil degrees at Jawaharlal Nehru University in New Delhi; and her Ph.D. from University of Waterloo in Ontario, Canada. Her scholarly interests include comparative-historical sociology, cultural theory, ethnic relations, social inequalities, gender, and social movements.

Abu Sesay is Vice-Chancellor and Principal of Njala University (Sierra Leone). He holds a Ph.D. in crop physiology and plant physiology from Iowa State University. He has taught at the University of Botswana, the University of Swaziland, and the University of Sierra Leone, and has had Visiting Scientist/Researcher appointments at The University of Nottingham (UK) and Iowa State University. Before being named Vice Chancellor and Principal of the University of Njala, Dr. Sesay was the Dean of the Faculty of Environmental Science, Vice Principal, and Head of the Department of Biology at of Njala University College of the University of Sierra Leone. Dr. Sesay has more than 45 refereed journal papers, conference papers, abstracts, book reviews, and book chapters. He is a member of the Crop Science Society of America, the American Society of Agronomy, the International Bambara groundnut Network (BAMNET), the Agricultural Society of Sierra Leone, Conservation Society of Sierra Leone, and the American Society of Plant Physiologists.

Elizabeth Shepherd is the Education Intelligence research manager based at the British Council in Hong Kong. Prior to joining the East Asia team, she worked for the British Council in Washington, DC, managing the delivery of the UK-U.S. New Partnership Fund that established 31 bilateral and trilateral Higher Education strategic partnerships. She also managed the *Realising the Potential: UK – US Policy Forum*, October 2010, in partnership with IIE, Universities UK, and New York University. This forum brought UK and U.S. higher education leaders and governments together at the Institute of International Education in New York, NY, to discuss future collaborative strategies. Shepherd joined the British Council in 2006 as part of the Education Market Intelligence team, producing research for the Education UK Partnership and PMI2 teams in the UK. She specializes in both quantitative and qualitative research methods and now works on product development as part of the Education Intelligence team in Hong Kong with a focus on forecasting international student mobility, examining international student decision-making, and global and country-specific higher education trends.

Anthony Shull has seven years of experience working in business and eleven years of experience in higher education in multicultural environments in both the private and public sectors. He has focused much of his professional development in the regions of Latin American and East Asia. Shull, presently the Director of Global Programs in the College of Education at the University of Colorado, Colorado Springs, is responsible for the direction of the Office of Global Programs, a cash-funded initiative which oversees international programs, international partnering, international recruitment of educators/students, the Intensive English Program, Faculty-Led Study Abroad, and international certificate development. His areas of expertise are strategic planning, interdisciplinary project development/management, international partnership negotiation/development, ESL programming, and international program innovation.

Mary S. Spangler is the seventh Chancellor of Houston Community College. As a professor, administrator, and national advocate for higher education, she has devoted her career to community colleges and their students. She served as president of Los Angeles City College, the flagship institution of the Los Angeles Community College District, and as chancellor of Oakland Community College in Michigan. Under her leadership, HCC has reached out to Houston communities to make the college more essential to the city's success. In 2008, she was among 21 national higher education leaders invited to contribute an essay to *Letters to the Next President: Strengthening America's Foundation in Higher Education*. Presented to President Obama, the book provides advice on how American educational institutions can continue to educate our population in order to compete in the global marketplace. Dr. Spangler serves on the boards of the American Council on Education (ACE); Greater Houston Partnership; Texas Association of Community Colleges; BioHouston; and ETS's National Community College Advisory Council. She co-chairs the American College and University Presidents Climate Commitment (ACUPCC) and is a former board member of the American Association of Community Colleges (AACC). She was appointed to advisory councils and taskforces by Governors Napolitano (AZ), Davis (CA), Granholm (MI), Perry (TX), and Senator Hutchison (TX), and was the only community college CEO named to the National Governors Association *Innovation America* Task Force (2006-07). She holds a Doctorate in Education and Masters in English from the University of California, Los Angeles.

Susan Buck Sutton has recently transitioned from over three decades at Indiana University to return to her alma mater, Bryn Mawr College, as Senior Advisor for Internationalization. While in Indiana, Sutton served as Chancellor's Professor of Anthropology and also as Associate Vice President of International Affairs, with particular responsibility for IU's urban campus, Indiana University – Purdue University Indianapolis (IUPUI). Under Sutton's leadership, IUPUI was honored with the 2009 Andrew Heiskell Award from the Institute of International Education and the 2011 Senator Paul Simon Award from NAFSA. Sutton is currently President of the Association of International Education Administrators, past Chair of the International Education Leadership Knowledge Community of NAFSA, and on the Advisory Councils of the Internationalization Collaborative of the American Council on Education and the International Academic Partnership Program of the Institute of International Education. She has served as an advisor on internationalization to over a dozen colleges and universities and has published and given numerous presentations and workshops on the nature of international partnerships and on international service learning. Sutton is also past President of the General Anthropology Division of the American Anthropological Association, as well as past Editor of the *Journal of Modern Greek Studies*. As an anthropologist, Sutton's research has focused on migration, tourism, and community in contemporary Greece. She has published four books and over 60 articles, and her teaching has been recognized with over a dozen awards.

Luís Orlindo Tedeschi was born in Araçatuba, SP, Brazil. In 1987, he enrolled in the University of São Paulo campus of Piracicaba, SP, (Escola Superior de Agricultura "Luiz de Queiroz" – ESALQ/USP) to pursue a bachelor's degree in agronomy. From 1993 to 1996, he completed a master's degree in animal science and forage in the same institution. In August 1997, he began a Ph.D. degree program at Cornell University with a major in animal nutrition and minors in animal science and agricultural engineering. He studied modeling and simulation of nutrient fluxes and requirements of ruminants. In February 2001, he started a postdoctoral appointment at the Department of Animal Science of Cornell University, and in June 2002 he accepted a Research Associate position in the same Department to develop a mathematical model to improve individual management of cattle. In September 2005, he accepted an Assistant Professor position at the Department of Animal Science of Texas A&M University, and in September 2010 he was promoted to Associate Professor. He is also a member of the Intercollegiate Faculty of Nutrition. Dr. Tedeschi teaches ruminant nutrition and precision diet formulation for undergraduate and graduate students. He conducts research on energy and nutrient requirements of grazing and feedlot animals, growth biology and bioenergetics, chemical composition and kinetics of fermentation of feeds, modeling and simulation of decision support systems, evaluation of models, and Monte Carlos simulation. He has published more than 95 manuscripts in peer-reviewed journals and presented in more than 60 conferences and workshops worldwide on nutrition and modeling.

Hans Thamhain specializes in R&D and technology-based project management. He is a professor of management and director of MOT and Project Management Programs at Bentley University, Boston/Waltham. His industrial experience includes 20 years of management positions with high-technology companies: GTE/Verizon, General Electric, and ITT. Dr. Thamhain has written over seventy research papers and five professional reference books in project and technology management: *Management of Technology* (2005), *Managing Effectively in Technology-Based Organizations* (1997), *Project Management Operating Guidelines* (co-authored with Harold Kerzner, 1986), *Project Management for Small and Medium-Size Businesses* (co-authored with Harold Kerzner, 1985), and *Engineering Program Management* (1985). He is the recipient of the Distinguished Contribution Award from the Project Management Institute in 1998, the IEEE Engineering Manager of the Year 2000/2001 Award, and the Research Achievement Award from the Project Management Institute in 2006. He is profiled in *Marquis Who's Who in America* and certified as NPDP and PMP.

Art Tyler became the first Deputy Chancellor and Chief Operating Officer of the Houston Community College System in August 2007. Dr. Tyler is responsible for leading the daily operations of a system that includes financial, academic, student services and support, informational technology, and human resources. Dr. Tyler has had a leadership career in business and the military in addition to 14 years of administrative and leadership experience in community colleges. Dr. Tyler was the President of Sacramento City College; Special Trustee for Community College (Compton, CA); and Vice President – Admin and Finance, Los Angeles City College. Prior to starting a career in higher education, he had been a president, COO, and CFO of several electronic engineering and manufacturing companies. He served for more than 20 years in the United States Air Force and with Joint Military Commands. Before deciding to retire from the military, he served as the Antiterrorism Manager for the Air Force. He served as an advisor for two commanders responsible for U.S. activities in Middle

East. He has a BS degree in business from University of Maryland, and a master's degree with distinction in national security affairs vis-à-vis the Middle East from the U.S. Naval Postgraduate School, Monterey, CA. Dr. Tyler holds a doctorate in management and organizational leadership with a focus on community college leadership and organizational development.

Peggy Valentine is Dean of the School of Health Sciences at Winston-Salem State University (WSSU), overseeing educational programs in nursing, clinical laboratory science, occupational therapy, and physical therapy. She received a Doctor of Education degree from Virginia Tech, and a Master of Arts degree and Bachelor of Science degree from Howard University. Dr. Valentine has conducted research on homeless and minority issues. She has lectured extensively on minority HIV/AIDS issues to professional and lay groups nationally and internationally. She is past President for the National Society of Allied Health. She serves on the board of trustees for Novant Health Systems, the board of directors for the National Society of Allied Health, Sci-Works Board, and the Community Development Corporation of Winston-Salem, North Carolina.

Jennifer Nicole-Wong Wade has been a development analyst in the office of University Outreach and International Programs at the University of California, Davis, since May 2007. She is responsible for developing and implementing programs that identify, cultivate, and sustain UC Davis's relationships with its international alumni and scholars. She actively promotes the strategic, international, programmatic, and development goals of the Office of the Vice Provost, University Outreach and International Programs. Moreover, she coordinates and facilitates official UC Davis international travel of designated officials and provides leadership on the unit's marketing and communication strategies. She serves on several committees, including: the UC Davis Staff Diversity Administrative Advisory Committee to the Chancellor (2009-13) and will serve as the committee's chair for 2011-2013; Cal Aggie Alumni Association's membership committee (2008-2011); and the Asian Pacific American Systemwide Alliance at UC Davis, for which she has served as co-chair from 2009–2011. Prior to joining UC Davis, Wade developed programs and prepared California-mandated cost claims for school districts, community colleges, cities, and special districts. She earned her bachelor's degree in both managerial economics and communication in 2003 from the University of California, Davis.

Biwu Yang is a professor in the Department of Technology Systems, East Carolina University. He teaches in the field of data networking, information technology, and information security. He has served as the technology coordinator in all aspects of Global Academic Initiatives, including the Global Understanding project that involves more than 30 partner universities from more than 20 countries, and the Global Climate Change course including Brazil, China, India, Mexico, and the U.S. Since its inception in 2003, Dr. Yang has joined the team effort in developing global institution partners from countries around the world. His expertise in the data networking field helps to identify and deploy appropriate technologies for the global collaborative projects and courses. He coordinates the technology support issues with the technical support personnel from all partner institutions, including training, troubleshooting, and day-to-day operations.

IIE INFORMATION AND RESOURCES

OPEN DOORS REPORT ON INTERNATIONAL EDUCATIONAL EXCHANGE

The *Open Doors Report on International Educational Exchange*, supported by the U.S. Department of State, Bureau of Educational and Cultural Affairs, provides an annual, comprehensive statistical analysis of academic mobility between the United States and other nations, and trend data over 60 years.

WEBSITE: www.iie.org/opendoors

THE CENTER FOR INTERNATIONAL PARTNERSHIPS IN HIGHER EDUCATION

The IIE Center for International Partnerships in Higher Education assists colleges and universities in developing and sustaining institutional partnerships with their counterparts around the world. Major initiatives of the Center are the International Academic Partnerships Program and the IIE Global Partner Service.

WEBSITE: www.iie.org/cip

ATLAS OF STUDENT MOBILITY

Project Atlas tracks migration trends of the millions of students who pursue education outside of their home countries each year. Data are collected on global student mobility patterns, country of origin, as well as leading host destinations for higher education.

WEBSITE: www.iie.org/projectatlas

IIE WHITE AND BRIEFING PAPERS

IIE White and Briefing Papers address the changing landscape of international education, offering timely snapshots of critical issues in the field.

- Joint and Double Degree Programs in a Global Context (September 2011)
- Expanding U.S. Study Abroad to India: A Guide for Institutions (July 2011)
- Evaluating and Measuring the Impact of Citizen Diplomacy: Current State and Future Directions (July 2011)
- Building Sustainable U.S.-Ethiopian University Partnerships: Findings from a Conference (July 2011)

- What International Students Think about U.S. Higher Education: Attitudes and Perceptions of Prospective Students in Africa, Asia, Europe, and Latin America (June 2011)

- Expanding U.S. Study Abroad to Indonesia: U.S. Perspectives and Strategies for Expansion (May 2011)

- International Education as an Institutional Priority: What Every College and University Trustee Should Know (2011)

- The Value of International Education to U.S. Business and Industry Leaders: Key Findings from a Survey of CEOs (October 2009)

- Expanding Study Abroad Capacity at U.S. Colleges and Universities (May 2009)

- The Three-year Bologna-compliant Degree: Responses from U.S. Graduate Schools (April 2009)

- Promoting Study Abroad in Science and Technology Fields (March 2009)

- Expanding U.S. Study Abroad in the Arab World: Challenges & Opportunities (February 2009)

- Expanding Education Abroad at Community Colleges (September 2008)

- Educational Exchange between the United States and China (July 2008)

- Exploring Host Country Capacity for Increasing U.S. Study Abroad (May 2008)

- Current Trends in U.S. Study Abroad & the Impact of Strategic Diversity Initiatives (May 2007)

WEBSITE: www.iie.org/publications

IIE/AIFS FOUNDATION GLOBAL EDUCATION RESEARCH REPORTS

This series of books explores the most pressing and under-researched issues affecting international education policy today.

- Developing Strategic International Partnerships: Models for Initiating and Sustaining Innovative Institutional Linkages (October 2011)

- Who Goes Where and Why?: An Overview and Analysis of Global Educational Mobility (April 2011)

- Innovation through Education: Building the Knowledge Economy in the Middle East (August 2010)

- International India: A Turning Point in Educational Exchange with the U.S. (January 2010)

- Higher Education on the Move: New Developments in Global Mobility (April 2009)

- U.S.-China Educational Exchange: Perspectives on a Growing Partnership (October 2008)

WEBSITE: www.iie.org/gerr

IIE WEB RESOURCES

IIEPASSPORT.ORG

This free online search engine lists over 9,000 study abroad programs worldwide and provides advisers with hands-on tools to counsel students and promote study abroad.

WEBSITE: www.iiepassport.org

STUDY ABROAD FUNDING

This valuable funding resource helps U.S. students find funding for study abroad programs.

WEBSITE: www.studyabroadfunding.org

FUNDING FOR UNITED STATES STUDY

This directory offers the most relevant data on hundreds of fellowships, grants, paid internships, and scholarships for study in the U.S.

WEBSITE: www.fundingusstudy.org

INTENSIVE ENGLISH USA

Comprehensive reference with over 500 accredited English language programs in the U.S.

WEBSITE: www.intensiveenglishusa.org

FULBRIGHT PROGRAMS FOR U.S. STUDENTS

The Fulbright U.S. Student Program equips future American leaders with the skills they need to thrive in an increasingly global environment by providing funding for one academic year of study or research abroad, to be conducted after graduation from an accredited university.

SPONSOR: U.S. Department of State, Bureau of Educational and Cultural Affairs

WEBSITE: http://us.fulbrightonline.org

FULBRIGHT PROGRAMS FOR U.S. SCHOLARS

The traditional Fulbright Scholar Program sends 800 U.S. faculty and professionals abroad each year. Grantees lecture and conduct research in a wide variety of academic and professional fields.

SPONSOR: U.S. Department of State, Bureau of Educational and Cultural Affairs

WEBSITE: www.cies.org

PROGRAMS OF THE AIFS FOUNDATION

The AIFS Foundation

The mission of the AIFS Foundation is to provide educational and cultural exchange opportunities to foster greater understanding among the people of the world. It seeks to fulfill this mission by organizing high quality educational opportunities for students, and providing grants to individuals and schools for participation in culturally enriching educational programs.

WEBSITE: www.aifsfoundation.org

ACADEMIC YEAR IN AMERICA

Each year, AYA brings nearly 1,000 high school students from around the world to the United States. They come for the school year to live with American families and attend local high schools, learning about American culture and sharing their own languages and customs with their host families.

WEBSITE: www.academicyear.org

FUTURE LEADERS EXCHANGE PROGRAM (FLEX)

Established in 1992 under the FREEDOM Support Act and administered by the U.S. Department of State's Bureau of Educational and Cultural Affairs, FLEX encourages long-lasting peace and mutual understanding between the U.S. and countries of Eurasia.

YOUTH EXCHANGE AND STUDY PROGRAM (YES)

Since 2002, this U.S. Department of State high school exchange program has enabled students from predominantly Muslim countries to learn about American society and values, acquire leadership skills, and help educate Americans about their countries and cultures.

PROGRAMS OF THE AMERICAN INSTITUTE FOR FOREIGN STUDY

American Institute For Foreign Study

The AIFS mission is to enrich the lives of young people throughout the world by providing them with educational and cultural exchange programs of the highest possible quality.

WEBSITE: www.aifs.com

AIFS COLLEGE STUDY ABROAD

AIFS is a leading provider of study abroad programs for college students. Students can study abroad for a summer, semester, or academic year in 17 countries around the world.

WEBSITE: www.aifsabroad.com

AMERICAN COUNCIL FOR INTERNATIONAL STUDIES (ACIS)

For more than 30 years, ACIS has helped students and their teachers discover the world through premier travel and education. Teachers can choose destinations throughout Europe, the Americas, and Asia.

WEBSITE: www.acis.com

AU PAIR IN AMERICA

Au Pair in America makes it possible for nearly 4,000 eager and skilled young adults from around the world to join American families and help care for their children during a mutually rewarding, yearlong cultural exchange experience.

WEBSITE: www.aupairinamerica.com

CAMP AMERICA

Each summer, Camp America brings nearly 6,000 young people from around the world to the U.S. to work as camp counselors and camp staff.

WEBSITE: www.campamerica.aifs.com

SUMMER INSTITUTE FOR THE GIFTED (SIG)

SIG is a three-week academic, recreational, and social summer program for gifted and talented students. Students from around the world in grades 4 through 11 can participate in SIG Residential programs offered at university campuses across the country including Dartmouth College, Princeton University, Yale University, UC Berkeley, UCLA, Amherst College, Emory University, Bryn Mawr College, Vassar College, and University of Texas at Austin.

SIG operates under the National Society for the Gifted and the Talented (NSGT), which is a non-profit 501(c)3 organization.

WEBSITE: www.giftedstudy.org

CULTURAL INSURANCE SERVICES INTERNATIONAL (CISI)

CISI is the leading provider of study abroad and international student insurance coverage. Since 1992, CISI has insured over 1 million international students and cultural exchange participants worldwide.

WEBSITE: www.culturalinsurance.com

AIFS INFORMATION & RESOURCES

The following resources are available for download at: www.aifsabroad.com/advisors/publications.asp

Diversity in International Education Summary Report

The Gender Gap in Post Secondary Study Abroad: Understanding and Marketing to Male Students

Study Abroad: A 21st Century Perspective, Vol I

Study Abroad: A 21st Century Perspective, Vol II: The Changing Landscape

Innocents at Home Redux – The Continuing Challenge to America's Future

Impact on Education Abroad on Career Development, Vol I

Impact on Education Abroad on Career Development: Four Community College Case Studies, Vol II